Writings of the Luddites

Writings
OF THE
Luddites

EDITED BY
Kevin Binfield

The Johns Hopkins University Press
BALTIMORE AND LONDON

The Johns Hopkins University Press
2715 North Charles Street
Baltimore, Maryland 21218-4363
www.press.jhu.edu

Library of Congress Cataloging-in-Publication Data

Writings of the Luddites / edited by Kevin Binfield.
    p.   cm.
Includes bibliographical references and index.
ISBN 0-8018-7612-5 (hardcover : acid-free paper)
1. Luddites—Sources.   2. Sabotage in the workplace—
England—History—19th century—Sources.   3. Textile
workers—England—History—19th century—Sources.
4. Riots—England—History—19th century—Sources.
5. Great Britain—History—1789-1820—Sources.
6. Regency—England—Sources.   I. Binfield, Kevin.
DA535.W75 2004
942.07′3—dc22   2003017426

A catalog record for this book is available from
the British Library.

Contents

List of Documents

❖   NORTHWESTERN

Foreword

THE LUDDITE DISTURBANCES OF 1811-12 have long held a
place in the public imagination unmatched by any other episode during
the industrial revolution. Yet these disorders formed only part of a continuum
of popular protest against new technology in the industries concerned. Frame
breaking, characteristic of East Midlands Luddism, had a long history in the
hosiery trade, while attacks on cloth finishing machinery, the focus of Yorkshire
Luddism, had disturbed the woolen industry in both the West of England and
the West Riding of Yorkshire from the 1790s. In Lancashire new cotton spinning
technologies had met with violent resistance in 1768 and 1779, while weavers'
battles over wages had led to widespread violence in 1808. Nor did antimachinery
disturbances end in 1812. Renewed attacks on both stocking frames and finishing machinery took place in both the Midlands and the West of England in 1816,
while the extensive power loom riots in Lancashire in 1826 proved far more violent than earlier Luddite actions in the county, mobilizing whole communities
across the region, something Luddism failed to achieve. Moreover, the Swing
riots of 1830 in southern England, many of which targeted labor-saving machinery, extended over a far wider geography than Luddism and resulted in much
harsher retaliation by government. Yet it is the Luddite disturbances that catch
the imagination and retain a firm, if inchoate, grasp on popular historical understanding. In this, history reflects the impact that Luddism made at the time.

One reason for this was the ubiquity of the name. Previous labor struggles
had failed to give rise to a name or an emblem that stuck. Those involved had
rarely given themselves a title and were generically labeled by the authorities

simply as "depradators," "the disaffected," or, more frequently, "the mob." Yet
the machine breakers of 1811–12 were referred to almost from the start as "Luddites," the name they gave themselves. This self-depiction as the followers of "Ned
Ludd," who was soon promoted to "General," merits some consideration. After
all, the perhaps apocryphal Ned was, at first sight, hardly a heroic figure. An apprentice stocking-frame knitter, he had, the story ran, been criticized for making
his hose too loose. He was therefore instructed to "square his needles," namely
to adjust the mechanism of his frame. Ned allegedly took this instruction liter-
ally and, with a hammer, flattened the entire workings. Frame breaking certainly
characterized the East Midland disturbances in 1811, but the targets were only
the "wide" frames that produced "deceitfully wrought" hose, not frames in general. Naming oneself after such a figure at the least indicates a sense of irony and
self-deprecation that is remarkable, perhaps reflecting the way in which Burke's
scornful ascription of the common people as "the swinish multitude" was turned
into a badge of honor by plebeian radicals in the 1790s. Certainly, in no time Ned
acquired a fame that set him above a far more famous local hero:

> Chant no more your old rhymes about bold Robin Hood,
> His feats I but little admire
> I will sing the Atchievements of General Ludd
> Now the Hero of Nottinghamshire.*

Robin had famously robbed the rich to give to the poor and defended the weak
against arbitrary baronial power. But Ned Ludd epitomized the right of the poor
to earn their own livelihood and to defend the customs of their trade against dis-
honorable capitalist depradators. While Robin, a displaced gentleman, signified
paternal protection, Ned Ludd evidenced the sturdy self-reliance of a community prepared to resist for itself the notion that market forces rather than moral
values should shape the fate of labor. Ned Ludd was not only a symbol of plebeian
resistance; he was an ideological figure as well, one who reflected the deep sense
of history that underpinned the customary values of working communities in the
manufacturing districts.

---

*"General Ludd's Triumph," sung to the tune "Poor Jack": HO 42/119. This song
summarized the aim of the East Midland Luddites, and indeed the aspiration of many other
trades, namely that "full-fashioned work at the old fashioned price" should be "established by
Custom and Law." The capitalization of Custom and Law was original and deliberate,
signifying the importance of both to artisans everywhere.

The Luddite name, one might almost say the Luddite brand, proved fecund. As the outbreaks of industrial violence died down in the Midlands and new disturbances broke out in both the West Riding of Yorkshire and in industrial Lancashire, participants there took the name to heart and in turn pronounced themselves supporters of General Ludd. How far this reflected simple mimicry—we might wonder in this case why men in different regions and different industrial contexts saw fit to appropriate the name—or a calculated decision, we cannot know. But the choice proved effective. The authorities were in any case alarmed by the extension of the disorders, especially because they occurred against a backdrop of war with Napoleonic France. However, the spread of Ludd's name to new regions suggested to those in power that they faced a great conspiracy, one that threatened not merely new technologies and the property of those who introduced them but the very security of the state. Defining Luddism—fixing its character and understanding its generation and development—are, then, not merely arcane historical questions: they were questions of moment to the rulers of Regency England. In tackling these questions the historian is sent back to the texts. Here Luddism is comparatively rich in material, as Kevin Binfield's excellent collection shows. In these texts Luddism both defined itself and was defined by others.

The hallmark of Luddism, as with the Swing riots later, was the threatening letter. We might note that such letters were in no way a Luddite innovation. The pages of the eighteenth-century *London Gazette* demonstrate that the threatening letter had long been not only the recourse of the disgruntled but also a typical tool of effective negotiation in all sorts of labor disputes. Such letters enabled workers to present demands in a form that protected individuals from the sorts of employer retaliation that face-to-face meetings risked. Although historians have been inclined to see such letters as indicative of an essential weakness in bargaining position, this is not entirely true. Even skilled workers often conducted negotiations in this way. The croppers, highly organized into a combination, the Brief Institution, which linked men in the trade across the country, saw advantages in announcing their demands in this form to recalcitrant and hostile employers. But for outworking trades, such as the framework knitters and cotton weavers, the threatening letter provided their main means of dealing with employers who rejected customary practice.

The purpose of threatening letters was, of course, intimidation. In 1811-12, as in earlier years, they might well be supplemented by further sanctions. The

Wiltshire shearmen had made extensive use of incremental industrial violence in their campaign to resist finishing machinery ten years before Luddism. At first they supplemented their letters by cutting down sapling trees and by setting fire, in turn, to a dog kennel, six hay ricks, a stable, and a barn. They also broke a large number of windows. It was only when such minor demonstrations of force failed to ensure compliance with their demands that they progressed to attacks on mills and houses. And it was only when their campaign to safeguard the old legislation, which they believed protected their trades, had been effectively defeated that they had recourse to direct personal attacks upon the leading employers. This same pattern was repeated, if on a much larger scale, in the Midlands in 1811 and in Yorkshire in 1812.

Threatening letters, therefore, were in themselves a significant weapon. However, Luddite letters carried an additional power and authority, because Ludd's imprimatur suggested the presence of a coordinated force whose ultimate strength could not easily be discerned. This opacity of Luddism, the community solidarity that prevented the authorities from obtaining any effective information concerning the perpetrators of the attacks, the ubiquity of the name across so extensive a geography, and the way in which Ludd's men seemed to strike at will all reinforced the sense of alarm that gripped both magistrates and government ministers. In such a context Luddite letters created a cultural space filled both by protesters in enlarging their demands for change and by the authorities in their attempts to come to terms with what seemed to them a many-tentacled underground conspiracy.

Luddite letters, however, were by no means confined to threats to employers. A variety of proclamations, poems, songs, and other statements emanated from the pens of General Ludd himself, his lieutenants, and supporters. These articulated, Kevin Binfield argues, three essential styles of discourse: petitioning, seeking the support from the respectable classes and local and national authorities for the regulatory model that Luddites demanded; economic analysis, expounding a Luddite moral economy that asserted the rights of labor within a framework of custom, as seen in "Declaration; Extraordinary," a notice posted in Nottingham in November 1811; and political analysis, propounding the views of radical and even revolutionary politics. The Luddite "text" was rich and complex, varying from region to region and from context to context.

This brings the reader to the question of whether there was an "authentic" voice of the true Luddites, a question that continues to vex historians. As Kevin

Binfield demonstrates in this valuable collection, there were many authentic voices. And, because General Ludd's message was promulgated through oral and literary channels, the process of transmission allowed for further variation in both "text" and "reading." Binfield's reconstruction of the derivation of the song "Welcome Ned Ludd" shows this clearly. His researches show that the earliest version, "Well Done, Ned Ludd," proves to be in the handwriting of Charles Sutton, the editor of the *Nottingham Review*, a paper that initially tended to sympathize with the stockingers' complaints. Yet it seems unlikely, to this writer at least, that Sutton was the song's author. Rather, as a journalist he recorded the version that he had heard. Different versions, dependent on the preferences or memories of different singers, may have been recorded elsewhere. Other elements might have been changed according to the "reading" that other "recorders" placed upon the "text." Historians, too, are not innocent of slanting the reading, as Binfield indicates when examining the famous letter sent by the Yorkshire Luddites to "Mr Smith Shearing Frame Holder at Hill End Yorkshire." The readers of this volume may judge for themselves how far an inserted word changes the "meaning" of this source.

Given that there was no monolithic Luddite "movement" but a series of overlapping protests, Luddism allowed differing voices access to a wider community while deriving the legitimacy that was seen to come from General Ludd's reassertion of customary moral values. Ludd's imprimatur might therefore be called upon not only by those seeking what they saw as the reassertion of customary economic rights but also by those who demanded political rights as well. Here historians disagree most strongly, inasmuch as the text offers no easy delineation between "trade" and "radical" discourses. Here context was all. In the Midlands, the framework knitters saw in their "Charter" a legal bastion that they hoped might be supported by the authorities to safeguard their trade. Here too there were at least some employers who preferred customary regulation to a market free-for-all. In Yorkshire there was little hope that any support might be forthcoming from the authorities. In the wake of the repeal of the old woolen statutes in 1809, the croppers had only their industrial muscle to fall back upon. Moreover, they felt betrayed at the way in which their "rights" had been so cavalierly thrown over. With their campaign of direct action stalling, they may well have found the solutions of the radicals increasingly convincing. In Lancashire the weavers had long sought to effect a legal framework to safeguard their trade, without success. Here the local authorities showed no disposition toward compromise. Here, too, insurrectionary politics had struck deep roots since the later 1790s. Yet while we may posit a line from industrial action to insurrectionary politics, tracing such a route remains a matter for conjecture. On this question, the jury must remain out. The reader, like the authorities in 1811–12, is left to determine whether "Ludd" was in any respect a voice of commonality or merely a series of voices appropriating a common name.

Kevin Binfield's book marks a major contribution toward the study of Luddism. His assiduous collection and editing of texts allows, as he says, the Luddites to speak for themselves. But he does more than this. As a rhetorician and student of linguistics, he brings a new and critical eye to the texts, showing the ways in which the forms and nature of Luddite writings changed and were transformed over time and space. He also alerts historians to the need to reflect upon the modes and purposes of Luddite language and, in so doing, makes a valuable intervention in the ongoing debates about popular protest generally. This is a book to be welcomed with open arms.

Adrian Randall

Preface

T HOMAS LARGE, a Nottingham stockinger, was at work in London during late April 1812, seeking parliamentary support for a bill to provide relief
in the framework knitting trade. He wrote to Thomas Allsop and asked him to
save a letter that Large had written some weeks earlier. Nearly two hundred years
later, I am attempting to complete the task set for Allsop.

I decided to begin work on this book in 1992 after reading E. P. Thompson's
statement of purpose in *The Making of the English Working Class:* "I am seeking to rescue the poor stockinger, the Luddite cropper, the 'obsolete' hand-loom
weaver, the 'utopian' artisan, and even the deluded follower of Joanna Southcott, from the enormous condescension of history" (p. 12). At the time I was
writing a doctoral dissertation at the University of Nebraska on Percy Bysshe
Shelley and had been reading of Shelley's simultaneously generous and bitter attitudes toward members of the working classes and of scholarly commentary on
the same. Struck by Shelley's lack of familiarity with working-class discourse—
and the same lack in scholars of Shelley—I formed my own idea about the nature of the condescension of history and how to pursue my work in a manner
that at the very least does not impede the rescue that Thompson effects. I began
collecting texts by the Luddites a year later, minutes after submitting my completed dissertation to the Office of Graduate Studies. A short walk took me to
Love Library. Longer journeys followed, as I carried this work to two other institutions and to archives in both the United States and the United Kingdom.

In the course of collecting and compiling the materials for this book, I have tried to understand the lives and perspectives of the persons whose words I collect; however, every new letter revealed the distance between the Luddites and me. Even my younger days spent cleaning toilets, loading and unloading trucks, and changing hydraulic hoses inside garbage trucks, under the protection of laws governing wages and working conditions, afforded me no understanding of labor undertaken two centuries ago by persons who lacked such protections.

What you read in these pages is the result of a trail of debts extending from Lincoln, Nebraska, to Huddersfield, West Yorkshire, and dozens of places in between and off the path as I attempted to reduce that distance. The tremendous sense of obligation that I feel to the many persons who have helped me as I stumbled through researching and writing makes acknowledging them — by name, where possible — a pleasure. I hope that I have lived up to their assistance. All of the faults and shortcomings in this volume are my own.

Valerie Parry, Janet Snowhill, and Barbara Cook of the Dover Library at Gardner-Webb University helped me to locate archives and documents in the United States and the United Kingdom. This book would perhaps have ended as a frustrated wish had I never met them. Librarians and archivists in the United Kingdom never failed to be helpful. In particular, I thank the staff of the Public Records Office, Kew; Adrian Henstock, Christopher Weir, and the staff of the Nottinghamshire County Archives; Dorothy Johnston, Caroline Kelly, and the staff of the East Midlands Special Collections Library at the University of Nottingham; the staff of the Nottingham Central Library, Local Studies Library; Janet Wallwork at the John Rylands University Library at the University of Manchester; the staff of the John Rylands Library at Deansgate; Alain Kahan at the Working Class Movement Library in Salford; the Local Studies staff at the Manchester Central Library, especially Judith Baldry and Gordon Sharples; the staff of the Greater Manchester County Record Office; Michael Powell at Chetham's Library; the staff of the Derby Local Studies Library; Lesley Kipling and the staff of the Huddersfield Local Studies Library and the West Yorkshire Archives, Kirklees; W. J. Connor and the staff of the West Yorkshire Archives, Leeds; Jenny Cooksey of the Special Collections Department of the Brotherton Library at the University of Leeds; Jack Smurfitt of the Framework Knitters Museum at Ruddington; and the staff of the Leicestershire Record Office.

Stephen Behrendt and Paul Olson of the University of Nebraska provided guidance from the beginning of my work. Susan Staves of Brandeis University pointed me toward some important revisions of an early draft of the chapter on Nottingham Luddism. Joyce Brown, my department chair at Gardner-Webb University, and Gilmer Blackburn, former academic dean at Gardner-Webb, encouraged me, relieved me of committee burdens when they could, helped me to fund my research in the United Kingdom, and demonstrated that small-college faculty can conduct research despite heavy teaching loads. Paul Holroyd, of Halifax, shared much of his own research into radicalism in the West Riding.

I owe a different sort of debt to Robert Smith, past director of the Tennessee Governor's School for the Humanities, for permitting me to teach a course on Luddism in 1998, and to my students in that course. My undergraduate student assistants—Jeanna Ford, Nicole Hartis, Karen Brower, and Gary Mitchem—deserve special acknowledgment for helping me with bibliographical research at Gardner-Webb and for smiling as I rambled on about the complexities of Lancashire Luddism.

Funding for this project was provided by grants from the Academic Dean and the Faculty Development Committee at Gardner-Webb University, a Summer Stipend from the National Endowment for the Humanities, and a Murray State University Presidential Research Fellowship. Much of my travel would not have been possible had not Joyce Brown always managed to find for me additional summer teaching that paid for several trips to Britain. On those trips, my work was eased by a number of friends who housed me—especially, Meryl Hobbs and Mike and Sheila Spratt. I am also grateful to John Leach, of Marsden, who gave me a very fine tour of the Luddite-related sites in the vicinity of Marsden and Huddersfield. His sharing through weekly e-mails his experience of growing up amid that history made Luddism much more "real" to me and made writing the sections on Yorkshire Luddites wonderfully exciting.

Special thanks to Doug Armato, formerly of the Johns Hopkins University Press, and Michael Lonegro, the current humanities editor. Brian MacDonald improved my manuscript immeasurably with his excellent copyediting.

Others who have contributed directly and indirectly to this volume include Kate Ronald, Linda Pratt, James McShane, Richard Quinn, Roger Cognard, Tony Epp, Bruce Erlich, June Hobbs, Steve Jones, Malcolm Thomis, Adrian Randall, Michael Cohen, and Bill Foreman. Finny, Bear, Milford, Autumn, and Phillipsburg never failed to help hold down important papers on my desk.

My greatest debt is to my family for teaching me to value an education that I was extremely fortunate to receive, for exemplifying hard work, and for respecting my own work, which must seem frivolous and insubstantial compared with theirs.

With the greatest love and esteem, I dedicate all that succeeds in this volume to my parents, Glenn and Marie Binfield, and my friend Ramona Jean Smith.

Note on Texts and Citation

I MAKE NO CLAIM to have compiled a comprehensive and definitive edition of the Luddites' writings, although my aim has been to amass a comprehensive collection; I have selected between texts only when such selection was necessary for reasons of coherence and precision. The texts included in this volume and reproduced in their entirety range from original texts that appear, due to internal evidence or external circumstances, to have been written by Luddites to background texts and texts written by persons sympathetic to Luddism and its associated political and economic aims. The internal evidence for including a document in this collection might consist of a letter's being signed "General Ludd," the invocation of the name of "Ludd," or the writer's reference to Luddite attacks and threats in a manner typically used by the Luddites (for example, a threat to a master to remove machines or increase wages). External evidence is often provided by letters from public officials enclosing a threatening letter or a declaration of protest and identifying the document as associated with Luddism or with the larger "disaffection" complained of by the authorities of the time.

The concept of disaffection problematizes the selection of Luddite texts. Early in the Luddite protests, the authorities lacked a clear understanding of the protests as a coherent and unique movement or rising, so most of the early letters to the Home Office enclosing threatening letters and proclamations referred to the documents only as evidence of what they broadly named "disaffection." Furthermore, most of the categorization of the documents was the result of the early conception of disturbance formulated by the Home Office authorities. The system of cataloging used by the Home Office clerks did not allow for careful distinction between the types of domestic disturbances but facilitated the creation of an inventory based on geographical location (notably differentiating between protest in London and in provincial Britain). Consequently, what came to be known as Luddism some weeks into the protests was not regularly indexed or analyzed as a set of events separate from other "disaffection," particularly outside of Nottinghamshire, until well into the protests. Furthermore, for a long time after the Home Office Secretary Richard Ryder and Undersecretary John Beckett became aware of Luddism as a movement of sorts, the authorities continued to conflate other forms of riot and dissent in the Luddite regions with Luddite machine breaking.

Another type of "evidence" used in selecting texts, especially those written by Luddite sympathizers and associated protesters, is the evidence of affinity. That is to say, many documents of industrial protest during the Regency period might be understood to fall under the classification of "Luddite" by the fact of their appearing within the regions or addressing issues in the regions that saw violent labor action by textile workers during that time. Documents such as the July 1812 letter from "a well wisher" at Daypool to the secretary of state, preserved in the Home Office Papers at 42/125, might not originate in the West Riding (the part of Yorkshire that experienced nearly all of the Luddism in that county), but it treats matters of concern to the Luddites, indicates an affiliation of the writer with labor protesters, and employs a discourse similar to that of paradigmatically Luddite writing—reasons sufficient to include it among Luddite texts from Yorkshire. This is not to say that all marginal documents ought to be included among the productions of Luddism. As historians have indicated, some violence not connected to protests within the textile trade was threatened or carried out by persons who nevertheless invoked the name of Ned Ludd. Texts associated with those crimes are not collected in this volume of Luddite writings. One letter, written by Adam Wagstaff and thrown inside the door of Richard Dennis, employs Luddite discourse for a private purpose (a complaint against the continued employment of a particular "rouge," or rogue) unrelated to the stockingers' protests against the depression in trade and the threat of machinery. That letter and others like it have been omitted from this collection.

Authentication and attribution of anonymous texts are singularly difficult exercises. In this volume, the problem is quite specific—determining whether the texts contained herein are likely to have been the work of Luddite writers or their sympathizers. The most important criteria that have been applied in their selection have been the dates of the documents, their style and handwriting, and the compatibility of the documents with the aims and methods of the Luddites. The aims and methods can be ascertained from authorities' reports, the depositions of victims, the confessions of captured Luddites, and the documents themselves. Currently, these aims and methods are understood in terms of protests against hiring practices that resulted in the abatement of wages, increases in rents of machines used to produce or finish cloth, the use of machines that damaged a trade's reputation for quality, increases in the costs of provisions, and the denial of a political voice to those persons affected by the decline in wages and the increase in prices. I choose not to include documents that do not fall under one of those criteria. (Texts that provide background or prior models for Luddite writing are exceptions.) Searching for Luddite aims and methods in the documents themselves is a precarious endeavor, with the potential for expanding previously accepted notions of the aims and methods by reading into Luddism the ideas contained in the documents under scrutiny. In other words, every text that might be of Luddite origin has the potential to change the current understanding of Luddism, thereby shifting the criteria for evaluating whether the text under consideration is Luddite or not. Each new text is measured against a changing gauge. It is probably not possible to avoid the problems that I have just described, so I have attempted to explain in the headnotes the circumstances surrounding the production of each text, especially when texts might expand what we know as Luddism into areas of practice not previously known to be within the sphere of Luddism. The most obvious example is the incorporation of a letter to the McConnel and Kennedy Company in protest against hiring practices within the Lancashire spinning industry. The letter indicates that Luddite discourse was employed to protest the hiring of women as spinners, a grievance not previously understood to be significant within Luddism; however, the general aim of the letter, to protest against wage abatement, fits the larger pattern of Luddism.

Problems of versioning and stemmatic concerns over the Luddite documents are minimal. With few exceptions, the documents are in manuscript form. Most of the original materials appear to be in the handwriting and style of persons with a minimal education but nevertheless sufficient to write a threatening letter or a lengthy broadside proclamation, but some of the documents have been copied by Home Office clerks or, less frequently, provincial authorities. Occasionally, the fact that a document is a clerk's copy is indicated on the manuscript. More frequently, however, only the similarities in handwriting among a number of manuscripts provide indirect evidence that an unlabeled copy is in fact a clerk's copy. When a source manuscript is evidently a copy, I have mentioned so in the headnotes to that document. I have found no need to provide a stemma for any text within this collection because I have found no evidence that, with two possible exceptions, any of the source texts is a copy of a copy. Those exceptions are the Nottinghamshire song "Welcome Ned Ludd" and the Leicestershire letter of threat sent to Henry Wood. The problem of the song "Welcome Ned Ludd" was resolved by my having found an earlier version of the song, differently titled as "Well Done, Ned Lud," but that discovery leads to new difficulties, which, at this point, seem to be unavoidable. Specifically, the "Well Done, Ned Lud" version is in the handwriting of Charles Sutton, the editor of the *Nottingham Review*. Sutton was sympathetic to the Luddites, but the song does not provide enough material to judge whether Sutton is its likely author or merely a transcriber of a song that he saw or heard elsewhere. The problem of the 29 May 1812 letter to Henry Wood is that the only known source for the letter is a reward notice that reproduces the letter. No mention is made by the authorities whether the printed transcription was made from the original or from a copy.

Many of the Luddite writings make sense only in conjunction with each other, or perhaps with other, non-Luddite texts. Although I generally choose not to stray from chronology, I do attempt to indicate in the headnotes the relationships of documents to other documents located elsewhere in the volume. Occasionally in the headnotes, I have chosen to include or quote extracts from non-Luddite correspondence when the correspondence provides additional information on the matters treated in a Luddite document, indicates the attitude of the authorities or the recipients of a Luddite letter, or describes how the document moved from one set of hands to another. The supplementary documents also provide some sense of the similarities and differences between the styles of the Luddites and other writers, including the authorities and those non-Luddite working-class writers whose aims overlapped the aims of Luddism. Scholars who are interested in the discourse of the authorities might like to know that the largest part of the correspondence of officials and others from which the supplementary quotations have been selected are preserved in the Home Office Papers, series 40 and 42. The officials' letters are typically legible and clear. The exceptions are the correspondence of Huddersfield magistrate Joseph Radcliffe, whose frequently illegible papers are gathered in the West Yorkshire Archives Service, Leeds.

In the interest of unity and coherence, I have omitted some documents (such as most of the letters, broadsides, and minutes of meetings of the Framework Knitters Company) that might be relevant to a larger study of trade unionism and direct action within the framework knitting trade but which do not bear directly upon Luddism; however, documents extraneous to Luddism but which are related to or dovetail with Luddite concerns or which incorporate rhetoric that resembles that of Luddite texts have occasionally been included, either as quotations in the headnotes or as complete documents.

I have chosen to reproduce all of the documents verbatim and as closely resembling the original manuscripts as typescript will allow so that readers might study the varieties and peculiarities of Luddite grammar, punctuation, and orthography. The principle of verbatim reproduction extends even to the inclusion of intercalations and struck words. I have, however, deviated from the original punctuation in a couple of instances. I have substituted dashes for the marks that resemble something between short underscoring and dashes. Such marks occasionally functioned as periods, commas, or dashes in the handwritten texts and were typically ambiguously placed in their vertical position in each line. I have also substituted periods for short marks that resemble abbreviated hyphens placed at the end of sentences in the vertical position where a period ordinarily appears. Original authors' insertions appear in square brackets.

Persons not familiar with manuscripts of the eighteenth and early nineteenth centuries might be struck by the absence of punctuation, especially periods. Often, writers left a somewhat larger space between the word ending one sentence and the word beginning a new one. I have tried to preserve that spacing. What is more difficult to reproduce, given the absence of punctuation in most sentences, is an indication of the frequent conclusion of one sentence at the right edge of a page and the beginning of a new sentence at the left edge of the page on the next line. Occasionally, writers began that new line with a capitalized initial letter of the first word, but, more frequently, the next sentence or line begins without regard for capitalization, perhaps because capitalization was often not uniform in much working-class writing.

I have tried to cite the original sources of the works as clearly and as completely as possible. For decades, the customary practice of historians and cultural scholars had been to cite documents in the Home Office Papers thus—H. O. 42/119. I follow this practice, although it can be problematic. Some of the series contain documents with as many as three stamped numbers on individual pages, making determination of the proper fold number quite difficult. Some documents are missing fold numbers entirely. Still other documents have not been microfilmed, as my requests to view the original boxes allowed me to discover. In any event, I have tried to provide enough information so that the interested reader might be able to find the original documents in order to examine them, to correct any errors that I might have made in transcription, and to advance the study of working-class writing in general and of Luddite writing in particular.

With rare exceptions, all of the documents within this collection have been transcribed from the original version. In some cases, determining whether a version is original is difficult. Home Office clerks' copies are often labeled as copies, but many of the documents in the Home Office Papers appear to be in the handwriting of a person who writes frequently—in other words, someone who is not likely to have been a textile worker.

All of the Home Office and Treasury Solicitor's documents transcribed herein are out of copyright under the Copyright Act, having been anonymous or pseudonymous, or copyright has been waived, as in the case of official correspondence by civil servants to and from the Home Office. The Public Record Office is the custodian of the original documents from the Home Office and Treasury Solicitor's Papers. Documents from the Radcliffe Papers have been reproduced with the kind permission of the custodians of the papers, the West Yorkshire Archives Service, Leeds. The materials from the McConnel, Kennedy and Company Papers are reproduced by courtesy of the University Librarian and Director, The John Rylands University Library of Manchester. Letters from the Gott Papers appear by permission of Leeds University Library, the owners of the letters. Permission to publish extracts from *Miscellanies* is given by The Department of Manuscripts and Special Collections, University of Nottingham Library. Letters contained in the *Records of the Borough of Nottingham* are reproduced by permission of the publisher of the volume, the Nottingham City Council, Adrian Henstock, Principal Archivist.

Writings of the Luddites

Introduction

HOME OFFICE SECRETARY Richard Ryder received the following letter from Manchester shortly after the May 1812 assassination of Prime Minister Spencer Perceval.

> Every frame Breaking act you Make an amendment to only serves to shorten your Days   Theirfore you may Prepaire to go to the Divel to Bee Secraterry for M⸢ᵣ⸣ Perceval theire for there are fire Ships Making to saile by land as well as by Warter   that will not faile to Destroy all the Obnoctious in the both Houses as you have been at a great Deal of pains to Destroy Chiefe part of the Country   it is know your turn to fall   The Remedy for you is Shor Destruction Without Detection--prepaire for thy Departure and Recomend the same to thy friends
>
> your Hbl sert &c
Luddites[1]

The threat is anonymous, inflammatory, colorful, ungrammatical, and exaggerated. It shares those qualities with letters sent by Luddite protesters to employers in various textile industries during the previous half year, but, while retaining concern with machinery, it goes beyond the earliest Luddites' local, measured threats to destroy machines and takes Luddite writing to a point of visceral futility that many scholars would consider to be Luddism's logical extreme. This letter captures Luddism on a single page.

In the Midlands and the North of England from November 1811 to April 1817, the Luddites broke machinery, rioted against high food prices, and wrote threatening letters, proclamations, and verses. Of course, machine breaking, food riots, and threats were neither unique nor original to the Luddite movement. What Luddism provided was a centralizing eponym, the name of Edward ("Ned") Ludd, who was at various times titled General, Captain, or King. The name circulated widely and became a centralizing force largely through Luddite writing. The name was used to distinguish Regency-period machine breaking from early outbreaks of frame destruction soon after Nottingham lace manufacturer William Nunn reported to the Home Office that "many Hundreds Letters have been sent sign'd 'Ludd' threatening the Lives and to burn and destroy the Houses Frames and Property of most of the principal Manufacturers through the Post office." [2] Not all of the activities, however, were conducted by persons announcing themselves as members of General Ludd's army, and not all of the anonymous, threatening letters were signed "Ludd." We should begin, then, by trying to define Luddites and Luddite writing.

The problem is a textual-editorial version of that "problem of definition" posed by Malcolm Thomis at the beginning of his book, *The Luddites*. [3] Defining Luddites or Luddism, however, is not an unproblematic maneuver. For example, rather than initially providing direct definitions of Luddism, Thomis, J. L. Hammond and Barbara Hammond, and Brian Bailey chart the movement from its 1811 origins among textile workers in Nottinghamshire through its spread into Derbyshire, Cheshire, Lancashire, and Yorkshire to its conclusion at the gallows in front of Leicester Gaol in April 1817. Trade, region, and chronology narrow the activities that scholars might designate as Luddite.

The protesting workers whom we call Luddites varied from region to region and even within each region. The Luddites in Nottinghamshire, Derbyshire, and Leicestershire were framework knitters, also called stockingers, in both the hose and lace trades. There is very little evidence of persons who were not framework knitters participating in any attacks on the wide stocking frames that were the targets of Midlands Luddite protests and destruction. The Midlands saw both the first and last instances of Luddism—an 11 March 1811 protest in Nottingham followed by attacks on stocking frames in Arnold later that same day and the sending of threatening letters in Derby and Leicester in early 1817 following the execution of James Towle and others involved in the Loughborough raid of 1816. In the West Riding of Yorkshire, most Luddites were cloth dressers in the woolen industry, also called croppers; however, Luddite assemblies near Huddersfield regularly included members of other trades—saddlemakers and hatters, for instance.

Luddism there ran a course from a 19 January 1812 arson fire at Oatlands Mills to a series of threatening letters sent to officials and manufacturers in January 1813 in the wake of the execution at York of Luddites convicted of murdering a Marsden mill owner. Cheshire and Lancashire Luddites are typically said to have been cotton weavers; however, spinners, colliers, fustian makers, and women working in no textile trade at all were quite likely to be found in the midst of Luddite riots in Manchester and the surrounding cotton towns. Luddism in the Northwest began with threats made against Stockport factory owners in February 1812 and ended with the 27 August 1812 acquittal of thirty-eight Luddites accused of illegal oathing.

Luddism must also be defined according to its activities and aims. In all three of the Luddite regions—the Midlands, Yorkshire's West Riding, and the vicinity of Manchester—Luddites sought to put an end to the manufacturers' use of certain types of machinery. More precisely, the Luddites opposed the use of machines whose purpose was to reduce production costs, whether the cost reductions were achieved by decreasing wages or the number of hours worked. In the Midlands counties of Nottinghamshire, Derbyshire, and Leicestershire, the "obnoxious" machines (in Luddite parlance) were wide knitting frames used to make cheap and inferior articles in the lace and stocking trades. In Yorkshire, the croppers opposed the use of shearing frames and gig mills in the process of finishing woolen cloth. In the Northwestern cotton districts surrounding Manchester (Cheshire, Lancashire, northern Derbyshire, and Flintshire), weavers in particular sought to eliminate the steam-powered looms that were driving down wages in the cotton trade.

In all three regions, the Luddites used threats against manufacturers and destructive attacks on machines, shops, and factories to realize their goals. Not surprisingly, the efforts to destroy machinery were accompanied by threats against the local officials who attempted to prevent the coercion of the manufacturers and the destruction of their machines. In the Midlands, Luddism worked in tandem with union-like negotiations to pressure hosiers. Frequently, in the Manchester area, attacks on the steam-powered looms coincided with food riots. In both Manchester and Yorkshire, machine breaking went side by side with political radicalism and, at times, arms raids and the administration of illegal oaths.

Definitions by period, location, occupation, and activity are obviously helpful for concentrating attention on a group whose membership is small enough to be manageable, but those definitions do little to illuminate the margins of an active population, the membership of which was already economically and politically marginalized, was spread widely across several counties, and was experiencing cultural instability wrought by industrialization, famine, economic depression, and war. Where do we place a spinner from Flintshire who, in May 1812, wrote a letter to absentee mill owners in Manchester demanding that they raise wages at a Holywell mill and "had better be content with a moderate profit, than have . . . mills destroyed"? What additional significance is to be found in the fact that the Flintshire writer backs the threat by alluding to the Luddite attacks on power looms in Stockport during the previous month? Is it possible to find in that letter a discursive continuity that joins the Flintshire letter to other writing that is more obviously classified as Luddite? If so, what would that discursive continuity signify about the character of Luddite protests across regions and trades?

One important, preliminary question remains: what terminology should be used to refer to those activities? Although my focus is on understanding Luddism as a discursive continuity, I use the terms "Luddism," "riots," "movement," and "protests" throughout this book. The various historians of Luddism have their own preferred terms, including risings, riots, campaign, disturbances, agitations, movement, revolt, or rebellion. Each term reflects a bias and structures the ways in which readers are led to think of the Luddites. Let us consider just a few examples.

To Hammond and Hammond, the term "campaign" ascribes a purposiveness to Luddism and an almost political equality with the governmental and industrial forces that the Luddites opposed. Considering Luddism to be a "campaign" with "aims," Hammond and Hammond can interpret it as generally progressive and minimally violent but also subject to the plots, designs, and subterfuges of a government that feared and sought to discredit it. Frank O. Darvall refers to the machine breaking as the Luddite "disturbances," which helps him to place Luddism among the other instances of public disorder that he studies. To E. P. Thompson, Luddism remains "Luddism," a transient, though developing ideology that shared some features with a larger, underground, nationwide (or perhaps kingdomwide) process of class formation with the insurrectionary potential to counteract the combination of capitalism and unreformed government. "Luddism" has become the conventional term, despite the troubling hint of attributing a monolithic character to a very diverse movement. Malcolm Thomis employs the term "Luddism," too, but prefers "machine breaking" so as to check the idea that Luddism was a coherent, revolutionary movement and to distinguish genuine Luddism (that is, the breaking of certain textile machinery) from the food riots, arms raids, politics, and other activities that often accompanied the breaking of machines. Like Thompson, John Dinwiddy prefers the term "Luddism" for its ability to convey the impression of an ideology developing not toward revolution but toward a realization among the working classes of the need to participate in democratic reform. Adrian Randall also seems to prefer "Luddism" for its ideological, though perhaps not revolutionary, significance—that is, to define resistance to industrial change and the loss of social cohesion. Most recently, Brian Bailey employs the term "rebellion," but, in his final chapter, he dances from "campaign" to "movement" to "agitation" in an attempt to fix upon a fitting characterization while avoiding the implications of settling upon one. It appears that Bailey uses the term "rebellion" to situate the Luddites somewhere between an angry mob and an organization of purposive revolutionaries.[4]

Many of these terms entail complications, if only because some of the historians using them attempt to represent a Luddite totality based to a significant extent on the secondhand information of spies, manufacturers, soldiers, constables, magistrates, and government officials. The problem of representation applies to many studies of working-class life generally. In *The Handloom Weavers*, Duncan Bythell writes:

> Like any group which fights a losing battle, the cotton handloom weavers and their problems became an almost forgotten bad dream as soon as they lost their place in the social and economic structure. . . . And in common with other long-vanished groups of poor, ill-organized and badly-educated working men, the weavers left very few literary remains in the form of letters, diaries, notebooks, or memoirs which might give in their own words an indication of their complaints and aspirations. As a result, they must largely be seen through the eyes of outsiders—journalists, employers, magistrates or politicians—who interested themselves in the weavers' problems, and whose views have proved more able to survive.[5]

Bythell's pessimism about the representation of resistance to economic change is founded on the difficulty of finding texts written by members of the laboring classes. The difficulties are not insurmountable. Amid the mass of correspondence and documents that found their way into the Home Office Papers, county records archives, the collected papers of manufacturers and officials, and broadsheet collections in town libraries, the form and content of resistance can be discovered, and from that morass the words of the historical losers can be re-cuperated in such a way that a continuous rhetorical thread might be discerned.

Luddite writing is as various as it is intense, and the writings that are col-lected here have resisted my early attempts to offer totalizing critiques and broad generalizations. The variety has led me to think in terms of a continuity, but not a totality, in Luddite writing. Exploring Luddism's discursive continuity avoids the problem of defining Luddism as a purposive campaign, opportunistic hooliganism, or some other totality in between; however, it also risks blurring material distinctions, facilitating arbitrary and shifting categorizations, and re-ducing Luddism to "text" in such a way that we might ignore or overlook the unique material realities that impel the various Luddite writers and charge their writings with motives and patterns.

Despite the variety, Luddite discourse can be understood as a more or less continuous practice deriving from one forceful exercise of naming—the cre-ation of the eponym "Ned Ludd." Luddism is also a discourse with a small num-ber of centralizing features that pertain even when the name "Ludd" is absent. Commonality in surface features such as threatening language and anonymity is obvious, but various contextual and intertextual features are more important. First, Luddite writing typically is aware of its place in relation to a larger array of activities of resistance to industrial practices, and it recognizes the similari-ties between activities within the array. Second, it refers to those other activities, thereby presenting a discursive and active continuity to readers then and now. Third, it presents itself in opposition to a network of oppressive economic prac-tices by manufacturers, merchants, and public officials. The following prelimi-nary sections treating Luddism in the Midlands, the Northwest, and Yorkshire attempt to sketch the continuity of Luddite rhetoric and its variety, and to ad-vance the thesis that Luddite writing takes its shape from the discursive contexts of the different regions and the rhetorical needs of the movement's writers.

There is good reason to ascribe to the Luddite writers an intention to present themselves as participants in a continuous discourse. Luddism is distinct from other movements or disturbances or riots in that the writers of the movement named themselves and their movement through their embracing the eponym "Ned Ludd." The authorities, manufacturers, and journalists attempted to im-pose other labels—"disaffected," "depredators," "Jacobins"—but the labels failed to stick because Luddite texts superseded the language of the authorities. The

Luddites were the losers in their fight, but their "linguistic legacy" is formidable and indelible, as Randall has noted.[6]

That linguistic legacy has not been examined to the extent that it might be. Although the period of Luddism was brief and its range geographically limited, it produced a significant body of writing—primarily ballads, chalkings, manifestos, and, of course, anonymous letters. It is true that the exploits of the machine wreckers have inspired several authors, even though the writings of the Luddites have not. The results of inspiration have included a number of novels (among them, Charlotte Bronte's *Shirley*, Phyllis Bentley's *Inheritance*, G. A. Henty's *Through the Fray*, and D. F. E. Sykes and G. H. Walker's *Ben o' Bills, or the Luddite*), a drama (Ernst Toller's *The Machine-Wreckers*), and recently an Internet "techno-opera" based on the Luddite song, "General Ludd's Triumph."[7] Late twentieth-century critics of culture and apologists for technology misappropriate the term daily. My web-surfing students regularly torment me with a "Luddite Purity Test" that they have discovered online.

The list of historians and historical scholars who have undertaken to examine Luddism is every bit as impressive: Frank Peel, John Russell, J. L. Hammond and Barbara Hammond, Frank Darvall, Malcolm Thomis, Robert Reid, Eric Hobsbawm, E. P. Thompson, George Rudé, John Dinwiddy, Craig Calhoun, John Bohstedt, John Rule, Adrian Randall, Alan Brooke and Lesley Kipling, Kirkpatrick Sale, and Brian Bailey. As a result of the historians' monopoly on Luddism, students of the events of 1811 through 1817 tend to understand the machine wreckers primarily as historical, economic, and political creatures (although this last designation is hotly contested). With few exceptions (Hammond and Hammond and Thompson most prominent among them), historians do not consider the Luddites as rhetoricians or, in the most extreme contrast, as writers of verse as well as swingers of hammers. Despite the influence of the linguistic turn upon historical and social studies, scholars typically fail to examine the writings for rhetorical qualities. My intention in compiling this book is to give a linguistic and rhetorical face to the Luddites, to let them speak for themselves, insofar as the passing of time has spared their writings.

Thus, this book is not a work of history but rather of rhetoric and textual recovery. By collecting and studying Luddite writing in its rhetorical, regional, and temporal variety, it provides readers with the means to consider Luddism through the words of the Luddites themselves, not just through the words of those authorities who reported on Luddism, even as they endeavored to suppress it. This book's concern with the rhetorical appeals, models, and values underlying the Luddite discontent distinguishes it from previous treatments by historians, who frequently read Luddism as a series of events either flowing to or from some point of economic or historical significance.[8] That limited mode of reading is made possible by historiographical views that acknowledge the existence of Luddite writing but treat it as if it were secondary evidence at best or, at worst, little more than silence—in John Bohstedt's words, the expression of "a rage of impotence."[9]

Writing to Huddersfield magistrate Joseph Radcliffe, Colonel Thomas Norton describes the behavior of Luddites hanged at York Castle during the first two weeks of 1812. Making a leap of judgment, Norton interprets the silence of the condemned men and, in doing so, reveals the consequences of the erroneous perception or construction of Luddite "silence":

> You know how the three Murderers died, and the five Men for Rawfold's Mill died precisely the same. The Chaplain told them it was his Duty to entreat them to confess. They *were silent*. He then told them he should take their *Silence* as confessions. They were still Silent on that Subject, but spoke Generally of their Sins. Thus in Fact tacitly allowing their Guilt as to the Offence they died for, but not doing so in Words. . . . Nor was one Word said by their People.[10]

Silence had economic and juridical consequences for the textile workers of the English Midlands and North who suffered from and resisted the use of machinery to drive down wages and to displace highly skilled laborers from their trades. Colonel Norton, for example, believed that he had discovered in the selective silence of the hanged Luddites a tacit confession of guilt, free of negotiation or qualification. Norton selected a silence and thereby neglected to notice what others who observed the hangings had noticed—that George Mellor, one of the three convicted Luddites, forgave his enemies in the crowd and wished them peace.[11]

Luddite silence has also had historical consequences in how the disaffected textile workers have been portrayed and in how their actions have been interpreted. My choosing in the opening pages of this book to resort to the words of one of those authorities who was engaged in suppressing the Luddite risings,

Colonel Norton, is emblematic and symptomatic of the historical consequences of Luddite silence.

In the field of meaning left vacant by the constructed silence of the Luddites, many historical and popular works distort Luddite intentions according to twentieth-century ideational preferences, in the same way that contemporary authorities interpreted them according to the fears, desires, and theories prevailing in Britain during the Regency period. One result has been a sort of critical cannibalism in which historians of Luddism and British labor movements feed on their own. E. P. Thompson, J. L. Hammond and Barbara Hammond, Malcolm Thomis, and others, despite their foundational work on Luddism and their pioneering research in the Home Office Papers (the single most valuable archive for studying Luddism), all have been taken to task in a series of disputes over the structure of history. The disputants have employed Luddism as an occasion or a moment for those disputes. John Rule, in his excellent introductory study, *The Labouring Classes in Early Industrial England, 1750–1850*, traces the disputes but fails to mention, except briefly, that few of the successive critics have added much in the way of archival materials to the debate over Luddism. Rule himself pays little attention to the Luddites' own writing.

All of the liberties, interpretations, and distortions are made possible by an uncritical acceptance of a dearth of Luddite texts—that is, by the construction of silence through historical strategies of ignoring, reducing, or rendering curious or impotent those Luddite texts that are known to exist. But the Luddites were not silent. They did not write for a historical record, and there is no indication that they believed that their words would outlast their purpose, but they were not silent. Although the Luddites did not produce the same quantity of letters, proclamations, reports, and reward notices as did the magistrates, army officers, spies, and manufacturers who opposed them and wrote about them, they did write and left a record of their values, perceptions, methods, and struggle.

This book is an attempt to gather into one volume those texts that fall along a continuous thread that we might designate "Luddite" and critically, though incompletely, to reconstruct some of the contexts within which Luddite rhetoric operated between the years 1811 and 1817. Insofar as is possible, I have attempted to place my own rhetorical interpretations at a distance from the Luddite documents themselves; nevertheless, I recognize that any attempt to sketch the discursive and historical contexts against which a reader might better understand each document is necessarily theorized. I hope that rhetorical and literary scholars in particular will scrutinize and correct any errors and inadequacies in contextualization that may have resulted from my own theoretical presuppositions.

LUDDISM has inspired a small but important body of scholarship, mostly in the field of history, as the following brief bibliographical sketch will indicate. One of the earliest accounts is Francis Raynes's *An Appeal to the Public, Containing an Account of Services Rendered during the Disturbances in the North of England in the year 1812* (1817), an account written largely but not entirely from the firsthand experience of Captain Raynes in leading troops who suppressed Luddism in the North. His account is useful for understanding Luddism from the perspective of an army officer, but it is limited to that single perspective and further limited by Raynes's choice to concentrate only upon the events of 1812 and 1813 in the North.

Other firsthand accounts appear in larger histories of trades in the regions. Gravener Henson's two-volume *History of the Framework-Knitting and Lace Trades* (1831) and William Felkin's *A History of the Machine-Wrought Hosiery and Lace Manufacturers* (1867) make brief mention of Luddism in the framework knitting trade and are useful for placing the protests within the context of the long history of trade relations and customs; however, the works treat only Midlands Luddism.

Secondhand histories began to be published in the late 1800s. The most famous is Francis Peel's *The Risings of the Luddites, Chartists and Plug-drawers* (1880). Peel's history has been criticized for its creative use of dialogue, but the work continues to be used as an important resource for understanding Luddism in the West Riding woolen industry. Shortly after Peel's work, D. F. E. Sykes and G. H. Walker published *Ben O' Bill's, The Luddite: A Yorkshire Tale*, a work that crosses boundaries between history and historical fiction. Like Raynes's *Appeal*, *Ben O' Bill's* concentrates solely on Luddism. Like Peel's *Risings of the Luddites*, *Ben O' Bill's* gives a dramatic account of the events surrounding the attack on Rawfolds Mill, but it could also be criticized for some creative liberties. Another work of local history, but in a documentary tradition, John Russell's article titled "The Luddites," gathered Luddite texts from the collection of papers in the estate of Richard Enfield, Nottingham Town Clerk after George Coldham.

In 1919 J. L. Hammond and Barbara Hammond published *The Skilled Labourer*, a work of British labor history that includes what is probably the first history of Luddism to be based on documentary evidence. They make excellent use of the Home Office Papers, still the best single archive for the study of Luddism. They also are the first writers to analyze Luddism region by region, thereby setting the tone for scholarship for the rest of the twentieth century. Although indebted to Hammond and Hammond, subsequent scholars have pointed out their interpretational bias, which includes a tendency to treat the Luddites as protounionists and to dissociate Luddism from revolutionary conspiracy and violence against persons.

Frank Darvall's *Popular Disturbances and Public Order in Regency England* (1934) is another history that places Luddism within a larger social context and uses documentary evidence. Though basic, Darvall's history is useful as an attempt to examine Luddism as a public, civil phenomenon. His history presaged later scholarly studies of Luddism as riot.

From the late 1950s through the 1970s, historical interest in Luddism increased. One documentary history, David Douglas's two-volume *English Historical Documents 1783–1832* (1959), contains some writing by Luddites and by textile workers bent on organizing to protect the trade and petition for parliamentary relief. Douglas's collection is selective and contains many errors in transcription, but it introduced culturally interested historians to the vast quantity of Luddite materials. More traditional works of history followed. In *Primitive Rebels* (1959), Eric Hobsbawn examined the Luddites as popular forces who sought to express grievances through means that twentieth-century scholars understood to be reactionary. In *Labouring Men* (1964), Hobsbawm treated the Luddites as part of a nascent working-class movement. Hobsbawm attempts to bridge a gap between labor history and Darvall's study of Luddism as public disturbance by developing the often cited term "collective bargaining by riot."

The most important treatment of Luddism from the mid-twentieth century comprises several sections of E. P. Thompson's *The Making of the English Working Class* (1963). Thompson places the Luddites in a line of development of working-class consciousness that had both economic and political components and was manifested in lawful and violent ways. Like Hammond and Hammond, Thompson makes a great deal of use of the documentary evidence available in a variety of archives. Unlike Hammond and Hammond, Thompson seems quite ready to accept that Luddism was part of an underground, but probably not nationwide, radical movement. Thompson's apparent readiness to welcome that possibility prompted a reply from Malcolm Thomis in his 1970 book, *The Luddites: Machine-Breaking in Regency England*. In *The Luddites*, Thomis makes a convincing case that Luddism was not a conspiratorial movement and that it lacked a clear leadership. Thomis's documentary history, *Luddism in Nottinghamshire*, followed soon after, in 1972. It draws heavily, even comprehensively, on the Home Office Papers, but Thomis only considers Luddism in the Midlands and overlooks other archival sources.

After the publication of Thomis's *The Luddites*, several books tried to popularize the history of Luddism. These include Douglas Liversidge's *The Luddites: Machine-Breakers of the Early Nineteenth Century* (1972), John Zerzan and Paula Zerzan's very brief overview *The Luddites: A History of Machine Breaking at the Dawn of Capitalism* (1976), Angela Bull's *The Machine-Breakers: A Story of the Luddites* (1980), and Laura Salvatori's *Luddism: A Revolution That Failed* (1983). None of the works contains much original research, and Bull's and Liversidge's books are aimed at a youth audience.

In a 1979 article, "Luddism and Politics in the Northern Counties," and a 1986 book, *From Luddism to the First Reform Bill*, John Dinwiddy makes the clearest attempt yet to locate Luddism accurately within a broader context of political action and the increasing awareness of the need for political action among the working classes at the time. Dinwiddy's work is important for its demonstration of the linguistic similarities between Luddism and Radicalism and for it cautious treatment in distinguishing real links for cases where only similarities exist. Dinwiddy sees Luddite politics as more reformist than revolutionary.

Two other works from 1986 examine Luddism in vastly different ways. John Rule's *The Labouring Classes in Early Industrial England, 1750–1850* contains an overview of prior histories of Luddism and an evaluation of those histories. Rule cautiously approves Thompson's interpretation of Luddism for its being in accord with popular tradition. Robert Reid's *Land of Lost Content: The Luddite Revolt, 1812* is a study of Luddism in the West Riding that draws primarily on the same resources as other histories in reaching a conclusion that heralds much of the late twentieth century's understanding of Luddism. Reid concludes that amid contradictory evidence of broader labor organization and local resentments, only one factor stands out as a cause of Luddism—the widespread and systematic use of technology. Reid's work heralds the most recent trend in the study of Luddism, interpreting it as a reaction against technological innovation and the incorporation of new technology into what had previously been manual trades.

Craig Calhoun's *The Question of Class Struggle: Social Foundations of Popular Radicalism during the Industrial Revolution* (1982) and John Bohstedt's *Riots and*

Community Politics in England and Wales, 1790–1810 (1983) initiated a trend toward understanding Luddism as a community phenomenon. Both authors examine the ways in which Luddism results from tensions manifested in local contexts with particular social structures and traditions. Both works are important examples of what can be done within the current field of cultural studies, but both works have limitations. Calhoun makes less use of primary documents than Bohstedt, and Bohstedt concentrates only upon Manchester. Neither writer pays much attention to actual Luddite writing.

Adrian Randall's *Before the Luddites* (1991) continues the trend toward localizing interpretation but Randall does not assume community as the operant locale. Rather, he treats Luddism in the woolen industry by considering the differences between trade structures in the West Country and Yorkshire. Randall's history is among the most important works of labor history in recent years, and he makes extensive use of primary sources, but his purpose is not to study Luddism proper but rather the pre-Luddite machine breaking in the West Country.

Liberty or Death: Radicals, Republicans, and Luddites, 1793–1823, by Alan Brooke and Lesley Kipling, examines Yorkshire Luddism as a part of a larger study of labor and radicalism in the decades following the French Revolution. Brooke and Kipling make good use of primary documents relevant to Luddism and quote from many of them, but presenting a large collection of Luddite texts from all Luddite regions is not part of their project.

For nearly twenty-five years after Thomis's *The Luddites,* no comprehensive treatment of Luddism itself was produced. In the 1990s, two writers undertook the task. Kirkpatrick Sale's *Rebels against the Future: The Luddites and Their War on the Industrial Revolution* (1995) examines Luddism across all regions. Sale quotes extensively from primary documents, particularly Luddite texts; however, *Rebels against the Future* advances the thesis that Luddism is primarily an antitechnology movement, and it ignores some Luddite texts that express wider grievances. In other words, a reader will find a rather narrow, albeit interesting, view of Luddism in Sale's book. Unfortunately, Sale has contributed to the very narrow perception of Luddites as technophobes—a misconception that has defined Luddism in popular and business periodicals and on Internet sites for the past decade.

Brian Bailey's 1998 *The Luddite Rebellion* is the most complete chronological study to date, though not a documentary history. Bailey concludes his study by denying that Luddism had a political agenda, reaffirming George Rudé's earlier remark in *The Crowd in History: A Study of Popular Disturbances in France and En-*

gland, 1730–1848 that politics was not intrinsic to Luddism but rather was intrusive. Besides exemplifying the condescension of history about which Thompson warned later generations of scholars, Bailey's conclusion is based on his assumption that politics means macropolitics. He attempts to chart the differences between Luddism in the different regions, but he lacks the sense of politics and protest as local, an approach that Calhoun and Bohstedt had already proved valuable.

Prior to Sale's *Rebels against the Future* and Bailey's *The Luddite Rebellion*, the trend in the study of Luddism had been toward considering the importance of communities in shaping or employing discourses that occurred across several communities and regions. This volume uses documentary evidence to continue that trend by demonstrating the varieties of discourse within the different Luddite regions. The volume contains texts that suggest that Luddism emerged in different regions as a labor movement uniquely suited to the exigencies of the affected trades in the different regions between 1811 and 1817 and shaped by the discourses prevalent in those regions. Furthermore, while presenting documentary sources region by region, this volume also expands the study of Luddism by considering the rhetorical influences and devices employed by the Luddites and their sympathizers.

ALTHOUGH THE HISTORIES that I have surveyed here range from adequate to excellent and are readily available, a brief, historical overview of Luddism is in order. The Luddites were artisans—primarily skilled workers in the textile industries in Nottinghamshire, Derbyshire, Leicestershire, Cheshire, the West Riding of Yorkshire, and Lancashire—who, when faced with the replacement of their own skilled labor by machines and the use of machines (operated by less-skilled labor) to drive down wages by producing inferior goods, turned to wrecking the offensive machines in order to preserve their jobs and their trades. This is not to say that the Luddites were the only machine wreckers. Because organized, large-scale strikes were impractical due to the scattering of manufactories throughout different regions, machine wrecking, which E. J. Hobsbawm calls "collective bargaining by riot," had occurred in Britain since the Restoration.[12] For example, in 1675 Spitalfields narrow weavers destroyed "engines," power machines that could each do the work of several people, and in 1710 a London hosier employing too many apprentices in violation of the Framework Knitters Charter had his machines broken by angry stockingers.[13]

Even parliamentary action in 1727, making the destruction of machines a capital felony, did little to stop the activity. In 1768 London sawyers attacked a mechanized sawmill. Following the failure in 1778 of the stockingers' petitions to Parliament to enact a law regulating "the Art and Mystery of Framework Knitting," Nottingham workers rioted, flinging machines into the streets. In 1792 Manchester weavers destroyed two dozen Cartwright steam looms owned by George Grimshaw. Sporadic attacks on machines (wide knitting frames, gig mills, shearing frames, and steam-powered looms and spinning jennies) continued, especially from 1799 to 1802 and through the period of economic distress after 1808.[14]

The first incident during the years of the most intense Luddite activity, 1811–13, was the 11 March 1811 attack upon wide knitting frames in a shop in the Nottinghamshire village of Arnold, following a peaceful gathering of framework knitters near the Exchange Hall at Nottingham. In the preceding month, framework knitters, also called stockingers, had broken into shops and removed jack wires from wide knitting frames, rendering them useless without inflicting great violence upon the owners or incurring risk to the stockingers themselves; the 11 March attack was the first in which frames were actually smashed. The grievances consisted, first, of the use of wide stocking frames to produce large amounts of cheap, shoddy stocking material that was cut and sewn rather than completely fashioned and, second, of the employment of "colts," workers who had not completed the seven-year apprenticeship required by law.[15]

Frames continued to be broken in many of the villages surrounding Nottingham. The *Nottingham Journal of* 23 March 1811 and 20 April 1811 reports several weeks of almost nightly attacks in the villages, all successful and carried out without the arrest of any attackers. The summer of 1811 was quiet, but a bad harvest helped to renew disturbances in November, when, as the story goes, stockingers assembled in the wooded lands near Bulwell and were led in attacks on a number of shops by a commander calling himself Ned Ludd.[16]

Letters from correspondents in the region to the Home Office report a number of riotous disturbances, including the burning of haystacks and "an anonymous letter received by a Magistrate threatening still greater acts of violence by fire."[17] Letters dated 13 and 14 November 1811 request that the government dispatch military aid because "2000 men, many of them armed, were riotously traversing the County of Nottingham." In December 1811 public negotiations between the framework knitters and their employers, the hosiers, some of which were carried out in the two Nottingham newspapers, failed to result in the return of wages, piece rates, and frame rents to earlier levels or in any satisfactory amelioration of the framework knitters' economic circumstances.[18] Frame breaking continued in the Midlands counties of Nottinghamshire, Derbyshire, and Leicestershire through the winter and early spring of 1812. It resurfaced in 1814 and again in Leicestershire in the autumn of 1816.

The first signs of the spread of Luddism to the cotton-manufacturing center of Manchester and its environs in Lancashire and Cheshire materialized in December 1811 and January 1812. Manchester Luddism was centered on the cotton-weaving trade, which had failed in an attempt to organize in 1808, and which was suffering from the use of steam-powered looms to decrease the wages of skilled weavers at a time of rising food prices and depressed trade. In Manchester, unlike Nottingham, the offensive machinery was housed in large factories. Luddite raids in and around Manchester tended to be carried out by large numbers of attackers and also often coincided with food riots, which provided crowds that were large enough to carry out the factory attacks and that came from a broadly distressed population ready to take action. Luddite activity continued in Lancashire and Cheshire into the summer of 1812 and blended into efforts to establish larger trade combinations and into political reform.

The factory owners and cloth merchants of the woolen industry in the West Riding of Yorkshire were the targets of Luddism in that county. Although West Riding Luddites represented a variety of skilled trades, the most active and numerous by far were the cloth dressers, called croppers, whose work was threatened by the introduction of the shearing frame. The croppers' work consisted of using forty- or fifty-pound handheld shears to cut, or crop, the nap from woven woolen cloth in order to make a smooth and salable article. They were threatened by two types of machines. The gig mill, which had been prohibited by law since the rule of Edward VI, was a machine that raised the nap on woolen cloth so that it might be sheared more easily. The shearing frames actually mechanized the process of shearing and reduced the level of skill and experience necessary to finish an article of woolen cloth, even though the machines could not attain the quality of hand-cropped cloth. From January 1812 through midspring, Luddite attacks in Yorkshire concentrated on small cropping shops as well as large mills where frames were used. In April Luddites began to attack mill owners and raided houses and buildings for arms and lead.

In all three regions, Luddites responded to the distressing concurrence of high food prices, depressed trade caused by the wars and by the trade prohibitions imposed under the Orders in Council, and changes in the use of machinery so as to reduce wages for the amount of work done. Luddite activities ended as a result of the rescinding of the Orders in Council, the suppression of the riots by the government's use of spies and the military, some wage and usage concessions, and some reduction in food prices.

I have said that I would like to avoid overtheorizing in treating the writings of the Luddites. At the same time, however, I have discovered, guided by the work of a number of scholars, that Luddite writing is best considered not as a totality but rather as a set of discourses generated under unique local circumstances. Four scholars in particular, working in three different disciplines, have developed approaches that guided me through my decision to arrange the texts by region and to discover in the following sections the local discursive circumstances that generated Luddite writing in each region.

In a chapter titled "Community in the Southeast Lancashire Textile Region," Craig Calhoun writes:

> Different sorts of communities were apt to be involved in different agitations, and involved in agitation to different degrees. This was partly because of the different strengths of social and material resources which they could bring to the support of their action, partly because of the different trades which gave their members economic interests, and partly because of the different social values which gave the members of those trades moral interests in one or another kind of agitation.[19]

Calhoun's examination of local custom as the basis of the formation of social structures that we eventually came to understand as class has influenced later considerations of Luddism, such as Adrian Randall's. Working at much the same time and in the same vein as Calhoun, John Bohstedt applied the idea of localization to his study of riots as events emerging from unique structures of community politics.[20]

Luddite language is quite varied. Dealing with that variety and the often contradictory discourses subscribed by the name of Ludd would be a difficult task but for the historical and literary models set out by Adrian Randall and John Mee. Randall argues that apparently contradictory forms of discourse in the resistance against machinery need not be compartmentalized: "These forms were in no way mutually exclusive. . . . Different methods were adopted singly or in combination as and when deemed appropriate both in the particular context obtaining at any one time and in the general context of that community's tradition and experience of previous conflicts of a similar kind."[21] Randall anticipates very important work by John Mee, who utilizes a version of Claude Lévi-Strauss's concept of *bricolage* to portray William Blake as a writer who, for practical reasons, appropriates and employs contradictory discourses, much like other working-class radicals and autodidacts.[22]

David Worrall has extended localization to the study of romantic-period discourse in his book *Radical Culture*. Worrall's structuralist method proves quite useful in examining the Luddite texts and reclaiming them from the margins of history. Worrall's most important lessons, I think, are that "there are no discursively marginal figures in *Radical Culture*" and that "Every ultra-radical utterance is already fully constituted elsewhere within the culture of its specific language system: there are no soliloquies."[23] Such ideas have made it easier for me to consider what the repeatability of Midlands Luddite discourse in the Northwest and Yorkshire means to the Luddites in those regions.

I say earlier that Luddism is generated not by conspiracy or the sudden emergence of class consciousness but rather by a single, forceful act of naming—the creation and appropriation of the eponym "Ned Ludd." Of course, in order to be just to the Luddite writers and keeping in mind the lessons of particularizing historians and cultural scholars, I must emphasize here that the forceful act of naming meant different things to writers in the different regions. In Nottinghamshire, Ned Ludd was a force generated wholly from within the framework knitting trade that perceived itself as constituted and sanctioned, although threatened. In Manchester, Ludd was a fairly unified set of resistances that could provide a focus for constituting new laboring populations in the cotton trades into a cohesive body capable of expressing its will to industrialists and a magistracy that sought to keep it unconstituted and weak. In Yorkshire's West Riding, General Ludd was a combination of law and local power that could be mapped onto a trade that recently had lost its statutory protections but that had not yet become impotent. The remainder of this introductory chapter examines the primary discursive features in the three Luddite regions and the unique characteristics that led to the varied significance of the eponym "Ludd" in the different regions.

Early in his book *Radical Expression*, James Epstein recounts one side of an exchange between Thomas Paine and Edmund Burke. In *The Rights of Man*, Paine demands of Burke a clear enunciation of "the Constitution." Defining a constitution as "a thing *antecedent* to government," Paine protests in the form of a question: "Can then Mr. Burke produce the English Constitution? If he cannot, we may fairly conclude, that though it has been so much talked about, no such thing as a constitution exists, or ever did exist, and consequently that the people have yet a constitution to form."[24]

The appeal to "the Constitution" was a master trope during much of the long eighteenth century. The Whig interpretation of history, which Herbert Butterfield demonstrates did much to unify a dangerously diverse English society, has obscured from the view of twentieth-century scholars the existence of a number of English subcultures with constitutive codes of their own, not isolated from the larger culture but rather paralleling and intersecting it. Constitutive rhetoric extended far beyond the argumentative appeals of the usual suspects—the Whigs, Tories, Jacobins, and Radicals, whose narratives are typically reproduced as the history of Great Britain during revolutionary, Napoleonic, industrial, and Reform eras. The subcultures grounded their claims, whether innovative or resistant, upon constitutive codes that gathered and named a collective body.

Some scholars have begun to note this diversity of codes, and the search for diversity has almost come to replace the latter-day whiggist search for unity. These scholars include Craig Calhoun in his reevaluation of Thompson's *Making of the English Working Class;* Iain MacCalman in his reconstruction of the "radical underworld" of revolutionary-era London; David Worrall in his discovery of the circulation and recombination of Spencean and other radical texts in the context of governmental surveillance; John Mee in his application of Claude Lévi-Strauss's concept of *bricolage* to William Blake's use of a variety of radical and millenarian discourses; and the contributors to James Vernon's *Re-reading the Constitution*, an effort to bring postmodern narrative approaches to bear upon nineteenth-century debates over the English "constitution."

Calhoun, for instance, recognizes the diversity and identifies community, in its local particularity, as "the crucial social bond unifying workers" during the early years of the industrial revolution.[25] Although many of the "reactionary radicals," as Calhoun calls them, were community-oriented, we ought not to ignore the codes, transcending and transecting communities, that constituted various groups—even those which cannot be subsumed under the term "reactionary radicals." Each of these groups sought validation in its own particular constitutive experiences, and these experiences derived from a larger mass of cultural values and presumably shared experiences. For example, the Whig government and its historians sought validation in the Glorious Revolution; the Yorkshire Movement sought it in Alfred the Great and the "ancient constitution"; the Tory-turned-Radical journalist, William Cobbett, sought it in the mores of his childhood, mores that defined an individual's relationship to the land.

Nevertheless, motives and occasions to innovate or resist, as well as the discourses that express or narrate those motives in action, are not created in or appropriated into a vacuum. Furthermore, motives and occasions have increasingly come to be understood as local, especially since Thompson's empirical-left perspective has come to define the study of eighteenth- and nineteenth-century British culture. The study of Althusserian structures, so well exposed by Thompson in *The Poverty of Theory*, has been supplanted by nontotalizing studies of narratives, voices, customs (even those held "in common"), and "community politics." Some of the historical and discursive studies mentioned in the previous section—the work of Calhoun, Bohstedt, Randall, Worrall, Mee, and Janowitz, for example—have been especially important to undo the damage done by totalization. They have revealed historical and discursive realities that are transgressive, contradictory, bifurcated, and embedded in local culture.

This section considers the utilization of constitutive discourses in the texts of resistance of the Midlands Luddites in ways that cross boundaries of law, custom, community, and trade. Like the discourses that Mee and Worrall examine, Luddite rhetoric is transgressive, mutant, and hybridizing; nevertheless, Luddite writing seeks and assumes a constitutive ground and makes use of originary documents, texts that create a myth of origins and impart legitimacy to the framework knitting trade and to activities undertaken in its defense. In short, I argue that the writers of the Luddite movement assume a model of selective culture that enables them to avail themselves of a text-oriented language of origination and constitution that parallels the language employed by radicals of the period and enables them to apply it as a metaphor for advancing their own local cause.

Like other groups, the textile workers of the English Midlands and North based both their daily vocational practices and their breaking of the machinery that was being used to drive down wages and produce cloth of inferior quality upon a group foundation—the customs of "the Trade," which Trade often takes the form of a governing body, both in its legitimate and covert forms. A Luddite letter from Nottingham (M13) illustrates such a trade discourse: "I do hereby discharge all Persons what soever from takeing out work called the Single Preess, or the two Coarse ole which is condemn by Law, any Persons Found so doing to the great----injuries of our Trade." The "Single Preess, or the two Coarse ole" was a type of knitting that produced an inferior article of hosiery or gloves that unraveled and lost its shape. The reputation of the entire trade, including that part of the trade that did not produce the two-course hole, would have suffered by association with the disreputable producers. The writer of the letter assumes the weal of the trade to be deserving of legal protection, and injuries to it, such as inferior knitting practices like the two course hole, are actionable under law. The existence of the Charter of the Company of Framework Knitters provided a memorial of legal origins for the stocking trade and allowed it to build its own constitutive texts, such as wage agreements and the Company Rule Books, on that foundation. Furthermore, the charter and the additional texts were interpreted and expanded according to custom and trade usage, along the lines of the model of "customary legality," a practice described by Adrian Randall in which custom interprets law.[26]

Custom provided the practical, everyday foundation for the framework knitting trade. It governed what knitting techniques ought to be employed, how journeymen and small masters negotiated for wages with hosiers and large masters, and how frame rents would be set. Although custom helped to ground the culture that gave rise to Luddism and defined its codes, in their writings the Luddites did not appeal merely to the customary, or to what J. G. A. Pocock calls "the immemorial."[27] Rather, they often sought validation for custom itself. Calhoun has argued that the "Luddite phenomenon was a movement which grew directly out of local community roots."[28] Indeed, custom does play a role in communal endeavors; however, in the case of the Nottinghamshire Luddites in particular, custom was extracommunal, in terms both of "origin" (if that word retains any significance) and of extension, evident in the texts produced by protesting workers in the stocking trade from 1811 through 1812—texts that have been consulted too infrequently.

Often, the Luddite writers sought validation for custom itself in originary documents of sorts. These documents served a "constitutional" purpose for the textile trades and, ironically, were created by Paine's "unconstitutional" English government. They include statutes regulating the trades by prohibiting colting, which is the hiring of workers who had not completed apprenticeships within a trade (5 Elizabeth cap. 4), prohibiting the use of the gig mill (5 & 6 Edward VI cap. 22), and limiting the number of looms any weaver could possess (2 & 3 Philip and Mary cap. 11).[29] In probably the best example of such validation, the framework knitters or stockingers, who launched the Luddite protests in Nottingham in 1811, justified their actions by referring to their own originary or constitutive charter, the 1663 Charter of the Company of Framework Knitters.[30] Previously, scholars had believed that no copy of the charter existed, so little consideration has been given to the derivation of codes from the charter and similar documents. However, inspection of copies of the charter, which are available in London's Guildhall Library archives and in the Report of the Select Committee on Petitions of the Framework Knitters, makes it possible to supplement what we already know of the framework knitters' primary constitutive document through the company's *Rule Book* (derived from the charter) and through the historical work of Gravener Henson, William Felkin, and J. D. Chambers.[31]

Although the charter founds a particular trade community, the extracommunal character of the charter is evident in two facts about it. First, by its origin in the seventeenth century and by its extension during the period of Nottingham Luddism, the charter and its derivative discourses were English nationalistic documents. Through the charter, the company was established to protect the English stocking industry against transplantation to foreign shores. Early attempts at transplantation almost smack of "industrial treason." William Lee, the inventor of the knitting loom, had removed his own frames and artisans to France, although most returned to England after his death. Other Britons conspired with foreign states to capture the industry—Henry Mead and Southcot Vaymouth with Venice, and Abraham Jones with Holland.[32] The charter and the Worshipful Company's rules provide for the punishment of such offenders. Furthermore, the most constitutionally "refined" of the trades that produced Luddism, Midlands framework knitting, was also the least insurrectionist. Founded to preserve an English industry, the charter perhaps tempered any revolutionary fervor that might otherwise have pulled Midlands Luddism outside of its nationalistic and legal-regulatory bounds. For instance, Midlands Luddism did not consistently produce Jacobinical threats in the way that Yorkshire Luddism—which lacked founding documents and a formal, document-based trade organization—

did from its beginning, as we find in a leaflet (Y4) distributed in Yorkshire early in 1812, in which "General Ludd Commander of the Army of Redressers" calls upon "all Croppers, Weavers &c & Public at large . . . to shake off the hateful Yoke of a Silly Old Man."

A revolutionary style in the Yorkshire proclamation is clear in both the substance of the argument ("crush the old Government & establish a new one") and in the totalizing tenor of the salutation, which combines into a single ideological entity ("Generous Countrymen") the interests of particular trades ("all Croppers, Weavers") with a general and unbounded "&c & Public at large." Although it would be difficult to demonstrate that the framework knitters' charter had a moderating influence on Nottinghamshire Luddism, I think that it is sufficient to demonstrate that moderation characterized the ludding of the framework knitters, who had a document that instituted, organized, and provided for the regulation of their trade and the addressing of grievances. In contrast, the more violent and insurrectionary croppers of West Yorkshire had no constitutive document and only one protectionist document—the very specific statute prohibiting the use of the gig mill. And that statute had been repealed in 1809.

Second, the codes and values embodied in the charter had been carried from London, the center of stocking manufacture in the seventeenth and early eighteenth centuries, to Nottingham and other Midlands communities during the middle and late eighteenth century. The masters and assistants in the stocking trade were aware of *national*, and not just communal, issues facing the trade. Migration from one community to another was one method by which the knitters participated in the new industrial economy, but the charter moved with them from one community to others and was invoked periodically as the binding force of the trade.

The charter is unusual as a constitutive document in that it designates economic (and what amount to legal and political) operants through the dispensation of King Charles II. The Luddites, however, do not necessarily appeal to the dispensation of the king but rather to the charter itself. We cannot know to what extent they may have been concerned about the risks inhering in what might appear to be a Jacobite appeal (the Stuart line having been deposed in the 1688 Revolution); it simply is beside the point. What is to the point is that the Luddites continued to locate their founding document in what was a living context linking their present to their past through a moral economy that was recognized and chartered by a king and empowered to regulate and sustain itself.

The nature of self-regulatory power is evident in the charter and the company's *Rule Book* and has also been outlined by J. L. Hammond and Barbara Hammond and by Chambers. Among the most important mechanisms were those specifically authorizing search, supervision, and legal standing to ensure quality of work. There were also mechanisms for prosecuting those selling substandard goods or undercutting prices, for licensing apprentices, and for preventing the flow to the continent of workers and machines.[33] As recently as 1808, the company brought a claim, decided at King's Bench favorably to the company, against William Payne, who had set up shop without being a freeman of the trade.[34] Both Henson and Chambers note the national-protectionist intentions underlying the charter. The mingling of trade, legal, and national-political languages and purposes in the charter make it interesting as a discourse event. Most important, its multiple purposes seem to have facilitated its use as law against law and its use to justify the violent breaking of the objectionable wide stocking frames used to drive down wages and produce inferior material—especially hosiery articles that were flimsy or lost their shape.

Trade claims were pursued through other avenues, too. In 1805 and 1809 the stockingers had negotiated higher piece rates with the large hosiers who employed them, and in 1811 Nottingham and Melbourne knitters wrote letters to the *Nottingham Review* reminding the hosiers of the earlier agreements.[35] Stockingers also asked hosiers for advice in petitioning Parliament. By 1813, after Parliament passed legislation prohibiting frame breaking and repealing many of the earlier laws that had constituted the codes of the Luddite subculture, the textile workers joined other artisans (unsuccessfully) to petition Parliament not to repeal the Elizabethan statute (5 Elizabeth cap. 4) that fixed apprenticeships at seven years and prohibited colting.[36] But the charter itself had established a system of self-regulation, running beside and sometimes intersecting (but usually not threatening) the larger legal system.

The charter was not merely a political document conferring legal rights over property to the knitters. Even the independent artisans working in the moral economy did not *own*, in an ordinary sense, the materials that were produced into cloth; the regulatory powers held by the Framework Knitters' Company are evidence of this. Each knitter did, however, have an *investment* in those materials by virtue of the charter. In this case, economic power and accompanying legal rights derive from a political assignation.[37] Often, the legal and trade languages are blended almost seamlessly, like the sketch of a gallows and the mention of the stocking frame in a March 1812 letter (M23) from "Genaral Lud's" headquarters to George Rowbottom, a Nottinghamshire hosier.

To investigate Luddite conceptions of trade law and societal law and the formation of a discourse of political and economic power, we might consider the legalistic vocabulary of stockinger self-regulation as it appears in a number of documents. Luddite declarations are especially good examples of the Luddites' appropriation of official discourse, repeated in the course of transforming the moral economy into a moral-economic polity.[38]

Although frame wrecking seems not to have taken place in Nottinghamshire between March and November 1811, it appears from the 1 January 1812 document titled "By the Framework Knitters, A Declaration" (M10) and the November 1811 "Declaration; Extraordinary" posted by "Thos Death" to "Edward Ludd" (M1) that a Luddite subculture had been forming and devising its own language of origination and continuation, despite the lull. The January "Declaration" (M10) is the more general of the two declarations, more clearly oriented toward affirming a system with regulatory powers: "[T]he Framework knitters are empowered to break and destroy all Frames and Engines that fabricate Articles in a fraudulent and deceitful manner and to destroy all Framework knitters Goods whatsoever that are so made." The Luddite writer conceives of the power granted by the charter to be so great, perhaps for reasons of primacy or of decentralizing custom, that the framework knitters empowered by the charter can nullify even an Act of Parliament, the law that made breaking frames a capital felony, that contravenes the charter. Under this conception, power devolves to the trades and falls under the regulatory powers of custom, thereby becoming permanent and legitimating the subculture against the larger nation.

The second Nottinghamshire declaration that is also useful for understanding the formation of a Luddite culture with a discourse of legitimation and power of its own is the "Declaration; Extraordinary" (M1). One of the more remarkable features of the "Declaration; Extraordinary" is its manifesting a democratic political and juridical structure within which the assembled "General Agitators" judge the guilt of a master, determine a penalty, and charge or authorize Ludd with the execution of that penalty and the distribution of the recovered money among the workmen. Devolved power, then, is even a feature within texts structured as Luddite-to-Luddite communications.

A democratic subtext also helps to explain the nature of the Nottinghamshire Luddite "judgment." The artisan tradition had provided for the levying of fines or forfeitures (usually of finished and unfinished goods) against trade members who violated the trade's rules. The violating members typically were masters, but artisans nevertheless, hence subject to government by the society and its rules. Even during the period of increasing social and professional distance between master and artisan in the late eighteenth century and the early years of the nineteenth, made possible by increased mechanization and by the replacement among the large masters of trade customs and usages by the accumulation of capital, artisans sought to enforce their rules against masters whom they still considered to be members of their society.

The language of the "Declaration; Extraordinary" is juridically legalistic; the document titled "By the Framework Knitters, A Declaration" (M10) is more political in its legalisms. Both address matters of jurisdiction, judgment, damages, forfeiture, and punishment in case of default, and the assignment of agency and surrogacy in enforcement. Although the Luddite writers did not make any direct attribution of their stylistic sources, in vocabulary and points of concern both declarations seem to be hybrids of legal and other governmental forms. Such forms were readily available within some of the established trades of the period. For example, an 1812 document, "The Articles to Be Observed by the Woolcombers," contains a number of forms, such as a "Form of an Address, To any master, or firm, who has employed men who have been divided," and a "Form of a Petition, To obtain redress of any grievances, &c." Many of the forms resemble the Luddite documents in style and vocabulary.[39]

Legal forms and models of writs and warrants for all varieties of offenses were readily available, too, in books written specifically for magistrates and clerks.[40] Another likely influence and model may have been the prince regent's "Proclamation," which was posted up and published in several newspapers in the Luddite regions:

By His Royal Highness the PRINCE OF WALES, A PROCLAMATION. *George*, P. R.

WHEREAS it has been represented that a considerable Number of disorderly Persons, chiefly composed of Stockingers . . . have for some Time past assembled themselves together in a riotous and tumultuous Manner, in the TOWN and COUNTY of the TOWN of NOTTINGHAM. . . . We, therefore, acting in the Name and on the Behalf of His Majesty, being duly sensible of the mischievous Consequences which must inevitably ensue . . .

from such wicked and illegal Practices, if they go unpunished . . . issue this Proclamation, hereby strictly commanding all Justices of the Peace, Sheriffs, Under-Sheriffs, and all other Civil Officers whatsoever, within this said Town and County of the Town of Nottingham . . . that they do use their utmost Endeavours to discover, apprehend, and bring to Justice the Persons concerned in the Riotous Proceedings above mentioned.[41]

The Luddite declarations employ not only a vocabulary similar to both the model warrant and the prince regent's proclamation but also a similar structure—a movement from representation of a grievance to rule to remedy to authorization. Even those letters making the most violent of threats, without offering the recipient an opportunity to reform or make a remedy, employ the representation formula. Henry Wood of Leicester (M34) is told that "It having been represented to me that you are one of those damned miscreants who deligh in distressing and bringing to povety those poore unhapy and much injured men called Stocking makers; now be it known unto you that I have this day issued orders for your being shot through the body with a Leden Ball." No conditions and no chance for redress are offered, but the representation formula remains intact.

Such vocabulary and structure seem to have been deliberately chosen by the Luddite writers in reliance upon the model of authority afforded by the charter, but the style depended upon the perceived power of the charter. We might contrast the style of an 1812 Nottingham letter (M15), written shortly after the stockingers had exhausted hopes of restoring the force of the charter:

> This is to inform you that if you do make any more two course Hole, you will have all your Frames broken and your Goods too, though you may think you have made your doom just I shall know how to break your frames, we will not suffer you to win the Trade will die first, if we cant do it just to night we will break them yet, and if we cant break them we can break something better and we will do it too in spite of the Devil.

The letter uses no official or legal model, makes no appeal to the charter or to negotiated prices, and is much more direct in its threat against a hosier. The document resembles much more closely the style of Yorkshire threats, which tended to rely on trade disapproval, unsanctioned by law, for its moral and persuasive force.[42]

Following the creation of the Nottingham Corporation Committee and the increased involvement of the national government in suppressing the risings, Nottinghamshire Luddism also became more political. A threatening letter sent to Prime Minister Perceval (M22), after introduction of the bill making frame breaking a capital crime, exemplifies the new Luddite tendency: "The Bill for Punish.g with death. has only to be viewd. with contempt & opposd. by measure equally strong; & the Gentlemen (who framd. it will have to repent the act: for if one mans life is Sacrificed,! blood for blood." The legal intervention was seen as a terrible affront to the charter and the devolving of juridical power to the trade, and Luddite resentment extended even to the local level. Members of juries were seen as collaborators with an enemy. In a 16 March 1812 letter (M27), a jury fore-man, Mr. Byrnny, is warned that he has been acting without the sanction thought by the Luddites to define his social duty: "[B]y Genaral Ludds Express Express Commands I am come to—worksop to enquire of your Character towards our cause and I am sory to say I find it to correspond with your conduct you latly shewed—towards us." By the time of the writing of the letter to Mr. Byrnny, the legal power of the charter had been replaced rhetorically by a "cause"; however, the structure of custom and the idea of the power to regulate economic behavior remained.

While the charter facilitated the emergence and continuation of a subcul-ture, the "official" legal and political discourses of the day provided the subcul-ture with models for its conduct and its rhetorical extension and participation in larger public life. The timing of the appearance of the two Nottinghamshire dec-larations suggests evidence of such modeling. The "Declaration; Extraordinary" (M1) uses a more focused legal vocabulary drawn, perhaps, from sources avail-able in late 1811. The January 1812 Framework Knitters' declaration (M10) pits sovereign against sovereign (Charles II against George III and the prince regent) and reward against reward, apparently parodying the prince regent's December 1811 proclamation.

The fact that the legalistic discourse appears to resemble or derive from offi-cial forms but also to contradict the official forms in intent may have caused scholars such as E. P. Thompson to concentrate their attention more on the di-rectly threatening letters as more uniquely Luddite; however, the double treat-ment of law is manifested in some other of the more familiar documents, too. One such document, the Luddite anthem "General Ludd's Triumph" (M14), is remarkable for its dual treatment of law. Early in the ballad, General Ludd is described as having "disrespect for the laws" and as outdoing Robin Hood in the material expressions of disrespect; however, later stanzas create an alternative-legal discourse—"guilty," "estate," "sentenced to die," "unanimous vote of the Trade," "executioner." We must inquire into the source of the blending of anti-legal and alternative-legal language, the blending of "Custom and Law." How, for example, did "the Trade," as an extralegal and even renegade institution, acquire the power to pass sentence? Furthermore, what role is served by the eponymic General Ludd?

First, the eponym "Ned Ludd" grows out of the framework knitters' experiences, mythic or actual. It is not, like a metonym, a gathering figure used to draw together an immaterial plurality into a material singularity. Wai Chee Dimock describes a metonym as a "a form of reduction, involving the telescoping of an immaterial order within a material embodiment."[43] The Midlands Luddite experience was very material in the sense that the mechanisms through which it was known and interpreted—the charter, the trade, and custom—were tied to the materiality of working life in an established and entrenched manner. In contrast to the metonym, the eponym expresses resentment specific to the trade, where that resentment existed. General Ludd is a singularity, but one that grows out of material existence in an almost organic sense. The eponym offers not a new gathering but rather a method of bringing renewed attention to a charter that had fallen into obscurity, perhaps even disuse. Although they needed a way to express grievances, the Midlands Luddites could not claim a new charter, but they needed new attention to the old one. The eponym provided a way of drawing that attention.

Second, at least part of the stanza is representational. We might remember the alternative governments proposed during George III's reign. These alternatives ranged from the "little senate" set up in every public house (noted in the *Leeds Mercury*, 6 March 1802) to Percy Shelley's nationwide caucus (in *A Proposal for Putting Reform to the Vote*) and Sir Charles Wolseley's "National Convention." The Luddite alternative differs from these in that the Luddites defined themselves by their trade and affirmed an already existing constitution that had been violated and corrupted by latter-day laws. Even when the force of the government caused some of the Luddite writers to rely less than before on an appeal to the charter, the style and structure of discourse emanating from the charter remained strong. The framework knitters' January 1812 "Declaration" (M10) states that the 1663 charter gives the knitters the right to break frames and further declares null and void the 1788 act making frame breaking a felony. It warns all hosiers, lace manufacturers, and frame owners that the Luddites would "break and destroy all manner of frames . . . that make spurious articles and . . . that do not pay the regular price heretofore agreed to by the Masters and Workmen. . . . [A]ll Frames of whatsoever description the Workmen of whom are not paid in the Corrent Coin of the Realm will invariably be destroyed."

Such political appeals have a dual nature, which helps us to understand the dual treatment of law in the "Triumph" and other texts. The declaration's citation of the charter suggests a self-contained and self-governing system of laws and constitutions, which must be construed as an alternative to the usurping system of laws of which the Frame-Breaking Act is part; however, another appeal is also at work. In the last sentence, the Luddite writer makes payment in the "Current Coin of the Realm" a standard of compliance. The double appeal affiliates Luddism with a legal tradition issuing from the Crown even as it exposes the abuses and injustices of a system controlled by the present government, even though the Nottingham stockingers stopped short of opposing the government itself, at least until Midlands Luddism had run through its first phase. Kenneth Brown notes, "There are no records . . . of Luddites turning against overt political targets such as town halls or magistrates' homes."[44] Yorkshire Luddism, of course, saw threats against Huddersfield magistrate Joseph Radcliffe, and Salford coroner Nathaniel Milne was threatened after he found no cause to prosecute a soldier who killed a Luddite, but generally the Midlands Luddites did not see government as enough of a threat to attack its physical structures. Rather, they seem to have thought themselves part of a culture that originated in, intersected, and at times overlapped the government. The originary appeal merely underscores the continuity of a sanctioned artisan tradition that only recently had been interrupted by industry and magistracy. In fact, even the Yorkshire song, "You Heroes of England" (Y19), in the course of attacking the industrial tyrants Cartwright and Atkinson, asserts no incompatibility between "the Rules of General Ludd" and "the laws of England."

Despite the affiliating language, the government perceived a threat in the discourse of alternative or parallel government, a perception evidenced by the words that a Home Office official wrote across the framework knitters "Declaration" (M10), saying that it "cannot be answered." It could not be answered because it was an anonymous document and was forwarded to the Home Office without an enclosing letter, but it also cannot be answered effectively in an ideological sense because it is neither entirely inside nor outside the system of English governance. Certainly, the people of the area considered the "Frame-Work Knitters Act as a protection against the *vagrant* laws."[45] Of the popular sympathy, Frank Darvall writes, "To make matters worse the population was so unanimous in sympathizing with the Luddites. No one would give evidence against them. No bystanders would stir a hand to stop the attacking parties or to warn the authorities. Many a householder in charge of the hated machinery was himself a sympathizer, if not an aider and abettor, of the attacking parties."[46] In this light, Luddism appears as a collective, perhaps even majoritarian, movement in many areas. Eventually, the government attempted to address this problem. The act of 52 George III, cap. 16, §3, extending the Act of 28 George III, cap. 55, required householders to give information of frame breaking to the frame owner and to a justice of the peace.[47] The new law had little effect. Nottinghamshire Luddism continued for a time until a number of arrests combined with a rise in wages to halt the machine breaking.[48]

By mid-1812, the continued complicity of masters and magistrates, the continued abuses on the part of the government, and the futility of collective bargaining by negotiation and riot forced even Nottingham Luddism to turn more and more to grand threats and desperate complaints. Whereas before Ned Ludd had served as the center of a discourse of moderation and constraint, yet nevertheless effective and demanding of the perceived rights of the trade, he later came to be seen in terms of an adversary, the prince regent. Nevertheless, Ludd continued to provide a discourse of morality and even patriotism, whereas the prince regent embodied and distilled all of the abuses that the Luddites found reprehensible and merited an enormous variety of threats, such as one from Nottingham (M36) written on 4 June 1812:

> The cry of your hard and unmoveable heart to the sufferings of your *Poor Starving* Subjects is gone into the eres of General Lud-Four thousand of his bravest Men (whoes lives are not worth keeping in this wretched period of your Reign) have sworn to revenge the wrongs of their countrymen and their own, if you dont stand still, and *think* and *act* differently to what you have done. . . . Take the advice of one who wishes well to his Country.

Ludd's posture in this letter is militant, but nevertheless it is restrained. Ludd seeks less to overthrow a government than to effect the repentance of the old one.

More militant documents than the letter to the regent were circulated, and can be found in the collection of Midlands texts, but the militancy typically was constrained by the figure of Ned Ludd. In one 1814 letter to the *Nottingham Review* (M44) General Ludd writes to the editor to describe the success of one of his sons, Ned, then serving His Majesty in the war against America. Part of the letter seeks to forget the troubles of the past. In fact, Ludd affiliates himself with the government, to an extent, but wields the imprimatur of his son's having served Britain against its American enemy in the recent war: "I am of opinion that all which I and my son have done in Nottingham and neighbourhood, is not half so bad as what my son has done in America; but then you now he has supreme orders, from indisputable authority, for his operations in America, and that makes all the difference."

Throughout much of its course, Midlands Luddism based its resistance to machinery on legal dispensations and the charter of their trade and devised a system of regulation that had effects both inside and outside of the trade, upon the larger culture as a whole. The 1814 letter to the *Review* illustrates what I believe characterizes many of the Midlands documents collected here—that the figure of Ned Ludd served as a discourse for concentrating public attention on a set of principles, previously sanctioned by the government but under threat at the time. Ludd is an eponym for a subculture, a selective trade culture, that grew out of a larger culture. The selected codes that founded and regulated the culture of framework knitters and facilitated its discursive extension into the larger culture were products of that larger culture. Studying the discourses of law and origination in Luddism makes clear that what the Midlands Luddites demanded was recognition by the larger culture, according to selected, but shared, codes. In the two other Luddite regions, the task proved to be different.

❖ NORTHWESTERN LUDDISM

The language of Midlands Luddism was grounded on a tradition of collective activity—specifically, the long-established trade of framework knitting, the trade's continued efforts to support wages and maintain the quality of articles, and its customary pursuit of negotiation through public mechanisms. When Luddite discourse migrated to the cotton districts of the Northwest, it did not enter a locale that was as prepared as the Midlands towns had been to incorporate a structured rhetoric of custom and law into an array of protest. It is true that Manchester and the surrounding cotton towns had their own traditions that defined Luddism in the cotton districts; however, as John Bohstedt demonstrates, the handloom weavers, whose interests were articulated most frequently in Northwestern Luddite writing, were a relatively new laboring population at the time that the Luddite risings commenced. Although they certainly had a sense of common right, they lacked the long-standing traditions of collective activity, organic identity, and social practice that would have been imparted by an ancient and communitarian trade, such as framework knitting, and would have enabled them to claim their customary rights through traditional procedures.[49]

When I speak of Northwestern Luddism, I refer to the Luddite activity in Manchester and its environs, including the cotton towns of Stockport, Oldham, Bolton, Wigan, Macclesfield, Holywell, and others. I am aware that my gathering the different Lancashire, Cheshire, and Flintshire locales under one label is misleading and reduces the effectiveness of my larger argument that Luddite discourse was locally determined; Luddism in Wigan differed from that in Stockport, for example. The smaller towns often had traditions of riot and protest that Manchester lacked, even though many of the towns shared with Manchester the same economic concerns that were causing tremendous suffering among the cotton weavers. John Foster points out that towns such as Oldham had "isolated groupings of families which provided at least some of the long-term continuity of language and direction."[50] Manchester had few such demographic traits that would have provided the kind of continuity enjoyed by Oldham and other towns; nevertheless, Manchester-area Luddism embodies a certain style that defines much of the writing in the region to such a degree that readers might be justified in considering the documents from towns in Lancashire, Cheshire, and Flintshire together (though cautiously) in terms of their shared features.

In this section, Bohstedt's theory of riot serves as the basis for an examination of the rhetoric of Northwestern Luddism. Bohstedt's theory develops the premise that riot is generated within a context of "community politics" and is defined by the presence or absence of traditions and institutions that govern collective activity and the resolution of conflicts in a particular locale. Certain communities, such as the towns in Devon with which Bohstedt illustrates his theory, had stable populations, long traditions of collective action, and community structures that facilitated negotiation. Under the "classic" model of riot exemplified in the Devon communities, negotiation was an integral part of a communal process of resolving economic, riotous disputes through the involvement of the general populace, the magistracy and constabulary, and the local gentry.[51] Although many of the components of the classic model of riot are missing in Midlands Luddism, the framework knitters of the Midlands counties can be construed as having enjoyed some of the essential institutions and features necessary for riot to progress along the lines of the classic model. Most importantly, the frame-work knitters had a long tradition of collective action through the existence since 1657 of a chartered and fairly active trade. That tradition gave them not only experience in resolving disputes but also a solidarity centered on a few clearly identifiable ideals held by the trade and clearly conveyed in the Midlands Luddite texts—adherence to negotiated wage agreements, a prohibition on the employment of unapprenticed workers, and maintenance of the stocking trade's high standards of manufacture.

Northwestern Luddism centered on the cotton handloom weaving industry, which posed special problems for popular protest. The cotton weavers of Lancashire and Cheshire were a relatively new industrial population, "recent immigrants into a new urban industrial world."[52] Bohstedt describes Manchester as a "town of strangers." Both the cotton trade and handloom weaving of cotton cloth were still recent industrial phenomena in Britain and Manchester by the beginning of the Luddite activities, but the number of weavers had grown quickly. Bythell remarks that "the recruitment of weavers for the new industry must have occurred on a massive scale" following the inventions of spinning devices and techniques in the 1770s that made possible the production of suitable cotton yarn.[53] The recent origins of the trade and the tremendous growth and migration in the Manchester region prevented the development of the stable communities necessary for traditions of popular protest to operate as they did in other parts of Britain.

What can be said about the framework knitters (and to a lesser extent the West Riding croppers)—that is, that their writing reveals that they tended to conceive of the hosiers and master clothiers as members of a trade but also as persons attempting to rise above that trade and its regulations—cannot be said of the cotton weavers. There were masters who had begun in the weaving trade, as the Middleton weaver and later Radical Samuel Bamford notes in his *Autobiography*, but cotton weavers tended to be employed by persons who had not themselves been weavers and by persons with sufficient wealth to participate on a commercial level in the cotton industry.[54] The "golden age" myths about weaving that drew so many people to the trade consisted largely of mythologized memory about high wages for people who required only a few weeks of training to become competent in the trade and of stories of a few persons who rose from weaving to manufacturing in the early years—narratives of realized potential such as those told later by William Radcliffe, who wrote that a "young man who was industrious and careful" and who had a bit of "courage" might set himself up as a manufacturer.[55] Such myths of prosperity were merely myths, according to Bythell: "The people best able to branch out on their own as manufacturers were those whose previous work had been sufficiently well-paid to allow some saving and had given them extensive and useful contacts with reliable weavers, master spinners, and merchants; warpers, reed makers, or agents and putters-out in particular, were the groups most likely to furnish aspiring new entrepreneurs."[56] The social origins of the manufacturers may have provided the basis for greater contact between weavers and manufacturers, but they also seem to have provided for greater social distance than that which existed between framework knitters and hosiers in the Midlands.

With the exception of the spinners, the cotton workers also lacked much of a union experience. The mule spinners are exceptional, having come to command an important position in the cotton industry, and have been called "an 'aristocratic' elite among members of the cotton trades."[57] They were fairly successful in forming combinations and in gaining wage concessions, but most of the cotton workers in the vicinity of Manchester had little fortune in attaining any group solidarity. The Union of Friendly Societies might have provided other Northwestern textile workers with a pattern of solidarity necessary for collective labor action, but the union (and subsequent attempts to revive it) failed before long, frustrated by the war, the Combination Acts, and fluctuations in the markets.[58] Similarly, the short-lived association formed by cotton weavers in 1799 was hindered by the passage of the Combination Acts later that year.[59] The procedures and institutions created by the Cotton Arbitration Acts made it even more difficult for cotton workers to effect any solidarity. By imposing from the outside a structure for resolving labor disputes, the acts removed from a very young industry the possibility of organic development—that is, of developing its own structures and traditions in a manner suitable to the trade and the community.[60] Even petitioning for governmental relief, a common discursive practice among weavers, would have externalized the weavers' sense of agency and efficacy.

Due to the nature of Manchester's government, the cotton weavers were also socially distanced from the magistracy. Bohstedt's account of Manchester's authority structure is instructive on this point. Manorial, parish, and commercial institutions attempted to cope with rapid growth through a set of practices unsuited to the municipality. Civic actions tended to be dictated by the interests of the propertied classes rather than by custom, patronage, or paternalism. The Manchester magistracy comprised mostly Tory clergymen, retired merchants, and some gentlemen who "had none of the family tradition, the patronage, or the experience that helped equip magistrates of the landed classes for governing—and for bargaining with rioters."[61] Even a measured desire for reform among many of the Manchester elite was not conducive to reciprocity and negotiation between classes. As Bohstedt remarks, "The laboring poor were *objects* of social policy, not political participants having a power to be reckoned with."[62] The exclusion of working-class Mancunians from processes of negotiation might have played a role in the replacement of price fixing during food riots by forms of symbolic expression. During a 31 July 1795 food riot, for example, "rioting took the form of a unilateral crowd action to punish dealers [by destroying food], rather than disciplined bargaining within a social and moral framework that included both magistrates and dealers."[63]

Without a trade history, long-standing trade institutions, relative social equality, sympathy from the magistracy, and (in the case of Manchester) community traditions, the weavers quite predictably eschewed the kind of threat bargaining that is so clearly and consistently evident in the Luddite writings of the Nottinghamshire framework knitters. Instead, the weavers of Manchester grounded their rhetoric on other, varied forms, and Luddism here entered a discursive field that was more complicated than in either the Midlands or Yorkshire. Three types of discourse surround Manchester Luddism. The first is petition. The second is a language of economic analysis that, although not macroeconomic in any real sense, does consider economic issues that extend beyond the rather confined purview of any particular trade. The third is Jacobinical language. Luddite rhetoric blended with each of these discourses, but all of them have in common a hierarchical perspective. Generally, Manchester-area Luddite writers tended to assume or engage a series of hierarchical tropes; in other words, they tended to look to the top, to those locations where power in a larger sense was more likely to reside. Threats to the prince regent, for example, are more common from Manchester-area writers than from Nottinghamshire writers.

In Manchester, the petition and reform were closely related. Like the weavers, the reform movement in Manchester made significant attempts to create an artificial collective. I do not mean to use the word "artificial" as a pejorative. On the contrary, the artifices of forming a community elicited from the people involved a great deal of creative social thought. Their tasks were several: to identify opportunities when collective concerns might be made evident to the population, to settle upon a language for making those concerns common, and to present the collective to those authorities who had to acknowledge it in serious terms. The need for external acknowledgment, so alien to the locales that Thompson describes in *Customs in Common*, was an overriding concern in Manchester. Given the governing structure of Manchester, the social matters that brought the new migrant populations together through petition and mass meeting could be addressed only by the authorities, only by persons extrinsic to the newly forming collective. The history of laboring-class self-help in Manchester has not yet been written. We can, however, infer from the Luddite and pre-Luddite Mancunian texts that self-help might have been possible, but the need for collectivity emerged at a time when only a limiting discourse of collectivity was available.

That most Mancunian of genres, the petition, could have served just that purpose—to draw together on one topic persons whose histories and dislocations otherwise impede the formation of a community. Petition, however, played an ambiguous, even contradictory role in constituting the weavers as a collective body. Petitioning and parliamentary reform, as discourses or as genres, looked outward to the government to address grievances and might actually have obstructed the development of a trade awareness sufficient to engage employers effectively in negotiations. Furthermore, the differences between the weavers in Manchester and those in the surrounding cotton towns (Bolton, Oldham, Stockport, and others) might also have prevented the formation of a collective identity. We frequently see, for example, addresses and petitions to Parliament from the various localities but very few from the cotton weaving trade as a whole during the years leading up to Luddism. Although the new migrant populations might have brought with them the desire for community and solidarity, the discursive culture that they entered permitted them to view solidarity only as a single face and single voice in order to plead for relief from the authorities. Metaphorically speaking, each face looked elsewhere for relief rather than to its fellow. Such petitions as the November 1811 "Humble Petition of the Clergy, Manufacturers & other Inhabitants of the Town and Neighbourhood of Bolton in the County of Lancashire" look to the prince regent to intervene in the diversion of grain from the production of bread to the production of alcohol:

Sheweth, That your Petitioners are principally engaged in the Cotton Manufactories of this County & situated in the centre of an immense Populations
of the labouring Poor. That your Petitioners have beheld & can bear testimony to the Patience with which the labouring Classes have borne their pri-
vations under the very reduced wages given in the Manufactories which have
for a long time scarcely afforded them the necessaries of life. That your Petitioners view with the deepest concern the rapid increase in the price of Grain
on the approach of Winter after a reported plentiful Harvest & when the
Manufactories afford no prospect of any increase of Wages. That your Petitioners conceive the increased prices of Grain to be in a great degree owing
to the consumption of it in the distilleries, whilst a plentiful substitute might
be found in Sugar of which there is a superabundant stock in this Country.
Your Petitioners therefore most humble pray that Your Royal Highness will
be graciously pleased to take into consideration the necessity of suspending
the distillation of Spirits from Grain until the Sense of Parliament on this
important subject can be taken. And your Petitioners will ever pray &c.[64]

The petition is interesting because it illustrates the tendency of Northwestern cotton workers to look outside of their own communities and other potential collective bodies for relief. It also illustrates the absence of the alternative:
why did the cotton workers and the concerned inhabitants of Bolton not exert
their energies to effect a rise in wages paid by the local cotton cloth merchants?
Self-constitution and communal regulation did not materialize in Bolton, even
throughout the Luddite risings.

Without some sort of constituting mechanism, the weavers risked remaining a
sociological and economic mass, not self-determined but rather objective. Strug-
gling to create a collective identity and to constitute themselves as an organized
body recognized by the clothiers, masters, magistracy, and the state apparatus,
the handloom weavers quite logically appropriated the genres and discourses of
other, established groups. As a genre, the petition offered a self-constituting
mechanism that might be understood as performative. Not only does the process of creating the petition draw together individuals into a petitioning body
and concentrates what might previously have been widely varied or unfocused
concerns, but also the petition itself incorporates the petitioners into a body, recognized and scrutinized by the government, especially the Home Office. Home
Office scrutiny was, during the period, the imprimatur of government recog-

nition. Even those bodies that were suppressed and prosecuted received some validation of existence by the attentions of the Home Office. This is not merely a historical or scholarly construction, wrought by the scholar's act of reading the record of the Home Office's scrutiny in the Home Office Papers; on the contrary, the Home Office validated such bodies by adjusting its activities to account for the new bodies. Out of the documents it collected, the Home Office wove a fabric of conspiracy, combination, and disaffection among the weavers and others. That fabric directed its surveillance and prosecutions, which had material effects on those petitioning bodies.

The rhetoric of the Midlands Luddites also provided the handloom weavers with a constitutive model. The framework knitters had exported—through the news, the reports of commercial correspondents, and the Luddite "delegates" the Home Office greatly feared—the language of a long-established trade in the process of resistance to economic oppression. The singular identity of a General Ludd presented collectivity and resistance. The difficulty inherent in the appropriation of Ludd's name was that in Ludd collectivity and resistance were intertwined. In Nottinghamshire, Ludd was an organic eponym, derived from and embedded in Nottinghamshire and framework knitting traditions. The weavers perhaps were unable to claim an alien tradition, even though they had hoped to borrow the legitimating function of Ludd's name. General Ludd did not function well as a petitioner. Absent their own trade traditions, the weavers had to resort to a broad range of self-constituting rhetorical strategies that they joined to the language of Luddism.

Although there would have been (and must have been) important differences between Manchester and the surrounding cotton towns, the differences do not show up very frequently in the surviving Luddite letters and proclamations from those towns. The ineffectiveness of bargaining and the tremendous distance between the elite and the working classes, distance so great as to preclude negotiation, defines Luddism throughout much of the Manchester cotton district. The weavers' recognition of that social distance and a larger socioeconomic order is exemplified in a number of Luddite texts from the Manchester region and led to the widespread use of a deflective language that expresses a grievance but redirects it to someone other than the likely target of any threatened physical violence.

Northwestern Luddite letters tend more than letters from the other regions to contain oblique threats. That is to say, Northwestern letters are more likely to be addressed to persons who are not threatened and are more likely to contain threats against third parties. I believe that the oblique threat is further proof of the Northwestern Luddites' awareness of a system or network of economic relations. Even though an appraisal of the personal guilt of the mill owners typically overrode any potential estimates of indirect economic responsibility of insurers, bankers, and cloth merchants, the awareness evidently existed. In two examples, the awareness ranges from the knowledge that employers are responsible for or have an influence over the hiring practices of factory overseers to the recognition that a fire protection provider would be interested to know that some of its insureds are at risk of an arsonistic Luddite attack.

In April 1812 the named owners of the largest spinning concern in the Manchester vicinity, McConnel, Kennedy and Company, received an anonymous letter (N4) containing compliments and expressions of respect to McConnel and Kennedy: "gent^m, we wish to Speake with respect to you because you have all ways Conducted your Selves to your spinners with that sevility and kindness which is a strong mark of your good Sence and humain harts and Cold wish to Serve you to the best of our power." The respect for McConnel and Kennedy is part of the background against which the writer registers grievances and obliquely condemns and threatens the company's overseers:

> [O]ur poor helpless Children have Hundreds of time's cryed unto us for bredds but a lass we had none to give them and we think it quiet inconsistent with Our duty as men as husbands and as fathers to Suffer our Selves to be ruined Any longer by a set of vagabond Strumpets and them Jibbet deserveing Raskals that is looking Over them, we will lud them to thare Satisfaction. . . . We sincerely hope Gentlemen that you will discharge the biches and take men in to your Employ a gain or they must take what they get[.]

Rhetorically, the tactic of indirect criticism and threat involves separating the responsibility for an abuse from the potential agency of the recipients who might be able to correct that abuse. The tactic would seem to be sound even if McConnel and Kennedy were not widely respected by their employees as kind and generous masters. Its effectiveness lies in imparting knowledge of a grievance and trusting that the recipients will redress that grievance even without having any threat made against them; were such a threat made, it might have caused the recipients to resist being bullied. The separation of threat from request also implies an understanding of the division of labor along hierarchical lines—that is,

between management and labor. Unlike the Nottingham and West Riding Luddites, the writer of this letter (like the writers of other Manchester documents)
does not think of the employers as masters or freemen, previously within the
trade but recently risen above their station.

The Luddite letter to McConnel and Kennedy is, however, rare. The rarity of
Luddite documents written by spinners might be attributed to the high demand
for cotton thread in several cloth industries—not just cotton weaving—throughout the period and the continued employment of spinners that resulted from the
demand.[65] A voluminous correspondence between McConnel and Kennedy in
Manchester and cloth manufacturers such as Samuel Cartledge, a Nottingham
hosier, indicates a healthy demand for cotton twist throughout 1812.[66] The spinners seem to have remained busy throughout the years of the Luddite risings,
although McConnel and Kennedy were under pressure to produce high-quality
yarn at cheap prices.[67]

Despite its being a rare Luddite letter written within the spinning trade, the
letter to McConnel and Kennedy is fairly characteristic of Northwestern Luddite writing in its rhetorical features. For one thing, the letter is directed to the top
of the industrial hierarchy. For another thing, the writer of the letter envisions a
wider economic reality than do the documents originating in Nottinghamshire.
More precisely, the writer includes the employers, McConnel and Kennedy, and
the objectionable employees in a matter that could easily be treated as either internal to the trade or wholly within the hands of the employers.

In the second instance, a Luddite letter from "Falstaff" directed to "Fire Office Agents" at Wigan (N5) informs the insurers that at least five of their insureds,
all owners of factories containing steam-powered winding machines, were likely
to be the victims of arson, due to a Luddite response to their oppressive labor
practices. Again, the rhetoric involves a separation of the responsibility for the
objectionable labor practice from the ability (and motive) of the recipients to
act as agents for the Luddites—an action that would also prevent harm to their
employers. This letter, perhaps more than any others, epitomizes the discursive features of Northwestern Luddism. Absent long-standing, stable trade and
community institutions for expressing and redressing economic grievances, the
Luddites of the region identified economic systems and networks that supported
or facilitated oppressive employment practices, and they availed themselves of
that knowledge to bring pressure upon their oppressors through legitimate
agents. McConnel and Kennedy and the Fire Office Agents act in the position of

mediating agent that magistrates occupied in areas, such as Devon, where more traditional forms of protest prevailed.

"Falstaff" concedes the distance between the group whose grievances he conveys and the manufacturers who are perhaps so distant that writing directly to them would be of no avail. The solution to the problem of discursive and social distance appears to be to write with a sense of the larger economic scheme that makes such distance possible. In this case, that sense extended to an awareness of the role of insurers in the system of cotton manufacture.

"Falstaff's" remonstrance, "it ill behoves Gen^m of Pro^y to . . . take away the Work of the Poor and therefore their Bread," appears to be an application of the language of paternalism and negotiation; however, the very scheme of address belies that appearance. Although the targets of the threat might be called "Gen^m," the intermediaries to whom the letter is addressed are not persons who play intermediate roles under a paternalistic system or even within a trade relationship. The commercial vocabulary of the letter is very basic, but its presence indicates that the writer recognizes either that such lexical overtures are necessary parts of threatening letters from the Manchester region or that the language of trade custom or of deference and paternalistic obligation would have no effect. McConnel and Kennedy and the Fire Office Agents are treated as magistrates of an economic system.

The sense of a larger economic reality requiring negotiation or engagement among a number of social levels or sectors is, I think, the single most distinguishing feature of Northwestern Luddism. Such an awareness grew out of the absence of a single organization of weavers, the readiness of political radicals to welcome into their fold new groups searching for redress of their grievances, and the failure of a magistracy to resolve the problems that resulted from industrialization and the spread of capitalism. I cannot be certain that the same pattern that John Foster discovered held for Oldham held true for Manchester, but the emergence of political radicalism as the primary discourse within which Luddite rhetoric was embedded or entwined (as was the case for the language of wage disputes in Oldham) suggests that the courses of development might be similar.[68]

Foster says of Luddism (although without mentioning the name and instead calling the risings "the troubles of 1812") that even the thousands of soldiers used to quiet the northern counties "were (not unnaturally) quite powerless against an opposition built so securely into the structure of the surrounding community."[69]

It might be more accurate to say that one reason for the relative powerlessness of the authorities was that the opposition in the Northwest was quite variable rather than embedded. The many facets of discontent, including those that Foster highlights in his study of Oldham, permitted the discourse of grievance and redress to take on several forms, appealing at one time to custom, at another time to natural rights, and at still other times to what Foster calls "a very special form of *trade union* consciousness." Foster's explanation of that consciousness complements Bohstedt's analysis of the wide-reaching character of Manchester Luddism: "If it was the defence of living standards that gave the radicals their position of leadership, its effective *practice* involved much more. It demanded the development of a coercive occupational solidarity extending to all sections of the labour community; a solidarity that was radically new, specifically illegal and in its practical application a direct challenge to state power."[70] In this passage, Foster might be overstating the threat to state power posed by the form of consciousness he describes, but his notice of the compass of the "occupational solidarity extending to all sections of the labour community" is valuable and quite in line with Bohstedt's account and with the substance of the Luddite texts from the region. The enlargement of Northwestern Luddite discourse to address political as well as local economic issues might have been in part the result of a kind of economic conflict that did not fit the "classic" model described by Bohstedt or was not accounted for by "the old controls" mentioned by Foster.[71] Certainly the disputes in the Northwest were not about trade reputation and the quality of manufacture (as was the case in Nottinghamshire) but rather about wages and prices. The "old controls" would have been out of place in a wage and price system.

The economic and political analyses of the petitioning weavers in the years leading up to Luddism and later of the Luddites and their sympathizers do appear to mark some familiarity with the economic ideas that were driving the industrial revolution in the cotton districts. The larger economic factors behind the decline in weavers' wages are part of the rhetorical calculations of the Manchester-area Luddite writers. Aware of the general depression in trade, the role of machinery in reducing wages and opportunities for by-occupations, and the government's role in joining economic and political positions so as to pursue wars that depressed trade in two hemispheres, the Luddite writers were as varied in their rhetorical appeals, addressees, and modes of threat as the economic-political system that confronted them. The wars provided a means of coupling the ruling classes with economic difficulties, including those caused or aggravated by industrialization and the abatement of wages. Manchester wall slogans from 1801 ("Peace or no King" and "Cheap bread or no King") and 1812 ("Peace and a Big Loaf," "No Mechenery no King," and "A Big Loaf or No King") demonstrate the rhetorical splicing of the ruling class, economic troubles, and the wars.[72]

In many of the Northwestern documents, questions of loyalty and social distance converge in texts that can best be described as radical or republican. The same radical strain that helped to shape the discourse of petition also provided a way for the Luddites to think of the connection between political and economic forces. At the same time, however, some radical language gravitated against any language of trade custom that might have emerged. A 6 May 1812 letter (N13) from "Thomas Paine" to Richard Wood, the boroughreeve of Manchester, illustrates that orientation. The writer refers to the 8 April loyalist meeting at the Manchester Exchange called by 154 persons, a "respectable committee of Gentlemen, who have sat in this town in aid of & for the information of the civil power." A group of reformers, most of whom were members of the merchant classes and led by a wealthy dissenter named Ottiwell Wood, opposed the meeting and published broadside proclamations titled, "NOW OR NEVER," asking the public to attend the loyalist meeting to voice their support for political reform. Anticipating possible violence, the Manchester Boroughreeve, Richard Wood, withdrew his permission to hold the meeting at the Exchange, citing an inadequacy of the building's stairs, but he was actually fearful of "an insurrection against society."[73] As the letter says, "Richard Wood You have been the cause of much bloodshed; you convened the people and did not meet them: you are therefore marked for punishment." The letter disavows "connection with machine breakers," even though its expressed aims are similar to those expressed by writers among the weavers engaged in Luddism in the Manchester region:

> I say we deny and disavow all, or any connection with machine breakers, burners of factories, extorters of money, plunderers of private property or assasans. We know that every machine for the abridgment of human labour is a blessing to the great family of which we are a part. We mean to begin at the Source of our grievances as it is of no use to petition, We mean to demand & command a redress of our grievances. We have both the will & the power.[74]

It would appear that expressed attitudes toward machinery, in this case at least, might actually distinguish between levels of respectability, at least in the minds of those members of the middle and working classes who opposed the monarchy and the government.

Just as frequently, however, radical and Luddite discourses blended well. One such letter (N8), forwarded to the Home Office by Reverend William Hay, invokes the name of Ludd to advocate radical, even revolutionary, ends. Signed "Eliza Ludd," the 30 April 1812 letter threatens an American-style revolution: "Doubtless you are well acquainted with the Political History of America, if so you must confess that, it was ministerial tyranny that gave rise to that glorious spirit in which the British Colonies obtain'd their independance by force of arms, at a period, when we was ten times as strong as now!"

Even more frequent exercises of the blending of the Luddite and the revolutionary were threats against the prince regent, some of which were cast into verse, as in a 5 May 1812 Flintshire letter (N10), which first complains of wages before threatening a Luddite juggernaut:

The poor cry aloud for bread
Prince Regent shall lose his head
And all the rich who oppress the poor
In a little time shall be no more
With deep regret, I write these things,
They'll come to pass in spite of kings.

But even with the yoking of two significant discourses, Luddism and radicalism, Northwestern disaffection remained muddled. No document illustrates that muddle better than the 30 April 1812 letter to Salford coroner Nathaniel Milne (N9). Written to protest a coroner's verdict of "justifiable homicide" by a soldier who had killed a Luddite during the raid on Burton's mill, the letter attempts to combine political and moral discourses in making a threat against Milne's life, but it incorporates an additional, confusing discourse in its use of one of Aesop's fables, "The Plague amongst the Beasts."

In his 1979 article titled "Luddism and Politics in the Northern Counties," John Dinwiddy argues that, although there is little evidence of any strong links between the Luddites of the northern counties and the political radical revolutionaries of the region and "there was no wholesale shift from industrial to political forms of activity," nevertheless "the crisis of 1812 was of some importance in the process whereby discontent in the northern counties acquired a major political dimension."[75] In his examination, Dinwiddy turns repeatedly to evidence of the blending of economic and political concerns in the petitions and addresses of radical and trade groups and in the reports of the government's spies operating in the region. Foster and others have already illustrated the concurrence of economic and political language in slogans and graffiti, but Dinwiddy's project is more promising, even if it does not follow through on its course of rhetorical analysis. Dinwiddy's remarks are qualified by his recognition of the political dimension of Luddism and of the efforts of economically distressed workers to seek relief from the government.

A study of Luddite rhetoric, however, suggests quite a different question: to what extent were the languages of Luddism and of political radicalism appropriated by different groups to express grievances that were not accounted for under any social model of the time and to constitute a group identity in a shifting social structure? And what exactly did the importation of Ned Ludd into the Manchester region afford to industrial, economic, and political protest in that area? The documents from the region incorporate such a wide variety of discourses that it is easy to imagine that Ludd could have been used as a concentrating device. In fact, in the Manchester region, the figure of Ludd is probably less of an eponym, generated from its own subculture, than a metonym, in the sense that the term has been used by Wai Chee Dimock. Dimock has appropriated the term from Kenneth Burke and George Lakoff to mark a cognitive movement encompassing instantiation and generalization. The term describes the reduction of an immaterial plurality to a material singularity. Burke's version of the trope "instantiates 'some incorporeal or intangible state in terms of the corporeal or tangible'; it is thus a form of reduction, involving the telescoping of an immaterial order within a material embodiment."[76] Dimock employs the trope to describe "a kind of cross-mapping, a cognitive traffic between two ontological orders, the immaterial here being invested in (and encapsulated by) the material in a generalizable relation: a relation of representative adequacy or logical inferability. . . . [I]t operates not only by instantiation but also by projection, not only by a play of salient details but also by a play of latent horizons."[77] The reduction of a group of textile workers, especially those without a long trade tradition, to a single eponym deserves scrutiny along the lines that Dimock suggests. In fact, reduction of any sort is problematic. Questions about the class and education of the Manchester Luddite writers are inescapable, considering not only their understanding of the systemic character of the difficulties they faced but also the frequent use by some writers of Latin quotations and other literary references.

Perhaps the figure of General Ludd is a "transclass" bridge (effective because imported from another region) between a systemic awareness and the expression of basic human suffering.

It would be difficult to argue that weavers in Cheshire and Lancashire copied the machine breaking of framework knitters in Nottinghamshire because a vocabulary and an eponym made that copying either possible or worthwhile. After all, ironworkers in Tredegar and workers elsewhere copied machine breaking but made no claims upon the name "Ludd." Nevertheless, some groups did not copy the machine-breaking tactics of the Nottinghamshire Luddites at all but did appropriate the language of Luddism. The spinners in Manchester and Holywell voiced no objections to the machines that replaced traditional cottage spinning, but they used the name of "Ludd" to denounce the hiring practices of their employers. I believe that what Ludd offered to the protesters of the cotton districts was a metonym that they hoped could concentrate a variety of discourses and enable the primary group of disaffected workers, the cotton weavers, to constitute themselves as a self-determining and articulate body.

❖ YORKSHIRE LUDDISM

The language employed by the Luddites of the West Riding of Yorkshire, particularly in the region surrounding Huddersfield, when compared with the discourse of Luddism in either the Midlands or the Northwest, presents a very different problem. In the previous section, I have tried to demonstrate that, due to the immaturity of the weaving trade and its lacking a long-established tradition, Northwestern Luddism assembled its rhetoric from a variety of customary, reformist, and revolutionary discourses, largely as part of an attempt on the part of the weavers to constitute themselves as a trade body acknowledged by employers and government. And prior to that, I argued that the Midlands Luddites used the languages at hand, law and custom, to mold a rhetoric that could effectively convey their grievances and make claims for redress based on their actual situation as a sanctioned, already constituted trade culture.

The Yorkshire Luddites comprised primarily the cloth dressers of the West Riding woolen industry, commonly called croppers. The croppers had fewer problems of self-constitution than the weavers had, and Luddism did not enter a discursive vacuum when it spread to the West Riding. Like the framework knitters, the croppers had been long-established as a trade. Even though they lacked

a crown sanction such as that enjoyed by the Worshipful Company of Framework Knitters, a mixture of trade realities and legal protections imparted to the
croppers a position and power that surpassed even that of the framework knitters. The cloth dressers' labor was invaluable and was protected not only by the
Elizabethan statute requiring apprenticeships in the woolen trades but also by
later laws prohibiting the use of the gig mill. Wool was so important to Britain that even the deregulatory impulses of MPs such as Nicholas Vansittart were
slow to have their effect upon the woolen trade. As late as 1802, nearly seventy
statutes continued to regulate the woolen industry.[78]

During the twenty years preceding the Luddite risings, the cloth dressers of
Yorkshire and the West of England had fought against the legalization of shearing frames and gig mills. They even had organized into a trade society that frequently appealed to statutory protections and sought additional regulation of
clothiers' business practices. In 1809, however, Parliament repealed some of the
statutory protections of workers in the woolen industry. Those repeals were followed by a decrease in the legal efforts of the croppers in the years thereafter,
particularly during the period of Luddism. In fact, Yorkshire Luddites placed
less emphasis than their counterparts in the Midlands and the Northwest did
on working in conjunction with a contemporary, lawful movement that sought
to undertake direct, peaceful negotiations with the cloth merchants and larger
clothiers or to influence Parliament to alleviate the depressed conditions in the
manufacturing centers. Nevertheless, despite the greater separation between the
different modes of labor action (that is, between legal-political and violent methods), Yorkshire Luddites appear, through their writings at least, to have recognized a complicity or connection between the governmental and commercial
forces that were combining to harm their trade interests. The problem faced by
the West Riding Luddites was how they ought to continue to think of and represent themselves as a constituted body after their legal protections and sanctions
had been removed by a government that was complicitous with the large capitalists who sought more control over the labor market. I believe that the Luddites'
recognition of complicity, along with the prior experiences of the croppers, explains a number of features of much Yorkshire Luddite writing—the variety of
rhetorical appeals, the tension between local and national orientations, the expansive character, and the importation of the language of Nottingham Luddism
for use in framing the entire discursive array.

In Yorkshire, Luddite language shifted from threats against employers for using shearing frames to threats against the local authorities for counteracting the machine-breaking campaign, which the Luddites believed was based on a just, righteous cause. Rather quickly, the focus in Yorkshire Luddite rhetoric on offensive machinery fell aside, though by no means out of sight, as the Luddites began to concentrate upon a political-economic system that was manifested locally in a highly visible and active form. The change in the focus of the Yorkshire machine breakers happened more quickly than it did in the Midlands. Furthermore, the rhetoric of Luddism in Yorkshire appears to have been more violent than in the other Luddite regions. The violent and expansive nature of Luddite rhetoric in Yorkshire arises from the cloth dressers' prior experiences with trade unionism and with methods of legal and forceful negotiations, and from the existence of an available legalistic discourse that could be used to advance some of the cloth dressers' claims.

Yorkshire Luddism has provided the material for one of the most extended debates on Luddism. E. P. Thompson relies to a significant degree on Yorkshire Luddism to draw his conclusions about Luddism's pivotal role in the development of class consciousness in England as the moment "of a crisis between paternalism and *laissez-faire*," as he says in his chapter titled "The Army of Redressers" in *The Making of the English Working Class*.[79] West Riding rhetoric reveals Luddism there to have been important in "marking a 'watershed' in economic and political allegiances."[80] Thompson's larger conclusions have come under scrutiny by later scholars. Malcolm Thomis has raised insightful questions about the singularity of purpose among the Luddites, thereby calling into question Thompson's observations. Although Thomis is among the least rhetorically and textually interested of the major historians of Luddism, his historiographical assumptions about the lack of singularity of purpose closely resemble a rhetorician's assumptions about a lack of univocality in the discourse of a movement. In reply to Thompson, Thomis outlines what has come to be called a compartmentalizing approach. He distinguishes between the legal, peaceful methods of withdrawing labor in protest over wages and the violent methods of the Luddites. Although Thomis does not condemn Luddite violence or relegate it to the category of vandalism (as Brian Bailey has done in his recent book), he nevertheless tends to cast Luddism as an ineffective expression of narrow trade interests largely because the Luddites employed methods that would prove futile over the next century.[81]

Thomis's own approach has come under attack by historians interested primarily in Yorkshire Luddism. In arguing against the compartmentalizing approach of Thomis and similar historians, Adrian Randall has pointed to the cloth dressers' remarkable successes resisting the introduction of machinery in the West of England and the West Riding, especially between 1792 and 1803. The compartmentalizing approach consists of distinguishing machine breaking from other forms of labor protest, and it further involves assuming what Randall calls a "teleological view of labour history." Although Randall's observations are also capable of being applied to Midlands Luddism (particularly because his analysis is based on a decentralized trade structure similar to the outworking structure of the framework knitting trade), they are directed toward an explanation of resistance to the introduction of machinery in the woolen trades, and they explain much about the rhetoric of Luddism in the West Riding. Randall argues persuasively that violence and threats worked in conjunction with strikes, community pressure, and recourse to the law in both the West of England and the West Riding. Randall's argument includes a warning: "Violence was selective, controlled and aimed at specific targets, supplementing and reinforcing the more orthodox sanctions of their combinations. We must firmly resist a simplistic imposition of nineteenth- or twentieth-century models of 'appropriate' trade union behaviour upon the actions and activities of eighteenth-century combinations regardless of their very different context and culture."[82]

Randall's work provides a useful starting point for this section on Luddite writing in Yorkshire. Randall, Craig Calhoun, and John Bohstedt have demonstrated that the different forms of Luddism grew out of regional particularities. Those particularities are evident in the rhetoric, but they thrived in the West Riding's "Domestic System" of woolen manufacture described by Randall. Any study of Yorkshire Luddite writing ought to begin by revisiting Randall's treatment of the organization of manufacture, of unionization, and of the cloth dressers' earlier successes in resisting mechanization of the West Riding woolen industry.

The West Riding woolen industry was relatively decentralized. In very few instances did large cloth merchants or gentleman clothiers control all stages of production. Rather, small master clothiers carried out a number of tasks and worked closely with their employed journeymen to produce an article of woolen cloth. Centralizing functions were carried out in the cloth halls in Leeds and Huddersfield. The one stage of production that remained independent even of the independent master clothiers was cloth dressing. Cropping shops and the croppers employed therein enjoyed more independence and status than most workers in the textile trades.[83]

For centuries, workers and small master clothiers in the woolen industry had enjoyed the regulation of that industry by a wide range of statutes. The most wide-reaching was 5 Elizabeth cap. 4, an act fixing apprenticeships in the woolen trades. The act had fallen into disuse long before the Luddite risings and was eventually repealed in 1813, but it had been widely perceived as preserving the status of woolen workers. A more narrowly focused act was 5 & 6 Edward VI cap. 22, "An Act for the putting down of gig mills." The cloth dressers relied greatly upon that act in pressing their cause in Parliament.[84] Statutes such as these had been the basis of the cloth dressers' objections to gig mills and other finishing machines. Even though the acts were repealed during the first decade of the nineteenth century, the cloth dressers had met with success in resisting machinery in a number of locales prior to repeal.

The cloth dressers already enjoyed a great deal of power and status within the woolen industry; in fact, Randall writes that the cloth dressers were "the most powerful labour interest in the woolen industry," primarily because they were essential in adding value to woolen articles. One cropper, asked in 1806 about the value of the trade, replied, "They can make a piece 20 per cent better or worse by due care and labour or the reverse."[85] Mechanization threatened the position of the cloth dressers, but those in the West Riding did not stand idly by when frames were introduced to the industry. During the two decades leading up to Luddism, the cloth dressers had pursued legal avenues of resistance to mechanization largely under the aegis of the Brief Institution. Randall describes the Brief Institution as having been established in 1796 in Yorkshire to prevent entry into the trade of cloth dressing by "illegal" workers. The Brief Institution's organizational structure mimicked the structure of the West Riding woolen industry. It served a largely communicative function and did not replace local societies of croppers

> but built upon them, welding them into a coherent whole. . . . It provided the means, far better than before, of scrutinising recruitment to the trade by issuing membership cards, of enforcing closed shops and of regulating the tramp system. It enabled information on disputes to be diffused more completely than before and, most important, it ensured that any employer standing out

against his workmen's demands faced the weight and financial resources not only of the local cloth dressers but of all the region.[86]

The Brief Institution might have provided the trade-unionist basis for some Yorkshire Luddite rhetoric, but the fact of early success in resisting machinery through violence was probably just as much a factor in structuring Luddite discourse in the West Riding. Pre-Luddite successes include the destruction of a Holbeck gig mill in 1799, forcing Benjamin Gott to take down a gig mill in Leeds in 1801, and the destruction by fire of Thomas Atkinson's Bradley Mills near Huddersfield in 1804. Indeed, a threatening letter sent from Huddersfield in September 1805 to the Royal Exchange Insurance Company bears witness to the blending of law and threat by earlier opponents of machinery in the region's woolen trade.[87] The blending of legal and violent methods had proved to be effective.

Additional incentives to take a violent line perhaps included the ambiguity of the law. Even the statute that the croppers relied upon to oppose the gig mill through legal means, 5 & 6 Edward VI cap. 22, did not unquestionably apply to the gig mills that the croppers opposed during the war years. One of the specified goals of the Yorkshire cloth dressers, contained in a bill drafted and brought forward by Mr. Brooke, MP, and others, was "To declare that the Act of Edw. VI. about gig mills applied to the present gig mills."[88]

The Yorkshire Luddites might also have been influenced to take a more violent line by the example of the failure of the purely legal, peaceful methods used by shearmen to oppose the introduction of the gig mill in Gloucestershire in the mid-1790s. The Gloucestershire shearmen engaged in few acts of violence and, while they did send threatening letters, the fact that the threats did not escalate into "outrages" probably diminished the rhetorical effect of the threats, and the gig mills became firmly and quickly established in that region. As Randall observes, "Here, then, we can see the fruits of what Thomis labels 'the labour approach.' Constitutional methods, petitions and attempts at negotiation proved impotent unless supported by direct pressure."[89] In rhetorical terms, in order to be effective, a threat had to be bounded materially on two sides—by material suffering and by physical action.

Randall and others have noted that the ideology of Yorkshire Luddism was developed in the many outlying cropping shops throughout much of the West Riding. We might expect that the discourse of West Riding Luddism would be primarily local in nature. Certainly, many of the threats reflect the localized and community-centered structure of the industry in that region. Although the Yorkshire croppers were removed from the central control of the cloth merchants and master clothiers, they remained engaged with their communities, and the Luddite writers assumed that such an engagement was typical. One letter, dated 27 April 1812, to Joseph Radcliffe (Y13), is replete with localized warnings: "With respect to this Watch and Ward Act, you are not aware of the additional, Oppression you are bringing upon your Tenants, and other Occupiers of Lands, and all for the sake of two Individuals in this District, which I am not afraid to subscribe their names, Mr Th^{s} Atkinson, & Mr Wm Horsfall." The letter to Radcliffe is primarily local in its concerns and methods of expressing concerns but, like other West Riding documents, should not be considered as evidence of Luddite insularity. On the contrary, a number of experiences of croppers and other workers within the West Riding impelled the Luddite writers to look outside of their own sphere for the causes of problems and the sources of solutions. Randall describes the Brief Institution as an organization that brought the Yorkshire croppers into closer cooperation with the West Country shearmen and taught them that neither their problems nor the solutions were entirely local. Similarly, Jacobinical and republican influences had been at work in Yorkshire since the French Revolution, as Alan Brooke and Lesley Kipling have demonstrated recently.[90] These different forces coincided in Yorkshire between 1790 and 1809, and they lent to Luddism in that region a set of tropes that might be understood for their expansive character.

When I mention tropes of an expansive character, I use the term to describe the tendency for the purview of Yorkshire texts to move outward from the local to the national, or even beyond that. Local clothiers such as Vickerman, Atkinson, and Horsfall and magistrates such as Radcliffe might be singled as targets for Luddite violence, as in a number of threatening letters to those and other persons. The destruction of a local mill containing frames might be celebrated, as in the song "Forster's Mill." However, the scope of causal analysis and of justification of the course of action often grew, sometimes line by line within individual documents, to encompass the community outside of the trade, the trade in other regions, other trades altogether, the kingdom, and relations between states.

A localist orientation is evident in several types of Luddite writing in Yorkshire. In most cases, the texts register the self-sufficiency of the members of the trade. Songs such as "T' Three Cropper Lads o' Honley" and "The Cropper's

Song" reveal that the Yorkshire Luddites had little need to construct heroism by the same means that the Midlands Luddites did (that is, by the use of comparison and outdoing schema, as demonstrated in the Nottinghamshire song, "General Ludd's Triumph"). "T' Three Cropper Lads o' Honley" (Y3), a song celebrating the reputedly cantankerous character of croppers, is set in that West Riding town, and is built on the old folktale about croppers' being so ornery and unruly that three recently deceased croppers are even evicted from Hell. "The Cropper's Song" (Y2), reputedly sung by a Luddite at the Shears Inn, Hightown, is a straightforward claim of cropper potency. It makes no efforts to legitimate the croppers' actions or to eulogize the croppers through comparison with other figures, such as Robin Hood. The croppers' character seems to have been sufficient, in the minds of some of the Luddites, to represent their resistance as a potent force:

> Come, cropper lads of high renown,
> Who love to drink good ale that's brown,
> And strike each haughty tyrant down,
>   With hatchet, pike, and gun!
> Oh, the cropper lads for me,
> The gallant lads for me,
> Who with lusty stroke,
> The shear frames broke,
> The cropper lads for me!

The allusions to renown and the croppers' reputations for ale drinking in the local public houses combine with the objection to shear frames to render a highly localized set of verses. Even the methods of redress are local:

> Great Enoch still shall lead the van.
> Stop him who dare! stop him who can!
> Press forward every gallant man
>   With hatchet, pike, and gun!

"Enoch" was the name that the Luddites gave to the great hammers that they used to smash the shearing frames. The hammers were named after Enoch Taylor, a metalsmith from the Marsden area who produced not only hammers but also the shearing frames that threatened the croppers' trade. The choice in the early weeks of Yorkshire Luddism to name the hammers "Enoch" marks a discourse of local containment and communal, internal regulation—that is, the idea that both problems and solutions can come from within a community.

Perhaps the cloth dressers' failures in the realm of political economy, specifically in their efforts to encourage Parliament to retain and expand the statutory protections for the trade, caused them to take less of an expansive view based on economic relations between the local woolen trade and national economic policies during the Luddite years. That is not to suggest that political-economic analysis did not find its way into Yorkshire Luddite texts but only that it shared a place with other analytical forms. Those forms were expansive, and the most basic level of expansion was from the trade to the community. "The Cropper's Song" works to situate the croppers as a central force within a local community—even as a moral, political force capable of identifying and punishing "each haughty tyrant." Other texts, such as an 8 April 1812 letter to Radcliffe signed "I ham for lud and the poor" (Y8), function in a similar manner, proposing that Luddite aims coincide with the aims of the poor of the community.

The Yorkshire Luddites held local cloth merchants and some master clothiers responsible for the introduction of shearing frames to the region's woolen industry, but they also recognized that the magistracy was complicitous in the introduction of machinery to the region. Huddersfield magistrate Joseph Radcliffe was a special target of Luddite threats, because he was entirely inimical to the idea that his position as a magistrate might require that he serve as a negotiator and as a guardian of the moral economy. The Luddites responded accordingly, with greater hostility for Radcliffe than for any official in any of the regions. (Radcliffe had little investment and few roots in the community, having come from Dobcross to inherit the magistracy.) More important, however, Radcliffe and other magistrates were targets because the Luddites inferred the connection between the political and the economic and commercial, and they saw it manifested on a local level. Such localization is also the prevailing discourse of many of the threatening letters sent to other officials in the region. A March 1812 letter (Y7) from "Genl Ludd's Solicitor" to Huddersfield magistrate Joseph Radcliffe even recommends to Radcliffe a sort of internal system of regulation based on collective responsibility among the local constabulary and magistracy: "PS you have Sir rather taken an active part against the General but you are quiet and may remain so if you chuse (and your Brother Justices also) for him, but if you either convict [a one], or coutinance the other Side as you have done (or any of you), you may expect your House in Flames and, your-self in Ashes. . . ."

One language available for treating the connection between the political and the economic would have been republican or reformist, but that language was employed only infrequently in the West Riding. More typical, the expansion to the level of community interest is accompanied by the inclusion of a discourse of morality, particularly in the threats directed at the officials. The political was the moral. In the 29 October 1812 letter to Joseph Radcliffe (Y21), the language of morality and moral struggle ("good and righteous," "glory," and "monsters") overrides even the language of political oppression ("tyrant" and "persicuteth") and completely replaces the juridical language of other West Riding documents. Law is no longer relevant to the struggle, as its logic has become entirely self-reflexive, dedicated to the persecution of the righteous and the good rather than to justice. Even the salutation sets that tone—"Unjust Judge."

The Yorkshire Luddites also availed themselves of the language of revolution, but often it was locally and regionally conceived, even amid some Jacobinical overtones. One example is a letter from March 1812 (Y4), addressed "To all Croppers, Weavers &c & Public at Large": "You are requested to come forward with Arms and help the Redressers to redress their Wrongs and shake off the hateful Yoke of a Silly Old Man, and his Son more silly and their Rogueish Ministers, all Nobles and Tyrants must be brought down." The letter advocates political violence on the national level, thereby recasting General Ludd as a political figure rather than as an artisan seeking to preserve a trade. Nevertheless, the address, "To all Croppers, Weavers &c & Public at Large," is localizing. The letter is one of the first of the Luddite documents from the West Riding to attempt to restage labor unrest in national, though not lawful, terms. Its language is geographically expansive, but, as in almost every instance of expansion in Yorkshire Luddite texts, the letter ultimately centers on the West Riding and its community dynamics. The address registers the expansion of the writer's purview beyond the cloth dressing trade to the larger community and joins croppers to other workers in the woolen trade and to the larger public.

Much expansion was quite political. The 9 or 10 March 1812 letter (Y5) from "Ned Ludd" addressed to "Mr Smith Shearing Frame Holder at Hill End Yorkshire" is probably the most indicative not only of the Yorkshire Luddites' blending of the languages of local trade and demotic concerns and political disaffection but also of the frequent Luddite pattern of localization, expansion, and return. Kirkpatrick Sale labels the letter "Luddism in a nutshell."[91] It begins as a fairly straightforward protest and threat directed at Smith for his use of machinery:

"Information has just been given in that you are a holder of those detestable Shearing Frames, and I was desired by my Men to write to you and give you fair Warning to pull them down." The local trade concerns continue for several lines: "[Y]ou will have the Goodness to your Neighbours to inform them that the same fate awaits them if their Frames are not speedily taken down as I understand their are several in your Neighbourhood, Frame holders." The writer mentions that a local, popular force, "the Army of Huddersfield," with twice as many more men sworn to the same cause in Leeds, are ready to "redress their grievances." The threat is locally revolutionary, confined to the woolen districts and thereby to the persons with some authority over the conduct of the woolen trade.

The first hint of a geographically larger revolutionary discourse in the letter appears shortly after the enumeration of the size of the "armies" of Leeds and Huddersfield, in the report that "the Manufacturers in the following Places are going to rise and join us in redressing their Wrongs Viz. Machester, Wakefield Halifax, Bradford, Sheffield, Oldham, Rochdale and all the Cotton Country," as well as Scotland and Ireland. The writer goes on to identify the government, specifically the "Hanover tyrants" and "that Damn'd set of Rogues, Percival & Co to whom we attribute all the Miseries of our Country," as the cause of the miseries in the woolen trade, and to "hope for assistance from the French Emperor in shaking off the Yoke of the Rottenest, Wickedest and most Tyranious Government that ever existed" and (ironically) establishing a republic.

The movement within the letter from local, trade concerns to republicanism and finally to violent rejection of peaceful petitioning is accomplished by a triple maneuver that plots the Luddites' course toward violence, disavows the methods of the past, but nevertheless hints at the connection between the peaceable and the violent methods. Much of this can be seen in the concluding lines of the letter. The writer professes a hope that "The House of Commons passes an Act to put down all Machinery hurtful to Commonality, and repeal that to hang Frame Breakers. But We. We petition no more that won't do fighting must." E. P. Thompson's transcription includes an emendation, an inserted "till": "We will never lay down Arms [till] The House of Commons . . ."[92] Similarly, Sale inserts "until."[93] The added word, "till," determines the meaning in a manner consistent with Thompson's thesis that an underground revolutionary network existed during these years, but Thompson uses editorial license to enhance that meaning. The hope for parliamentary protection continues, just as it had prior to the statutory repeals of 1809, and Thompson's emendation suggests that continuity;

however, through the emphatic two-word sentence, "But We," and the repetition of "We" at the beginning of the next sentence, the Luddites' petitioning to secure parliamentary protections is severed from action by the Commons. It is not entirely clear whether the Luddite writer retains a hope for parliamentary processes, spurred on by violence, or whether the conditionality implied by Thompson's "till" has been forsaken. The republican sentiments of the first part of the letter would seem to indicate some faith in governmental action but not in the government at the time. The writer is vague about the scope of the "fighting." It could be local, against the constabulary and clothiers, or it could be kingdomwide. In any event, continuity and scope must be considered together.

Determining the proper scope for the letter is important. Malcolm Thomis argues that "there seems every reason to suppose that it [the letter] was a stirring and joyous playing with words rather than a serious call to arms or an accurate statement of Luddite numbers and intentions."[94] Through its particularized grievances, the letter appears to appeal to the local, customary rights that Thompson has described so well, except that those rights are recognized on a larger scale, perhaps as a matter of a principle ("hurtful to Commonality") that Thompson interprets as an "ancient right" or "a lost constitution."[95] Sale, in his typically forward-looking and cautionary manner, would read the letter as a statement of a set of human rights, communally understood. Sale translates "commonality" as "the common people in general," but he recognizes, consistently with Thompson, Calhoun, and Randall, that what the Luddite writer calls "commonality" is manifested in "particular communities long established and much cherished."[96] Nevertheless, all of this occurs within an enlarged scope ("put down all Machinery hurtful to Commonality") that encompasses the Luddites and their special concerns ("and repeal that to hang Frame Breakers") without unduly limiting the discourse to those concerns ("all").

Sale's judgment of the letter as "Luddism in a nutshell" perhaps should be qualified, even though he tries not to deviate from the line established by Thompson, who preceded him in assuming the larger significance of the letter.[97] The temporal continuity and contingency assumed by both Thompson ("till") and Sale ("until") are consistent with their enlarging (but I would not say totalizing) interpretations, but the interpretations of the letter depend to a significant extent on the editorial emendations. Without the insertion, the rhetorical effects of continuity and contingency are diminished. Instead, reading the letter as it appears in the manuscript, we find a break between Luddite and parliamentary actions. The break is accentuated by the curt "But we." The letter returns to machine breaking in Yorkshire, to the futility of the petitioning by croppers and other woolen workers that preceded the repeals of 1809, and to the redressing of grievances by a plural, first-person collective ("we," Ned Ludd's "redressers") rather than a kingdomwide abstraction alone, whether it be government or revolution.

Kingdomwide revolutionary discourse provided not so much a practical orientation for Luddite rhetoric as a parallel structure on a more general level to accentuate the gravity of local grievances. Jacobinical rhetoric might also have complemented threats of local violence and actual violence in the same way that law, industrial action, and violence worked together in both the West of England and in the West Riding prior to 1809, as Randall has described.[98] In the case of the croppers, however, the legal, peaceful methods did not coexist with the violence but rather antedated it. This fact distinguishes Luddism in Yorkshire from that in the vicinity of Manchester, where petitioning coincided with violence and was, as I have argued, part of a larger attempt by the weavers to constitute themselves as a body. In Manchester, any mention of petitioning in a threat or a posted paper signaled that the weavers were constituting themselves in several dimensions and spheres of action. In the Yorkshire letter to Mr. Smith, mention of the rejection of petitioning signals that the already constituted body of croppers has decided to break with its recent past in order to secure its long-held rights.

The break with petitioning has special importance, given both the croppers' prior use of it and the fact that petitioning was a legal form of trade action. Many petitioners from those distressed years simply sought relief for suffering, though without making claims under any specific legal protection. The Bolton petition of 11 November 1811 to the prince regent is just such a petition. No protective statute or customary privilege is cited. On the contrary, only an account of suffering and its cause is brought to bear against a customary and legal practice— the use of grain to distill alcohol even when bread is scarce.[99]

Many other petitioners based their claims on legal or customary rights, and petitioning did not bar an interpretative impulse. Randall explains that,

> The West of England woollen workers and master clothiers and journeymen of Yorkshire alike clearly expected Parliament to uphold the existing legislation or to modify it where appropriate, "keeping in view the uniform policy of the state." They did not necessarily intend that the existing law should be

enforced to the letter. The crucial factor was how custom had interpreted the law and what boundaries of enforcement various communities accepted and felt to be right.[100]

Randall employs the term "customary legality" to describe an attitude by which custom and law functioned complementarily in the woolen districts. It is not clear whether under the concept custom was viewed as preceding law and serving as its founding basis or whether custom followed, interpreted, and extended law. Perhaps the distinction is arbitrary. In any event, custom and usage within a trade community was seen by the cloth dressers as extending beyond legality in the "distinct form of words." Rather, the customary legality that prohibited the shearing frames, regarding which the law said nothing, was defined in 1806 by Randle Jackson, the counsel hired by the cloth workers to represent their interests, as a prohibition "in spirit and in fact."[101]

Even though custom was a mode of discourse that looked backward to ensure the rights of the community against the individual, thereby hindering full-fledged capitalistic market practices, it coexisted in Yorkshire Luddite writing with radicalism. That coexistence complicates an analysis of the writing and suggests that Yorkshire Luddite writing occurs at and reflects a moment in the temporal and numerical orientations of labor organization. There may be something to be said for Thompson's emphasis on the centrality of the Luddites in the making of the English working class. The Yorkshire region, for example, had passed through a period of radicalism in the years prior to Luddism. For example, documents that came into the possession of Joseph Radcliffe in 1802 were influenced by the outlined radical aims of the United Britons. One document especially, a pamphlet titled "Tyrants tremble the people are awake," makes natural-rights arguments for individual liberties.[102] Randall also remarks on the democratic and individualistic ideals of the master clothiers in the West Riding and notes that the ideals were shared by many journeymen who aspired to become masters themselves one day:[103]

The structure and *mentalité* of the West Riding woolen industry lent itself better to such ideas than did that of the West of England. The Domestic System's strength lay in its multiplicity of independent petty-producers and in the way in which their values, expressed in the cloth hall, the small workshops and cropping shops, were shared widely by the journeymen who worked alongside them and who had aspirations to join their ranks. . . . The ethos of the

Domestic System therefore reflected a society of small capitalists, conscious of personal rights and liberties and jealous of any encroachment by the large merchant capitalists whose role, they believed, should be confined solely to selling and not manufacturing cloth. . . . The ideas of Paine could find a conducive home in a culture such as this one, especially among those small master clothiers who found their modest businesses increasingly unable to compete with those of the nascent master manufacturers and also among the journeymen weavers and croppers whose hopes of social mobility and social security were being eroded by the advent of machinery. . . . The Painite ideal of pettyproducer independence reflected and ratified their view of the Domestic System, only now with the rise of mechanisation ceasing to appear secure and protected."[104]

Randall goes on the assert that many of the ideas of Jacobinism "were at many points congruent to the community *mentalité* of the West Riding."[105] Absent a constitutive discourse upon which claims might be grounded, Paine's attack on the constitutions that supported a government that denied protections to the trade would have had a special effect. The opposition of the French to the British government might have had a similar effect.

In the West Riding, as in much of Britain, the French enjoyed the good wishes of many of the inhabitants. In 1798 a Huddersfield man, John Taylor, was reported to Joseph Radcliffe for toasting " 'Success to Buonoparte and his undertakings' in front of recruiting parties in a public house in Huddersfield."[106] Sympathy for the French continued through much of the first decade of the 1800s. In 1800, James "Citizen" Gledhill of Battyeford composed "A patriotic song for the 14th of July 1800 being the anniversary of the French Revolution." Brooke and Kipling report that two years later the song was still in the possession of Edmund Norcliffe, a member of the United Britons.[107] Documents associated the United Britons were also discovered in the West Riding in 1802.[108] (Those same documents were found ten years later at Foster's Mill following a Luddite raid.)

One important question remains. By 1812 the woolen industry was suffering tremendously from the combined effects of reciprocal economic embargoes— Napoleon's Berlin Decrees and the British government's Orders in Council. Why would a Luddite author express a desire for the assistance of Napoleon, one of the leaders responsible for the depression of trade? I believe that the answer lies in the numerical orientation of many of the Luddite writers of the West Riding. Only in the West Riding do the Luddite writers boast of numbers. The address "To all Croppers, Weavers, &c & Public at Large" mentions that "Above 40,000 Heroes are ready to break out, to crush the old Goverment & establish a new one." The letter to Mr. Smith warns that one of General Ludd's lieutenants will be dispatched with 300 men and that "2782 Sworn Heroes" are ready to act. Numerical threats pervade Yorkshire Luddite writing. The tactic might be traced back at least as far as 1801, when a letter was sent to Joseph Radcliffe claiming that his life was in danger and that "500000 are redey boys yea & stedy Boyss."[109] It could be argued that the numerical tactic grew out of the democratic politics of Yorkshire during the preceding years and provided one method by which a member of a disaffected group (a Luddite, for instance) was able to make a representational claim.

A related tactic works in a letter to Joseph Radcliffe (Y8). The writer offers ironic congratulations to Radcliffe for his work in suppressing Luddism. The trope of popular disapproval, related to the numerical claims contained in other writers, is accented by a measure of formality that resembles but contrasts with the actions of the forty thousand weavers of Manchester, who raised a penny subscription to give to Joseph Hanson a gold cup.[110] Radcliffe's reward is not, however, a gold cup: "[I] think the medalon soon to be given to sutch villons as you is a ledon ball with powder."

These rhetorical tactics demonstrate that the Luddite writers of the West Riding might have been less concerned with constituting a community or a subculture through their writing than they were with representing that community to the authorities and cloth merchants. In this way, they more closely resemble the Midlands Luddites than those of the vicinity of Manchester. Unable to appeal to laws that recently had been repealed, and lacking (as Thompson points out) the old paternalistic interventions in wage and price markets, there remained for the croppers a relatively clear avenue—unionization, or an organizational process that resembled unionization. The Brief Institution had provided a model; however, the Combination Acts barred the public realization of that apparatus. The result, as Randall implies, was bifurcation. Randall cites a 14 August 1799 letter from William Barlow, a spy for the government, to R. Ford: "There has been more persons turned Jacobin within the little time that has elapsed since the bill was passed than for a year before."[111]

There were other Jacobinical influences at hand in the West Riding. John Baines, described so well in Peel's and Sykes and Walker's accounts of Luddite deliberations in the Huddersfield vicinity, was a Paineite, and Huddersfield had a long republican tradition. This context suggests that arguments from natural rights and the rights of man would have been ascendant in Luddite writings from the West Riding. In fact, at times they are, but perhaps not as much as we might believe. In the letter "To all Croppers, Weavers &c & Public at Large" (Y4), the writer advocates a Jacobinical revolution: "[A]ll Nobles and Tyrants must be brought down. Come let us follow the Noble Example of the brave Citizens of Paris who in the Sight of 30,000 Tyrant Redcoats brought A Tyrant to the Ground. by so doing you will be best aiming at your own Interest." The letter to Mr. Smith (Y5), however, distinguishes an English revolution from the French Revolution, claiming not to follow "the Noble Example of the brave Citizens of Paris" but rather desiring the assistance of "the French Emperor." English nationalism actually seems to be foregrounded in the letter to Mr. Smith. The Luddite writer does not seek to follow a French model but rather professes a willingness to accept French assistance in causing England to progress to a "just Republic." There is probably very little unconscious irony involved in the letter. In fact, the contrast of external assistance in the Mr. Smith letter with external example in the letter "To all Croppers, Weavers, &c & Public at Large" suggests that different Luddite writers considered different rhetorical options and kept them separate to some degree. The writer of the letter to Mr. Smith, for example, does not confuse the French revolutionary example with the assistance of Napoleon.[112]

Despite the early saturation of Yorkshire by Jacobinical discourse, Luddite texts are not themselves replete with such statements, tending more toward expressions of communal and customary grievances and ideals. In contrast, Luddite discourse was weakest in Manchester, where radicalism and its Paineite rhetoric of individual rights remained most pervasive throughout the Luddite years. Although republican sentiments might be expressed, communal notions predominate in Yorkshire Luddism. The language of moral outrage remains clearer than any Paineite or revolutionary rhetoric in many of the texts. More frequently than not, the first-person plural of many Yorkshire Luddite texts, the insistent "we," captures the value of "commonality" that was defended in the March 1812 letter to Mr. Smith (Y5). Paineite, Jacobin, and related ideas complicate the picture of Luddite discourse in the West Riding, but it still is possible to envision how those ideas coexist with others. The rest of this section is devoted to understanding that coexistence and how those ideas came to be contained under the umbrella of Luddism.

The Yorkshire croppers had available to them a highly developed discourse of petition, political engagement, Paineite political-economic analysis, trade organization, and threat. Given the vast array of linguistic resources at hand, it is surprising that they chose the language of Luddism, borrowed from the Midlands, to express their grievances. Certainly, the weavers and spinners of the cotton districts surrounding Manchester would have desired the constitutive effects of Luddite rhetoric, but what did the croppers have to gain from Midlands Luddism? More precisely, what did they have to gain from appropriating a discourse that had emerged in a different trade, in a different region, and under different conditions of production?

The croppers had experienced some success in preventing or slowing the incorporation of gig mills into the woolen manufactures some years before; however, the rescission of protective statutes in 1809 removed the possibility of utilizing what Randall calls "customary legality" as a mode of thinking and as a method of rhetorical appeal. Midlands framework knitters had experienced no similar direct erosion of legal protections. In fact, as indicated previously, the framework knitters had conducted successful legal actions against offending masters as recently as 1808. Midlands Luddism, then, might have provided to the disaffected croppers a still potent legal language that could be mapped onto the Yorkshire croppers' experiences and goals, and that could express the croppers' grievances in a language that had some rhetorical grounding not only in communally approved action but also in the sort of legality that the croppers had recently lost.

The mapping can take a number of forms. At times, only the name of General Ludd is appropriated to signal a singularity of purpose and a militancy in Luddite resistance. At other times, however, the Yorkshire writers employed a more highly developed device that might be called the Nottingham trope or an appeal to Nottingham. The trope involves describing Luddite disaffection in Yorkshire as having been authorized in Nottingham.

The clearest instances of the more highly wrought form of mapping appear in two letters from the vicinity of Huddersfield purporting to have originated in Nottingham. The first (Y7) is a 20 March 1812 letter from the "Soliciter to

General Ludd" to "Mr Ratcliffe" at "Millsbridge." Radcliffe is warned of a "judgment" likely to be filed against him:

> Take notice that a Declaration was this Day filed against you in Ludd[s] Court at Nottingham, and unless you remain* neutral judgment will immediately be sign[d] against you for Default, I shall thence summon a Jury for an Inquiry of Damages take out Execution against both your Body and House, and then you may Expect General Ludd, and his well organised Army to Levy it with all destruction possible.

The legalistic language within the letter coincides precisely with the Nottingham trope. Law and legal authority reside in Nottingham, and the authorization of a remedy for disaffection is typically treated as a process resembling legal proceedings. It imparts to the threatening letter a legitimacy that extends beyond the West Riding community. Nevertheless, the threat makes clear that the enforcement of the judgment will be felt locally.

The letter also bridges two other gaps. In the first case, legal discourse is joined to threats of armed activity in the statement that General Ludd's army will execute the judgment of Ludd's Court. The joining serves to counter the execution of governmental policies and the preservation of law and order by the army in the north of England during the Luddite risings, but the countering is not Jacobinical. The "Solicitor" writes that Ludd's Court is governed by equity, an English legal concept. In this case, the Nottingham trope mitigates the force of revolutionary threat by emphasizing Ludd's continuity with English law.

Second, the remainder of the letter contains a passage that recalls the cloth dressers' earlier efforts to petition Parliament:

> [T]he Cloth Dressers in the Huddersfield District as spent Seven Thousand Pounds in petition Government to put Laws in force to stop the Shearing Frames and Gig Mills to no purpose so they are trying this method now, and he is informd how you are affraid it will be carried on to another purpose but you need not be apprehensive of that, for as soon as ye Obnoxious machienery is Stopd or Destroyd the Genearal and his Brave Army will be Disbandd, and Return to their Employment, like other Liege Subjects

Again, the letter attempts to contain the threat and to assuage any fears of a larger, Jacobinical purpose, this time by professing a desire for trade protections, so that the laws no longer have to be preserved and enforced out of Notting-ham.[113]

The second letter to employ the mapping of a Nottingham discourse onto West Riding trade concerns is a 1 May 1812 letter from "Peter Plush" writing from Nottingham to "Mr Edward Ludd" at Huddersfield (Y14). Peter Plush writes,

> By order of Genral Ludd sener the levetinent colonel and every rank of oficers in the generales servece in the town and county of Nottingham I am reqested to expres the hye sence of honer We entertan of the meritoreous movment you and your forses have so gallantly mad in the neborood of Hudersfield to secure the rites of our poor starving fellow creturs.

The Nottingham trope differs in this rather late Yorkshire text. The letter is writ-ten in a congratulatory vein and, unlike the letter from General Ludd's "Solici-tor," takes the form of a military commendation, but the letter preserves the notion that authorization for Luddite activity emanates from Nottingham.

The letter concludes in a nationalistic but also republican vein that makes clear that Ludd has had to claim the discourse of morality as his own because the government has failed as a guardian of justice and equity:

> I am futher otherised to say that it is the opinion of our general and men that as long as that blackgard, drunken whoreing fellow called Prince Regent and his servants have any thing to do with government that nothing but distres will befole us there foot stooles. I am further desired to say that it is expected that you will remember that you are mad of the same stuf as Gorg Gwelps Juner and corn and wine are sent for you as wel as him.

The Peter Plush letter moves beyond the language of judgment into a language approaching but not quite realizing republicanism.

The rhetorical appeal to Nottingham enables the Yorkshire Luddite writers to join their number to a larger "we," comprising disaffected textile artisans in a number of trades and locales. The numerical and geographical threats of com-bination and correspondence would have been useful to Yorkshire writers who were seeking to reestablish their potency in the wake of the repeals of 1809. The Nottingham trope was also complex in a temporal sense. The legalisms of Not-tingham Luddite writing, appropriated by West Riding Luddites, harken back to a time when the textile trades enjoyed legal protections. But the croppers' protections had vanished, so any rhetorical borrowing of legal claims had to be undertaken with care. The Midlands Luddites enjoyed the long-established sanction of the crown, contained in the Charter of the Framework Knitters, but that sanction had recently been validated by the King's Bench in 1808 and had not yet been repudiated by the government. The Nottingham trope was simultaneously ancient and timely.

The figure of General Ludd ultimately served as an organizing principle that enabled disaffected English workers to think in terms of both the locality and the commonality of their difficulties. Even the Nottinghamshire General Ludd who congratulates the Huddersfield Luddites emphasizes the local nature of their problems. Even the leader of the Army of Redressers seeks to recruit the local populations of Huddersfield, Leeds, and the other northern towns into service. In almost all of the texts, including those with rhetorical appeals to nationalism, the local is emphasized, despite the lessons of the Brief Institution to consider national causes.

Nevertheless, even to its end, Yorkshire Luddism exhibited its bifurcation. Imprisoned in York Castle in November 1812, George Mellor turned his mind to petitioning Parliament for reform, writing to Thomas Ellis (Y22), "I have heard you are petitioning for a Parliamentary Reform and I wish these names to be given as follows," and sending a list of some thirty names. Weeks after the execution of Mellor and the other Luddites in January 1813, letters to officials in the vicinity of Huddersfield mentioned Mellor and threatened vengeance, death, and destruction to those opposing Luddite aims. As throughout the period of Luddism in Yorkshire, these letters reflect the Yorkshire Luddite propensity to make use of whatever discursive tools were conveniently at hand.

Midlands

M IDLANDS LUDDISM comprises the machine breaking, letter writing, and related forms of protest that occurred in Nottinghamshire, Leicestershire, and Derbyshire. Most of the machine breaking occurred in Nottingham and its vicinity, and most of the Luddite texts also originated in the Nottingham area between November 1811 and April 1812 and again briefly in the autumn of 1814 and summer of 1816.

The division between the lawful and the machine-breaking strands of Luddism, assumed by historians since E. P. Thompson, both facilitates and complicates the selection of Luddite documents. On the surface, the division of texts seems to be more clear in the Midlands than in the North, where writers from the affected trades rarely signed their names to letters and proclamations that sought to open public, nonsecretive avenues for resolving wage, usage, and price disputes. In the Midlands, however, anonymity was rather exceptional. The framework knitting trade, as a recognized public body that openly negotiated with masters through named representatives, provided the Midlands Luddite writers with an established rhetoric and with neatly delineated and commonly desired material goals. The grievances, the rhetorical strategies and appeals, and even the cadences of the writing of both the lawful and Luddite groups are frequently similar, but the fact that representatives of the Company of Framework Knitters and the local and branch committees signed their names to publicly disseminated documents creates the appearance of a dissociation from the anonymous, or eponymous, violent strand. Compared with Luddism in the North, where a mingling of constitutional and violent discourses is obvious and ubiquitous, the division in the Midlands between lawful writing and Luddite writing rings of artificiality.[1]

Midlands Luddites were also less interested in kingdomwide political reform than their Northwestern counterparts. In Nottinghamshire, Luddite writing remained comparatively, though by no means completely, differentiated from other forms of written protest actuated by different motives, especially political ones. George Rudé goes so far as to insist that the political language was "intrusive rather than intrinsic" to Luddism.[2] The Luddite texts themselves probably do not support Rudé's broad claim or Thompson's related claim of a division, but rather they indicate a range of languages and rhetorical tactics centered on the existence of a form of trade consciousness. Intending to reflect what I believe to be a focused continuum of discourses, I have chosen to include several other texts, including signed documents, that share formal, ideological, and strategic features with anonymous Luddite writings.

MI ❖ November 1811: Posted "Declaration; Extraordinary" by "Thos Death" to "Edward Ludd," Nottingham

The Home Office is the most important archive of Luddite letters, but a collection of papers in the estate of Richard Enfield of Bramcote, discovered during the early years of the twentieth century, also contains some of the same documents in the Home Office Papers. These papers, primarily letters and proclamations dating from 1811 and 1812, have been compiled and reproduced by John Russell in his 1906 article, "The Luddites." Some appear to be originals, but most are clearly copies. Unfortunately, it is necessary to rely on the Home Office versions for dates and other information regarding the circumstances of reception or composition.

Luddite declarations, proclamations, and posted notices provide good examples of the Luddites' appropriation of official discourse, repeated in the course of transforming the moral economy into a moral-economic polity capable of taking action on behalf of a community and a trade against manufacturers who were supported by the government. Although frame wrecking seems to have tapered off in Nottinghamshire from the end of March through October 1811, it appears from the declaration here (dated November 1811) that a Luddite subculture had been forming despite the relative quiet. The declaration, like the Luddite anthem "General Ludd's Triumph," indicates that the historian's traditional reliance on texts descriptive of events may be inadequate to an understanding of a working-class culture, the formation and operations of which are often undocumented. A rhetorical analysis of the values manifested in the text here and others like it may prove effective as supplements in increasing our understanding of Luddite writing and the subculture that produced it.

One of the more remarkable features of the declaration is its manifesting a political structure in which the assembled "General Agitators" determine courses of action, charging or authorizing General Ludd with the execution. Such "democratic" markers might recall earlier, similar features of the New Model Army. Other Luddite documents, such as the 1 May 1812 Yorkshire letter from "Peter Plush" on behalf of General Ludd to the Huddersfield Luddites, indicate a hierarchy descending from the West Riding version of General Ludd, who "otherises" Peter Plush to convey certain thoughts to the Huddersfield agitators.³ The purpose of the declaration might explain its more democratic appearances: it is intended to be presented to the offending manufacturer, revealing to him the popular, widespread sense of injustice. Given such a rhetorical project, a democratic subtext would be appropriate.

Recognizing the democratic subtext also helps to explain the true nature of the Luddite "judgment." The artisan tradition had provided for the levying of fines or forfeitures (usually of finished and unfinished goods) against trade members who violated the rules of the trade. The violating members typically were masters, but artisans nevertheless, hence subject to government by the trade, the Framework Knitters Charter, and its rules. Even during this period of increasing social and professional distance between master and worker made possible by industrial capitalism, workers sought to enforce the rules against masters whom they still considered to be members of their trade.

The writer of the declaration took care to make the document resemble an official proclamation through mimicking the language of legal writs and through the physical presentation of the lettering. For example, the first three lines appear in larger characters than the body of the declaration and through underscoring the writer attempts to reproduce typographical effects of official, printed proclamations. Substantive revision, evident in the striking of the more colloquial "get rich" and its replacement by the more formal "gain riches," indicates the writer's preference for elevated constructions appropriate for the language of law.

The declaration follows immediately a copy of a 15 November 1811 outletter from Home Office Undersecretary John Beckett to High Sheriff Thomas Wright at Norwood Park, Nottinghamshire, informing Wright that a squadron of the 15th Dragoons will be dispatched to Nottingham in response to the violence. Beckett's letter provides no additional information about the text.

H. O. 42/119. A version also appears in John Russell's "The Luddites," *Transactions of the Thoroton Society* 10 (1906): 53–62, as Facsimile C, facing page 59, with no additional information about the document.

❖   ❖   ❖

<u>Declaration; Extraordinary.</u>
<u>Justice.</u>
Death, or Revenge.
To our well-beloved Brother, and Captain in Chief, Edward Ludd.

Whereas, it hath been represented to us: the General Agitators, for the Northern Counties, assembled to redress the Grievances of the Operative Mechanics, That Charles Lacy, of the Town of Nottingham, British Lace Manufacturer, has been guilty of divers fraudulent, and oppressiv, Acts—whereby he has reduced to poverty and Misery Seven Hundred of our beloved Brethren; moeover, it hath been represented to us that the said Charles Lacy, by making fraudulent Cotton Point Nett,[4] of One Thread Stuff, has obtain'd the Sum of Fifteen Thousand Pounds, whereby he has ruine'd the Cotton-Lace Trade, and consequently our worthy and wellbelov'd Brethren; whose support and comfort depended on the continuance of that manufacture.

It appeareth to us that the said Charles Lacy was actuated by the most diabolical motives, namely to ~~get rich~~ gain riches by the misery of his Fellow Creatures, we therefore willing to make an example of the said Charles Lacy, do adjudge the said Fifteen Thousand Pounds to be forfeited, and we do hereby authorise, impower, and enjoin you, to command Charles Lacy to disburse the said sum, in equal shares among the Workmen, who made Cotten Nett in the Year 1807, within ten Days from the Date hereof.

In default whereof, we do command that you inflict the Punishment of Death on the said Charles Lacy, and we do authorise you to distribute among [the party]

you may employ for that purpose the Sum of Fifty Pounds, we enjoin you to
cause this our Order to be presented to the said Charles Lacy without Delay,
November 1811--By Order Thos Death[5]

M2 ❖ 8 November 1811: Threatening letter from "Ned Lud" at Nottingham to
"Mr H" at "Bullwell"

This letter is one of the earliest Luddite documents from the vicinity of Nottingham. Even in its early stages, Nottinghamshire Luddism employed a legal
style (indicated in this letter by words such as "execution" and "Forfeit"). "M^r
Bolton," the "Forfeit" whose name is cited in the letter almost as a form of prece-
dent, is probably the Arnold hosier whose frames were broken during the first
round of Luddite attacks of March 1811.[6]

The document is in poor physical condition. The addressee's name is illegible due to bleeding of the ink, but the long name of more than ten characters
begins with "H," and the town seems to be Bulwell. The recipient may have
been Edward Hollingsworth, an unpopular Bulwell hosier, whose frames were
destroyed on 10 November 1811 despite his having prepared for the attack, during
which one Luddite (John Westley or Westby or Wesley) was killed.[7]

The letter, sent from Nottingham to Bulwell, might serve as partial refuta-
tion of the argument made by R. A. Church and S. D. Chapman, who attempt to
resolve the problem of the apparent division among the framework knitters between the machine-breaking and the "constitutionalist" branches. Church and
Chapman argue that the effective division was between town and country stockingers. The lower-paid country workers were supposed by Church and Chapman
to have been more resentful, desperate, and prone to violence than their town
counterparts.[8] This letter and others indicate that much of Luddite discontent
did issue from Nottingham, even when the threats were made against masters
outside of the town.

The letter appears without any enclosing correspondence and with damage to
the document in several places. I have retained the original format of the letter,
particularly line breaks, to show the position of lacunae caused by bleeding and
tearing.

H. O. 42/118.

❖ ❖ ❖

M^r H[illegible]
at Bullwell

S^r,

Sir if you do not pull don the Frames
or stop pay [in] Goods^9 onely for ~~work~~
~~extra~~ work or m[ake] in Full fashon
my Companey will [vi]sit y^r machines
for execution agai[nst] [y]ou--
Mr Bolton the Forfeit--
I visit^d him--

Ned Lu[d]
Kings [illegible]

Nottingh^m---Novemb^r 8 1811

M3 ❖ 27 November 1811: "Address of the Plain Silk Stocking-Makers to the
Gentlemen Hosiers of Nottingham"

The anonymous public writings of the Luddites share many rhetorical features with the named public writings of the framework knitters and members of
other trades. Typically, even the lawful, signed publications do not make clear
whether the authors write as agents of the Company of Framework Knitters or
as an ad hoc collective. In November 1811 the *Nottingham Review* carried two addresses to the gentlemen hosiers of Nottingham from a group of stockingers.
One of the addresses, "From the Framework-Knitters," written shortly after the
commencement of the November breakings, appeals to the compassion of the
hosiers, to their desire for commercial advantage and community prosperity, and
to their fears of frame breaking ("suitable defence" and "We wish to live peaceably and honestly by our Labour"). Whereas the address "From the Framework-
Knitters" is unsigned, the "Address of the Plain Silk Stocking-Makers" is signed
"WILLIAM CRUMP, Secretary, In behalf of the Plain Silk Stocking-Makers."
Crump's signature is followed by a list of fifty-two hosiers who signed an agree-
ment to pay their employees an advance of sixpence per pair of hose. When the

two addresses are considered together, as their original proximity to each other requires, the tension between publicity and anonymity simultaneously complements and displaces the eponymy typical of the pieces signed "Ludd," usually as a defender of "the Trade." The tension further reflects the dilemma that the hosiers and the authorities must have faced: with whom were they to negotiate? Officials sought, above all, to preserve the peace, and the "classic" model involved a process of negotiation and compromise.[10] Typically, the magistrates and landed gentlemen would bargain directly with persons who were known to them. In the case of Nottingham Luddism, the ambiguity centering on naming and namelessness cast an element of doubt into any negotiation. Officials and hosiers could not be certain that any compromise with the named members of the trade could satisfy the demands of the unnamed members. The unsigned "Address from the Framework-Knitters" must surely have complicated matters even more by insinuating a link between the signed "Address of the Plain Silk Stocking-Makers" immediately below it in the *Review* and the anonymous or eponymous Luddite threats circulated throughout the region at the time.

Nottingham Review, 29 November 1811, printed on the front page. (The same documents appeared in the *Nottingham Journal* but not in such a prominent position.) A copy of the *Review* was forwarded to the Home Office, where it appears in H. O. 42/117.

❖ ❖ ❖

ADDRESS
OF THE PLAIN SILK STOCKING-MAKERS
TO
THE GENTLEMEN HOSIERS OF NOTTINGHAM,
WHO HAVE AGREED TO GIVE

An advance of Sixpence per Pair

FOR THE MAKING OF BLACK SILK HOSE.

GENTLEMEN,—Gratitude is an Attribute imprinted upon the Human Heart by Deity himself; and for us not to acknowledge your Favor on the present occasion, would render us unworthy of your future regard, and justly expose us to the scorn of every honest and humane Man, who might be made acquainted with your present attention to our interest. It is therefore with peculiar satisfaction that we return you our Thanks for your ready condescension in attending to the solicitations of those Persons that waited upon you, on our behalf, to obtain the advance above specified. Indeed, whoever contemplates for a moment the present situation of the Stocking-Makers, with the alarming price of every necessary of life staring them in the face, will sympathize with their sufferings, and the sufferings of the Families, and will readily join with them in giving Thanks to those of their Employers, who attend to the amelioration of their piteous Condition.

Gentlemen,

Believe me your very humble and obedient Servant,

WILLIAM CRUMP, Secretary,

In behalf of the Plain Silk Stocking-Makers.

Nottingham, Nov. 27, 1811.

N. B. The following is a List of those Gentlemen Hosiers, who have Signed the above Advance: — [11]

Lawson and Sons
J. and I. Lawson
Brocksopp and Parker
E. Chatteris
Thos. Kelk
Beardsmore and Sons
T. Galloway
W. Meats and Sons
Barwick and Christian
N. and J. Cox and Co.
Simon Skidmore
For Mr. Eaton, *Rich. Satter-thwaite*
Child, Cosens, and Co.
Saml. Clark
Scorer and Acomb
James and Neal
Saml. Barlow
G. and S. Nichols
Geo. Gibson and Son
Hancock and Wakefield
Hall, Northage, and Hardwick
Wilks and Armfield

Kewney and Richardson
Wm. Howitt
Berridge and Tarratt
For L. B. Mason, *W. Smith*
J. Rawson
For Berridge and James, *Rich. Shaw*
Radford and Stones
R. Hopper
Thos. Jackson
Turner and Smith
Geo. Carey
Edmund Wright and Co.
Strahan, Theaker and Co.
J. Billins
G. L. Cox and Son
W. Walker
Morley, Wilson, and Morley
Holmes, Edenborough, & Stenson
Trentham, Trentham, and Martin
G. and J. Ray

Geo. Pickering

G. and J. Mills

Pope and Co.

J. Lightfoot

Thos. Jerram

James Pritt and Co.

R. and S. Cheetham

Green and Gill

Dove, Gill, and Co.

Richd. Smith and Co.

A Pledge of the same nature has been given by several other Hosiers, whose Names are not annexed.

M4 ❖ 28 November 1811: "An Address from the Framework-Knitters to the Gentlemen Hosiers of the Town of Nottingham"

Nottingham Review, 29 November 1811, printed on the front page.

❖ ❖ ❖

AN ADDRESS

FROM THE FRAMEWORK-KNITTERS

TO THE

GENTLEMEN HOSIERS

OF

THE TOWN OF NOTTINGHAM.

GENTLEMEN,—At a time like the present, so big with Calamity and Distress, we think it right to solicit your Advice, Aid, and Direction, as we know no Reason why our Business, which is looked upon as the staple Trade, and principal Support of the Community at large, should be exposed to so many Evils, without any suitable means of defence; or if any, why not brought forward into exercise. As we have nothing in view but a reciprocal Advantage in the Trade, both for ourselves and you, and a mutual good Understanding in all our Actions, we solicit your Advice, Aid, Direction, and Support, in this time of our Calamity and Distress, and we think we have a humble Claim upon you for it. On account of the great rise of all the Necessaries of Life, a Man that has full employ, with all his industry, and a Woman, with all her care and economy, can by no means support a Family with any degree of Comfort. If this is the Case (which it really is) how deplorable must the situation of those be, that have but a small portion of Employ, and at very low Rates; but still worse, what must the situation of those be that have none at all, which is the Case with INCALCULABLE NUMBERS at this time.–Destitute of all the Comforts of Life, our only acquaintance is pinching Poverty and pining Want. We wish to live peaceably and honestly by our Labour, and to train up our Children in the paths of virtue and rectitude, but we cannot accomplish our wishes. Our Children, instead of being trained up by a regular course of Education, for social life, virtuous employments, and all the recipro-cal advantages of mutual enjoyment, are scarce one remove from the Brute, are left to all the dangerous Evils attendant on an uncultivated Mind, and often fall dreadful Victims to that guilt, which Ignorance is the parent of. But, Gentle-men, we forbear, as we think it would be insulting both to your judgments and feelings, were we to attempt a description of all our Calamities, which you so well know, and which we so much experience. Our request, Gentlemen, is that you will favor us with your best Advice, respecting as Address to Parliament, for the better Regulation of our Trade, and means of defence against future Imposi-tions. Being well assured that the most suitable means lie in the compass of your breasts, we wish to pay all deference to your superior judgments, and are now waiting for your decision, which we hope you will favor us with as soon as pos-sible; that if it meets your views, the Business may be conducted peaceably and in good order, to our mutual Comfort and Advantage.

November 28, 1811.

M5 ❖ 16 December 1811: Proclamation, "Ned Lud Gives Notic, to the Coperation," Nottingham

Although some letters merely hint at violence, most Luddite threats were ex-aggerated; however, especially in Nottinghamshire, the exaggerations were more often than not rhetorical responses intended to counter some official action. For example, the regent's offer of a reward of fifty pounds begat a parodic Luddite reply—a reward of fifty bullets for any informer (Rutland to Ryder, 5 January 1812, H. O. 42/119). On 11 December 1811 a committee consisting of public offi-cials and large manufacturers was formed by the Nottingham town corporation, thereby politicizing the conflict. The committee was to operate in secret to quell the risings and had two thousand pounds at its disposal.[12] In December 1811, while the stockingers were seeking a negotiated settlement with the manufacturers, the government dispatched troops to Nottingham at the urging of members of the newly formed "Corporation Committee," as it was called. The notice here urges the Corporation Committee to call a meeting to pursue negotiations, which had been the aim of the earlier open letters published by stockingers in the December 1811 Nottingham newspapers, but the arrival of soldiers changed the bargaining position of the framework knitters. The Luddite response was to recognize the fact of politicization on the local or civic level and to exaggerate their own power, thereby seeking to force negotiations. This is the first Luddite document that threatens violence on a civic scale as a demonstration of Luddite power and determination. In fact, by the end of the letter, the threat of violence intensifies and broadens through defiance of a national institution, the military, and through the closing, "no King."

The document is undated in Russell and has no accompanying information about the recipient, but it certainly is the letter described in a reward notice in the *Nottingham Review*, 27 December 1811: "Resolved Unanimously—That this Corporation do agree to pay a Sum not exceeding £500 . . . to any Person or Persons, who may give such Information of the Authors, Writers, Publishers, or Senders of . . . a wicked and inflammatory Paper, addressed by way of Notice to the Corporation, under the fictitious Name of Ned Lud, delivered at the Police Office on the Evening of the 16th of December Instant . . ." [13]

Russell, "The Luddites" Facsimile D, facing page 61.

❖   ❖   ❖

Ned Lud Gives Notic, to the

Coper^{a}tion,

if the Coperation does not take means to Call A

Meeting with the Hoseiars about the prices Being——

Droped Ned will asemble 20000 Menn together in a few Days

and will Destroy the town in Spite of the Soldiers——

no King——

M6 ❖ 20 December 1811: Address of the Plain Silk Hands of Derby

Two weeks after the open letters from the hosiers and the stockingers appeared in the *Nottingham Review*, the Plain Silk Hands of Derby published in the *Review* their own open letter. The biblical epigraph comes from Luke 10:7, in a passage in which Jesus instructs his followers on disseminating the Gospel, comparing their work to a harvest. Among other things, Jesus tells his followers that he sends them forth "as lambs among wolves" (Luke 10:3) and that they should undertake their work with an attitude of peace (Luke 10:5), but the passage also contains a threat against those who refuse the missionaries' overtures: "But into whatsoever city ye enter, and they receive you not. . . . it shall be more tolerable in that day for Sodom, than for that city" (Luke 10:10–12). Given the double message of the biblical passage, the epigraph imparts to the address a tone that is dynamic, moving from overtures of peace to the threat of violence.

Nottingham Review, 20 December 1811.

❖ ❖ ❖

"The Labourer is worthy of his Hire."

At a General Meeting of Plain Silk Framework-knitters, held at the Fox and Owl Inn, Derby, December 9th, 1811, to take into consideration the increasing Grievances under which they labour, it was unanimously Resolved, that every means in their power should be employed to stop the progress of future Impositions upon their Manufacture, and that a Statement of their Case be once more submitted to their Employers, with an application for immediate Redress.

Gentlemen Hosiers,

GALLED by the pressure of unprecedented times, we cannot any longer remain indifferent to our common interest as men. As a body of ingenious artizans, employed on materials of great value; pent up in a close shop fourteen or sixteen hours a day; (a confinement prejudicial to many constitutions), having under our constant care machine confessedly difficult, from the construction of its principles, to preserve in good condition, and allowed to be one of the first productions of British genius; devoting our time and abilities alone, to adorn the rich and great, we conceive ourselves entitled to a higher station in society; and that, in point of emolument, we ought to rank with mechanics of the first eminence. If the position be admitted that one calling is more respectable than another, surely the making of Silk Stockings is an employment, both in point of value and elegance of the article, highly respectable; and considering our manufacture is consumed alone by the opulent, it ought to produce a competence adequate to the just wants of our families.

About thirty years ago, a Silk Stocking-maker obtained a decent subsistence; but since that time we have had to contend with two great drawbacks upon our necessary comforts, the one is imposition upon our manufacture, the other a tripled augmentation in the price of nearly every article we consume. That has crept upon us by a slow and imperceptible motion; this by bold and rapid strides; each at once aiming the blow that has laid us prostrate beneath every other mechanic in this part of the empire.

To prove that we have imposition upon our manufacture, we must advert to its originally established order, that has, till now, stood inviolate for nearly two centuries. By its established order, we mean the gauges of our frames: by these alone we ascertain the quality of a silk stocking, and in proportion to the number of gauges, our wages have been regulated for nearly two hundred years; these always remaining sacred between the employer and his workmen. In most articles of plain silk, one shilling for two extra gauges was generally given; that is to say, from a 24 to a 26 gauge, one shilling extra; from a 26 to a 28 gauge, one shilling extra, and so on in proportion. Is it not an imposition then to be compelled to make 24 work on a 26 gauge, for the price of a 24 gauge? Is it not a still greater imposition to be compelled to make 24 work on a 27 or 28 gauge, without a remuneration? As the price stands at present, we are losing from nine-pence to one shilling and nine-pence per pair, the quality of the work being nearly equal to the gauge. That these impositions exist we presume no Hosier will take upon him to deny; neither do we pretend to charge any individual amongst them as being the author of them. We are at a loss to know where to fix the stigma (too much blame being due to ourselves for not watching better over the trade) as each striving to manufacture on the lowest terms, makes us little better than mere engines to support a jealous competition in the market. The average earnings of plain silk hands are indeed too well known to you, to be a very small pittance for the maintenance of a wife and two or three children; they do not exceed 10s. 6d. per week: if some average 13s. per week, this will do very little for a family. Three shillings at least must go for house-rent and taxes—one shilling for coal—one shilling and sixpence for soap and candles, for himself and family; and if he has a wife and three children he must have one stone and a half of flour, which is at least six shillings more; here we see the poor fellow has left three shillings and sixpence to provide all other necessaries of life.

Is it not very discouraging to us to know that the shoe-maker has doubled his wages within the last twenty years, that the tailor has done nearly the same, and the labourer who had about that time six shillings per week has now eighteen shillings? Whenever any other class of mechanics turn out for an advance of wages, so far as we are concerned in the consumption of their particular manufacture, it has a direct tendency to diminish our's; while at the same time the price of our labour, to our great mortification, is fatally doomed to be stationary. If a mechanic in any branch of business either increases his hours of labour, or takes a piece of work extra to what he has been accustomed to do, justice, reason, and honor, demand an adequate remuneration. But alas! how far different this with a Silk Stocking-maker! Instead of our wages increasing with the price of provision (which ought to be the case under every civil government) we are generally making stockings one shilling under their real quality. The time is now come when it is impossible for us to go any longer in a contented condition, under present circumstances. The imperious dictates of human nature impel us to raise up a manly voice in our own behalf: governed by every principle of right towards you, acknowledging that due deference to your superior station, yet loudly calling your attention to our present case. Much encouraged by the late address to the trade, from the Gentlemen Hosiers in Nottingham, we avail ourselves of this auspicious moment, fully believing that you see the necessity of an amelioration of our wretched condition. Hedged in by a combination act, we cannot say to you as a public body, that we demand an advance of wages, but we can say that JUSTICE DEMANDS that we should receive a remuneration for extra labour: this is all we want, and until it is obtained, nothing but complaints will be found to exist amongst us.

It cannot reasonably be expected that we shall obtain a full remuneration for the impositions on our manufacture AT ONCE; probably this will be a work of some time: therefore we have fixed upon SIXPENCE per pair on all sorts of silk hose; at the same time observing that we consider this a very paltry consideration indeed, compared with the alarming high price of provisions, and the repeated advances all other mechanics have received in their wages. This *partial* remuneration for extra labour, as we may justly call it, we have every reason to believe may on your part with great ease be ceded; knowing some little of men and things, we certainly conclude that not one pair less of silk stockings will be worn. If a poor man is obliged now in give three shillings and sixpence more for a pair of shoes than he did in time past, is it unreasonableness that a gentleman out of his fortune should give sixpence extra for a pair of silk stockings, when at the same time there is a shilling extra in labour upon them? Instead of complaining, we might suppose he would rather say, 'Let the ingenious live.'

During the last twenty years, while provision has been so rapidly advancing, we have seen it our duty frequently to petition you for an advance in wages. In the year 1805, we attained twopence per pair: although you certainly granted us a favor, we were very much disgusted with the smallness of the advance. You told us if you raised the price of our labour, (and you always tell us so) the French would undersell us in the market. Considering the high repute of British manufacture, we have reason to hope this would not be the case; an allowed preference always being given to it. And we observe that a branch of commerce that must be spun out of our very bowels, to support a competition with the trash produced by the French manufacture, rather than its being an ornament to our national glory, is a curse to us as individuals; and makes us regret the day that ever doomed us to be Plain Silk Stocking-makers.

Gentlemen, there is every reason in the world to prove that a remuneration ought and must take place. Several Hosiers in this town have openly avowed its necessity. The high price of provision is on our side, reason, honer, morality, philanthropy, necessity, justice, your own interest, as being accountable to the Almighty, the practicability of the case, the combination act, and the general sufferage of mankind; all declare that we ought to be remunerated for extra labour.

Gentlemen, being invited by some of you to state our grievances, we have used great plainness on the subject; well knowing that this will prvail, when acts of violence would render us detestable to mankind.

In order to prevent any future imposition on our manufacture, we have drawn up the following Statement, by which we mean to abide.

RESOLVED—That all Hose shall be marked with the Figures in the Welt according to what they are.

Women's Jacks.	Men's Jacks.		Price of Women's.		Price Men's.	
			S.	D.	S.	D.
24 ... 120 ... 128		24	3	0	3	4
26 ... 128 ... 138		26	3	9	4	1
28 ... 138 ... 150		28	4	8	5	2
30 ... 150 ... 162		30	5	8	6	2
32 ... 162 ... 174		32	6	8	7	2
34 ... 174 ... 186		34	7	8	8	2
36 ... 186 ... 198		36	8	8	9	2

24 narrowed down 1 plain, 14 jacks in women's, 16 in men's, 4 bindings in in women's heels, 5 in men's, 5 bindings in in women's bottoms, 6 in men's.

26 narrowed down 1 plain, 15 jacks in women's, 17 in men's, 5 bindings in in women's heels, 6 in men's, 6 bindings in in women's bottoms, 7 in men's.

28 narrowed down 2 plain, 17 jacks in women's, 19 in men's, 6 bindings in in women's heels, 7 in men's, 7 bindings in in women's bottoms, 8 in men's.

30 narrowed down 2 plain, 19 jacks in women's, 21 in men's, 7 bindings in in women's heels, 8 in men's, 8 bindings in in women's bottoms, 9 in men's.

32 narrowed down 2 plain, 21 jacks in women's, 23 in men's, 8 bindings in in women's heels, 9 in men's, 9 bindings in in women's bottoms, 10 in men's.

34 narrowed down 2 plain, 23 jacks in women's, 25 in men's, 9 bindings in in women's heels, 10 in men's, 10 bindings in in women's bottoms, 11 in men's.

36 narrowed down 2 plain, 25 jacks in women's, 27 in men's, 10 bindings in in women's heels, 11 in men's, 1 bindings in in women's bottoms, 12 in men's.

24 and 26 half size, 4 jacks--28 and upwards 6 jacks.

Any alteration in the above width to be paid for accordingly.

We expect and trust the above remuneration for extra labour, together with these regulations, take place on the 1st of January, 1812.

From the Derby Committee of Plain Silk Hands.

M7 ❖ 21 December 1811: Letter from "Ned Lud" at Nottingham to the Corporation Committee at Nottingham

Like the preceding "Ned Lud Gives Notic" paper, this letter addresses the activities of the Corporation Committee in Nottingham. And, like other letters written later, it links the Corporation Committee with Spencer Perceval, indicating that the Nottinghamshire Luddites had begun to envision a connection, or at least an operational affinity, between the local authorities and those in London. The predominant focus by the Luddite writers on the Nottingham Corporation Committee suggests that, despite mention of national political figures, the increasing political consciousness remained local in nature, in contrast to the heightened concern with national policy exhibited by the Yorkshire and, to an even greater degree, Northwestern Luddites, as well as in later letters from the Midlands.

Transcript 3 in Russell, "The Luddites" 61.

❖   ❖   ❖

Gentlemen

I prosum you are desireus of A sitiation hin the fugoffis[14] and you may Rest ashured nothing shall be wonting hon My part to procure you the sitiations you Apply for but I doubt I shall not be able to provide for you all in the fugoffice, as som of you willnot alltogather be wiling To stop there hon A Count of the dangeours Desorder you seem to Laber hunder, it aperes from the simtoms of youre desorder that another full moon or two will make som of you fit objects for the Hous in snenton Fields, but if it shud plese devin provedenc to render any of you unfit to discharg the dutys Which Mr. Coldham has imposed hon youre Commitey befor the 12th of february 1812 I will get Docr. Willis[15] to atend hon you but At the A bove date Mr. Willis will be wanted at Saint Lukes[16] as it may be Expected he wil have Ocation to meet King Percevell and the rest of youre Coleges there.

I am yours faithfuly

Ned Lud ———

Nottingham

December the 21 1811

M8 ❖ 23 December 1811: Posted proclamation signed "By order of King Ludd," Nottingham

This signed proclamation appears in the Home Office Papers, with no enclosing letter, and as Russell's Transcript 2. Russell remarks, "No date but published 23 Decr. 1811." That date is provided in the version in the Home Office Papers in the handwriting of a Home Office clerk, although the document itself appears not to be a clerk's copy. Thomis, too, provides a date of 23 December 1811.[17] The date follows two official actions, both of which were announced in the *Nottingham Journal*, 28 December 1811, several days after their being introduced. One was an offer by the prince regent of rewards and pardons for persons giving information against the machine breakers. The other was a decision by the Nottingham mayor and council to form a Corporation Committee, funded with two thousand pounds and appointed the task of quelling the Luddite "outrages."

H. O. 42/118; Transcript 2 in Russell, "The Luddites" 60. It is reproduced in Malcolm Thomis, *Luddism in Nottinghamshire* (London: Phillimore, 1972), 18.

❖ ❖ ❖

⟨Home Office version⟩

I do hereby discharge, all manner of Persons, who has been, employ'd by me, in giveing any information, of breaking Frames, to the Town Clerk, or to the Corporation Silley Committee—any Person found out, in so doing, or attempting to give out any information, will be Punish'd with death, or any Constable found out making any enquiries, so has to hurt the Cause of Ned, or any of his army, D E A T H (by order of King Lud)

⟨Russell version⟩

Ned Ludd

Proclamation

I do hereby discharge all manner of Persons, who has been employed by me in giving any information of breaking frames to the Town Clerk or to the Corporation Silley Committee, any person found out in so doing or attempting to give any information, will be punished with death or any Constable found out making inquiries so as to hurt the cause of Ned or any of his Army, Death

By order of

King Ludd[18]

(with the Prince & 2

Thousand Pounds   2 Hundred Pounds Reward.

at their Ace.)

———————————————————————————————————————

M9 ❖ 27 December 1811: Address of the Framework Knitters of Melbourne

One week after the publication of the address of the Plain Silk Hands of Derby, the Framework Knitters of Melbourne published a similar address to the gentlemen hosiers, reminding them of earlier wage and rate agreements.

Nottingham Review, 27 December 1811.

❖ ❖ ❖

Melbourne, December 23, 1811.

THE Framework-Knitters of this peaceable and hitherto undisturbed Town, were very much rejoiced to hear that the Gentlemen Hosiers were taking into their consideration to redress the Grievances the Workmen labour under; and to establish a respectable, regular, and permanent Price, for the making of the different Articles belonging to that extensive and respectable Branch of ENGLISH COMMERCE: In consequence of which, the Framework-Knitters of this Town thought it indispensably necessary to hold a Meeting, for the purpose of stating the Prices they wish to have for the different Sorts of Work that are making at this Place. And it is hoped that the Gentlemen Hosiers will not think the Statement unreasonable, as we do not wish for any addition to the Price that was settled by One Hundred and Thirty-nine honorable Hosiers, on the 7th of May, 1805, and published in the Nottingham Review, on the 6th of December, 1811. And as there are different Sorts of Work making in this Neighbourhood at the present Time, not known at the above Date of 1805, it has been thought necessary to state a Price to those Sorts of Work, and it is hoped that the Gentlemen Hosiers will readily agree to the Statement, when it is considered that it is Sixpence per Yard lower than it was Two Years ago, in the Derby Ribbed Double-looped Piece Work.

THE STATEMENT IS AS FOLLOWS:
DERBY RIBBED DOUBLE-LOOPED CORD.
24 *Gauge* .... 1*s.* 9*d.*
26 .... 2*s.* 0*d.*
28 .... 2*s.* 0*d.*
GERMAN RIBS.
21 *Gauge* .... 1*s.* 9*d.*
24 .... 2*s.* 0*d.*
BERLIN PIECES.
White Worsted ...... 2*s.* 0*d. per Yard.*
Light Drab .... 2*s.* 2*d.*
Dark Drab .... 2*s.* 3*d.*
Dark Blue .... 2*s.* 4*d.*

The Journeyman's Price for making the Berlin Pieces, at this place, is 1*s.* 6*d.* per Yard, as the Yard in taken in and measured at the Warehouse; and the whole of the extra Price we have, from the Warehouse, for Colours.

M10 ❖ 1 January 1812: Posted proclamation titled "By the Framework Knitters, A Declaration"

After a December busy with anonymous and open letters and proclamations, a "Declaration . . . was stuck up at Radford on y first of Jany 1812." The most remarkable feature of the proclamation is its appeal to the authority of Charles II. It is interesting that the writer of the proclamation appeals to the authority of a monarch at roughly the same time that the great reformer, John Cartwright, writing to the *Nottingham Review* (17 January 1812), urges workers to conceive of making their own laws: "With regard to those who trade or who toil for wealth, of for subsistence, from the highest merchant down to him who works the loom, you cannot but have observed how little, *while at their ease*, they are disposed to recollect that they have "any thing to do with the LAWS but to obey them." Cartwright observes that if "they themselves would have made the LAWS, this would have prevented the calamity [of low wages and high prices]."

In contrast to Cartwright's argument for self-determination and electoral reform, the declaration merely summons a limited power granted to the stockingers by a monarch of a deposed line. Cartwright grasped the limitations of a royal indulgence. He even professes a suspicion of Magna Carta in a letter published in the *Nottingham Review*, 27 December 1811:

That charter only scorched arbitrary power, but did not put an end to it. Tyranny again soon reared its head, vexing and pillaging the people, and but too often shedding their blood. . . . When, however, the people became once more *unanimous*, the asserter of divine right thought it time to flee. . . . The people then having elected another King, *peacably* obtained the Bill of Rights. But by the oversight of some, and the trickery of others, this charter again was lamentably defective.

Despite Cartwright's warning about royally granted charters and dispensations, addressed specifically to the frame wreckers of Nottinghamshire, the Luddites continued not only to break the frames but also to appeal to the Framework Knitters Charter granted by Charles II, as later Midlands documents show.[19]

Considered in the larger discursive context existing in Nottingham at the time and the Luddite propensity for rhetorical appropriation and *bricolage*, the Luddites' appeal to a royal discourse is reasonable. The Nottingham authorities buttressed their own local notices with associated royal discourses. For example, in the *Nottingham Review*, 27 December 1811, the mayor and the common council published their resolutions immediately beside the prince regent's proclamation and reward notice, evidently hoping that some of the regent's cache would carry over from one column to the adjacent one.

Sent to the Home Office by Robert Baker, probably on 3 February 1812, labeled "A True Copy." That version now appears in the Nottinghamshire Archives M 429, pp. 31–32, which is my source. A copy taken by a Home Office clerk was cataloged in H. O. 42/119. As Hammond and Hammond note, the "Declaration" "received the official endorsement: 'This letter cannot be answered'."[20] The heavily emended H. O. 42/119 version of the "Declaration" has also been transcribed with further emendations in David C. Douglas, ed., *English Historical Documents*, 12 vols. (New York: Oxford University Press, 1969), 11:531.

❖   ❖   ❖

⟨Nottinghamshire Archives version⟩

By the Frameworck Knitters

A+Declaration.

Whereas by the Charter, granted by our late Sovereign Lord Charles the Seacond by the Grace of God of Great Brittain France and Ireland the Frame Worck Knitters are Impowre'd to breake and Distroy all Frames or Engines that fabricate Articles in a fraudilent and Deceitfull manner and to distroy all Frameworck Knitters Goods Whatsoever that are so made—And Whereas a number of Deceitfull Unprinciped and Interguing Persons did Attain An Act to be passed in the twenty Eight Year of our preasent Sovereign Lord George the third Whereby it was enacted that Persons, Entring by Force into any house Shop or Place to Breake or Distroy frames should be Adjudged Guilty of Feloney, and as we are fully Convinced that such Act was Obtain'd in the most Fraudilent Manner Interesting and Electionering manner and that the Honourable Parliment of Great Brittain was deceived the Motives and Intentions of the Persons Obtained such Act we therefore the frame worck knitters do hereby declare the aforesaid Act to be null and void to all Intents and Purposses, Whatsoever as by the passing of this Act Vilinous and Impassing persons Are Enable to make Fraudilent and Deceitfull Manifactory's to the discreadit and utter ruin of Our Trade. And Wheareas wee declare that the afore Mentioned charter is as much in force as tho no such Act had been passed and we do hereby declare to all Hosiers lace Manufactirou's and properieters of frames that we will break and distroy all manner of frames Whatsoever that make the Following spurious Articles and all Frames Whatsoever that do not pay the regular prises heretofore Agree'd to by the Masters and Worckman all point nett frames making single press and frames not working by the rack and rent and not paying the price regulated in 1810 Warp frames working single yarn or to cource all, Not working by the rack not paying the rent

And prises regulated in 1809 Wereas all plain Silk frames not making worck according to the Gage, Frames not making the work according to Quallity whereas all frames of whatsoever discription the worckmen of which Are not paid in the current Coin of the realm will Invarioably be distroy'd Whearas it as been represented to Frame worck Knitters that Gangs of Bandittys have Infested various parts of the Country under pretence of Being Complyed of Breaking of frames and hath Committed divers Robbereys uppon any friends and Neighbours I Do hereby offer a reward of 1000 pound to any Pirson that will give any Information at my Office I have I have Got two Thousand pounds as Seacret money any Person that will Give any Information of the Villiannary and False Rumers of the Frame brakers, any one that will come forward may depend upon the Greatest secresey and the same reward.

Given under my hand this first day of January in one thousand Eight Hundred an Twelve

NED LUD'S OFFICE

God protect the Trade. Sherwood Forrest

⟨Home Office version with Douglas's emendations indicated in nn. 21-26⟩

BY THE FRAMEWORK KNITTERS.
A Declaration.

Whereas by the charter granted by our late Sovereign Lord Charles the Second[21] by the Grace of God [King] of Great Britain France and Ireland, the Framework knitters are empowered to break and destroy all Frames and Engines that fabricate Articles in a fraudulent and deceitful manner and to destroy all Framework knitters Goods whatsoever that are so made And Whereas a number of deceitful unprincipled and intriguing persons did attain an Act to be passed in the Twenty Eighth[22] Year of our present Sovereign Lord George the Third[23] whereby it was enacted that persons entering by force into any House Shop or Place to break or destroy Frames should be adjudged guilty of Felony And as we are fully convinced that such Act was obtained in the most fraudulent interested and Electioneering manner And that the Honorable the Parliament of Great Britain was deceived[24] the motives and intentions of the persons who obtained such Act We therefore the Framework knitters do hereby declare the aforesaid Act to be Null and Void to all intents and purposes whatsoever As by the passing of this Act villainous and imposing persons are enabled to make fraudulent and deceitful manufactures to the discredit and utter ruin of our Trade. And Whereas we declare that the aforementioned charter is as much in force as though no such Act had been passed. And We do hereby declare to all Hosiers Lace Manufacturers and proprietors of Frames that We will break and destroy all manner of Frames whatsoever that make the following spurious Articles and all Frames whatsoever that do not pay the regular prices heretofore agreed to[25] the Masters and Workmen - All point[26] Net Frames making single press, and Frames not working by the rack and rent and not paying the price regulated in 1810 - Warp Frames working single Yarn or two coarse hole - not working by the rack, not paying the rent and prices regulated in 1809. Whereas all plain Silk Frames not making Work according to the Gage - Frames not marking the Work according to quality Whereas all Frames of whatsoever description the Workmen of whom are not paid in the Corrent Coin of the Realm will invariably be destroyed. Whereas it hath been represented to the Framework knitters that Gangs of banditti have infested various parts of the Country under the pretence of being employed in breaking of Frames and hath committed divers Robberies upon our Friends and Neighbours I do hereby offer a reward of one thousand pounds to any person that will give any Information at my Office. I have Gave two thousand Pounds as secret money any person that will give any Information of those villainous and false rumours of the Frame Breakers (any one that will come forward may depend upon the greatest Secresy and the same reward.

Given under my hand this 1st day of January 1812.
God protect the Trade.   Ned Lud's Office
                                                           Sherwood Forest.

M11 ❖ [Before 5] January 1812: Solicitation letter from "Edward Lud" to "Gentlemen All," Loughborough

Luddism was not an extortionist movement in the ordinary sense, but the frame breakers did solicit subscriptions to support their efforts (and, later, they collected arms from private homes). In the crime wave that accompanied Luddism, some extortionist threats and thefts were attributed to machine breakers, but they typically took care to police their own ranks.[27]

This note is a version of the letter referred to by stockingers William Davenport the Elder and William Brown, examined in Leicestershire regarding events around Loughborough of 5 December 1811. The note "purported that the Stockingers were to contribute towards the Support of Ned Lud's Army who wo^d come himself--This Examin^d understood that if he did not give something his Frame wo^d be broken" (H. O. 42/119). The Davenport and Brown depositions were forwarded by Lieutenant Colonel Rutland to the Home Office with his enclosing letter, dated 5 January 1812.[28]

The words of the January 1812 Loughborough letter of solicitation transcribed first were recollected by another examinant, Thomas Gilbert, before examiners Richard Hardy and J. Dawson. A slightly different version of a solicitation note appears next and was recollected by another deponent, John Frearson of Ibstock, regarding events of 6 December 1811.

Gilbert version: H. O. 42/119. The letter has also been reproduced in a slightly different version in Frank Darvall, *Popular Disturbances and Public Order in Regency England* (1934; reprint, New York: Augustus M. Kelley, 1969), 72. Frearson version: H. O. 42/119.

❖   ❖   ❖

⟨Gilbert version⟩

Gentlemen All—Ned Lud's Compliments unto you and hopes you will give a trifle towards supporting his Army as he well understands the Art of breaking obnoxious Frames: If you comply with this it will be well, if not, I shall call upon you myself Edward Lud.

⟨Freason version⟩

[F]our Men came to his House one of which offered him a Paper the purport of which was I Ned Lud to frameworkknitters all calling for Assistance which this Examinant understood to mean Money threatening to break the obnoxious frames that worked at an under price or he should pay them a visit with his Army that the Paper with signed - Ned Lud - at the bottom.

M12 ❖ 10 January 1812: "Address of the Plain Silk Hands, to the Gentlemen
Hosiers," Nottingham

The 27 November 1811 open letter from the Plain Silk Stocking-Makers to
the Gentlemen Hosiers involved in the silk branch did not have the effect hoped
for by the members of the committee who wrote and published it in the Nottingham newspapers. Six weeks later, another address followed. Its economic analysis
is much more precise and explicit than any analysis that appears in anonymous
Luddite documents, but the themes and grievances are substantively the same.

Nottingham Review, 10 January 1812. It follows immediately a list of resolutions, nearly identical to the earlier demands of the lace workers, entered into on 15 December 1811 "At a
respectable and numerous Meeting of the LACE MANUFACTURERS of the Town of
Nottingham."[29]

❖ ❖ ❖

THE ADDRESS

OF THE PLAIN SILK HANDS,

TO THE

GENTLEMEN HOSIERS,

CONCERNED

In the Manufacturing of Plain Silk Hose and Gloves.

GENTLEMEN—Urged by the pressure of the Times, and the Encouragement
of some of you, we beg leave to state the Grievances which many of us are labouring under; at the same time hope and you will call a Meeting of yourselves, to take
into your most serious Consideration the great Evils of which we complain—
Evils not only grievous to ourselves, but highly injurious to the fair and upright
Hosier; a statement of plain Facts need but little glossary to explain them, as
the making what is termed inferior Work on fine gauged frames, has destroyed
the comforts of our Families, is a fact too well known to be denied. By making
such Work on those frames, we are compelled to have finer Silk, and then if set
on the regulated number of Jacks, the Hose become too Small for the Size intended; to remedy this, we are ordered to widen our Frames by some four Jacks,
others eight, giving us 1d. for four, and 2d. for eight Jacks, as supposed Remuneration for extra labour. Here then let us examine the case as it really is, beginning with Women's 24 Work, which by your own Regulation, bearing Date the

14th November, 1809, is to be set on 120 Jacks. This work made from too fine a Gauge as above stated, if ordered to widen eight Jack, we receive 2d. extra, and then become the exact number of Jacks, with the same sized Silk and Quality, in *every shape*, (BUT PRICE,) as for Women's 26 Work, for which, when Chevened, the difference between 24 and 26 Work, is 10d. per pair extra; here our loss is 8d. per Pair, and in finer Work still more; and permit us to say, that in the case of Plain Silk Gloves, the Evil is not less grievous. Thus, while every Necessary of Life has been advancing to a great Amount, and all other Manufacturers have been raising their Wages, we are suffering a shameful Abatement.

Gentlemen, these Evils do exist, and loudly call for your interference. The distressed State of many of our Families, compels us to call upon you to rescue them from a State of little better than Starvation, well knowing without your aid, all our efforts will prove unavailing.

If, at your Meeting, you will condescend to listen to our Proposals to remedy the above Evils, by a Deputation from the Trade, or by Writing, we shall be ever thankful, and pledge ourselves to cease complaining, if we do not prove the existence of these and other Impositions.

By Order of the Committee,

WM. LOCK, Chairman.

WM. CRUMP, Secretary.

Nottingham, January 10th, 1812.

M13 ❖ [Before 14] January 1812: Posted proclamation by "Mr Pistol," Nottingham

It has become a commonplace that the Nottinghamshire Luddites were less concerned with the utilization of machines themselves (which had become part of the trade in Elizabethan times and which had displaced the hand-knitting trade) than with particular practices associated with wide-frame machines and inferior knitting techniques. These objectionable practices included the employment of "colts," that is, unapprenticed workers, and the manufacture of "cut ups," hose that were knit on wide frames (previously used to make pantaloons, which were no longer in fashion by 1811), cut, then sewn into stockings. These practices led to an abatement of wages, but just as important to the Nottinghamshire framework knitters was the damage to the reputation of their trade.[30]

"Mr Pistol," the writer of this proclamation, makes no mention of the abatement of "old prices" that we find raised in "General Ludd's Triumph," another Nottinghamshire document frequently cited by historians as a compendium of Luddite grievances, but the writer does threaten persons who produce an inferior and cheaper article made by a method called the single press or the two-course hole. The proclamation makes use of the same formula, "I do hereby discharge," as "King Lud's" proclamation of 23 December 1811 in H. O. 42/118. It is the "paper which has been lately discovered posted up by the Framebreakers," as it was described by George Coldham in a 14 January 1812 enclosing letter to the Home Office in H. O. 42/119.

H. O. 42/119; Russell, "The Luddites" Facsimile A.

❖ ❖ ❖

I do hereby discharge all Persons what soever from takeing out work Called the Single Preess, or the two Coarse [ole] ole[31] which is Condemn by Law, any Persons Found so doing to the great——injuries of our Trade such People so found out shall be shot any Persons will bring me information of the offenders shall receive a reward of one Guinea to be Paid be me, Mr Pistol
1812

M14 ❖ [Before 27] January 1812: Song titled "General Ludd's Triumph," Nottingham

Within their unique contexts, Luddite songs and poems performed special functions, most of which are evident in the works themselves. Some are celebratory or self-congratulatory. Others are inspirational, the literary equivalents of a fortifying pint of ale before a raid or a meeting in the forest or on the moor, as we know from Frank Peel's historical accounts. Still others lament hardship. Often, the functions are combined, as, for example, when the self-congratulation one would expect to find in a text celebrating an early successful factory raid appears in verses sung before a subsequent raid. In most instances, the verses operate within predictable rhetorical forms that are broader than the Luddite culture; nevertheless, the songs frequently reveal much about the values and strategies of Luddism and its discursive culture.

Sometimes referred to as the Luddite anthem, "General Ludd's Triumph" condenses almost all of the features of Luddite rhetoric into a few stanzas. It is so important that Thomis departs from his chronological organization to include the song as the first document in his collection of Nottingham texts, *Luddism in Nottinghamshire*. Thomis, Thompson, Hammond and Hammond, and Sale feature it prominently in their historical treatments of Luddism. Given such attention to the song, it is especially appropriate to examine Luddite balladry in the "Triumph."

The appearances in the poems of the singular "General Ludd," his various lieutenants and secretaries, and the plural croppers in "The Croppers' Song," which follows, constitute an important step in the formation of a variable but collective Luddite "identity." The formation of a collective identity was a problem for workers from diverse trades, in diverse locations, working in small shops employing only a few artisans. Both Thompson and Calhoun have attempted to address the matter by placing Luddite activity, in different ways, within a progressive pattern of development of a class consciousness. I do not attempt such an explanation. Instead, I remark on the rhetorical strategies and contexts of these works in order to understand their significance to Luddism as a whole and within the particular circumstances giving rise to each work (because Luddism was not a monolithic, uniform movement across all of the textile-producing regions).

"General Ludd's Triumph" is a Nottinghamshire ballad, evidently composed in January 1812 during the period of intense Midlands ludding, and reflective of the ideals of the framework knitters who broke wide stocking frames. The specific mention of personal property ("wide frames") as a target for Ludd's wrath suggests an effort by the writer to distance Nottinghamshire Luddism from ordinary constitutional or franchise politics. Constitutional reformers had been trying to intervene in (or perhaps appropriate the momentum of) Midlands Luddism; one such attempt can be found in Major John Cartwright's 27 December 1811 letter to the *Nottingham Review*. An attempt to distinguish action against property from political action also can be seen in another Nottinghamshire document, "Declaration; Extraordinary" presented earlier.

The focused, apolitical intentions of the writer of "General Ludd's Triumph" can also be understood in contrast to the intentions of Luddite writers in the west of Yorkshire. West Riding Luddism seems to have embraced some measure of political consciousness early in its development. Additionally, from the very beginning, Yorkshire Luddites selected as targets for direct action not only personal property (shearing frames) but the bodies and homes of authorities and factory owners to whom they attributed responsibility for the oppressive system. Midlands Luddism saw one attempt at personal violence against a master.

For the most part, the "Triumph" is celebratory, fitting the rhetorical form of the eulogy, but the form is certainly not pure. Eulogy typically employs humility tropes and "all sing his praises" topoi, but "General Ludd's Triumph" is distinguished by its legitimation strategies. Attempts at legitimation are clearly indicated by the discourse of law and "old prices"—simultaneously legal, economic, and moral codes, the violations of which by large hosiers have caused suffering. Legitimation is connected to character, too. Ludd's characteristic restraint and faith in the proper action and effects of the laws to mitigate suffering must be set aside in the face of repeated and unrelieved abuses, punctuated by the use of temporal-conditional markers such as "Till" and "Then." Legitimation is also tied to a popular, vaguely democratic sanction ("unanimous vote of the Trade").

By its ties to a popular "Trade" sanction, the strategy of legitimation has not only an externally persuasive function but also a rhetorically centripetal function. Through a vote (that is, through the collective and concentrating action of the diverse individuals working in separate shops but nevertheless constituting a "Trade"), a necessary univocality is achieved and is described in the "Triumph" in terms that the people of the textile-producing region around Nottingham can comprehend—an ancient "Trade" chartered by King Charles II. The appeal is simultaneously antiquarian and popular, thereby differing little from the arguments of the writers involved in the county associations during the 1770s and 1780s. Those writers had appealed to "Alfred" and to what they understood to be popular, local systems of governance—juries, hundreds, and tithings. Significantly, after a few months of the Regency, the Luddite appeal to Robin Hood, too, recalls the outlaw's purpose of defending both the people and the legal monarch.

According to Palmer, the tune, "Poor Jack," was composed by "the ultra-patriotic Charles Dibdin" and was borrowed, "cheekily," by the Luddite writer.[32] It can be found in various abridged or emended forms in most of the histories of Luddism. For example, Palmer's version contains not only orthographic changes but also some changes in word order, which make the piece sing less awkwardly but which also change the flavor of the Luddite song.

As is the case with most Luddite ballads, ascertaining an exact date of composition is difficult. The date of record in the Home Office Papers is given as 27 January 1812; however, that is the date on which Coldham and the special magistrates, Conant and Baker, posted the "Statement of Outrages" to London.[33] Perhaps "General Ludd's Triumph" was sent to the Home Office with the "Statement."

H. O. 42/119. The song follows, in what appears to be Nottingham Town Clerk George Coldham's handwriting, a 27 January 1812 letter from Coldham to John Stevenson, Mayor of Leicester.

❖ ❖ ❖

General Ludd's
Triumph

Tune "Poor Jack"

1

Chant no more your old rhymes about bold Robin Hood,
His feats I but little admire
I will sing the Atchievements of General Ludd
Now the Hero of Nottinghamshire
Brave Ludd was to measures of violence unused
Till his sufferings became so severe
That at last to defend his own Interest he rous'd
And for the great work did prepare

2

Now by force unsubdued, and by threats undismay'd
Death itself can't his ardour repress
The presence of Armies can't make him afraid
Nor impede his career of success
Whilst the news of his conquests is spread far and near
How his Enemies take the alarm
His courage, his fortitude, strikes them with fear
For they dread his Omnipotent Arm!

3

The guilty may fear, but no vengeance he aims
At [the] honest man's life or Estate
His wrath is entirely confined to wide frames
And to those that old prices abate
These Engines of mischief were sentenced to die
By unanimous vote of the Trade
And Ludd who can all opposition defy
Was the grand Executioner made

4

And when in the work of destruction employed
He himself to no method confines
By fire, and by water he gets them destroyed
For the Elements aid his designs
Whether guarded by Soldiers along the Highway
Or closely secured in the room
He shivers them up both by night and by day
And nothing can soften their doom

5

He may censure great Ludd's disrespect for the Laws
Who ne'er for a moment reflects
That <u>foul Imposition</u> alone was the cause
Which produced these unhappy effects
Let the haughty no longer the humble oppress
Then shall Ludd sheath his conquering Sword
His grievances instantly meet with redress
Then peace will be quickly restored

6

Let the wise and the great lend their aid and advice
Nor e'er their assistance withdraw
Till full fashioned work at the old fashion'd price[34]
Is established by Custom and Law

Then the Trade when this ardorus contest is o'er
Shall raise in full splendor it's head
And colting, and cutting, and squaring no more[35]
Shall deprive honest workmen of bread.

M15 ❖ Late January or early February (?) 1812: Threatening letter signed
"Remember Nedd Ludd" to "Mr Harvey," Nottingham

Like the 8 November 1811 letter, this letter is quite specific in stating a griev-ance and it refrains from making a direct personal threat (although, admittedly, there is some ambiguity in the clause "we can break something better"). These characteristics, together with the absence of political rhetoric and some corre-spondence to a frame-breaking episode outlined below, suggest that the letter was written during January or February 1812, before Midlands Luddism began to respond to the complicity of the government with the manufacturers. Mr. Harvey has not yet been identified, but he could possibly be the "Wolf" Harvey described by Gravener Henson or, more likely, Joseph Harvey, mentioned by William Felkin.[36] Both were Nottingham men involved in lace manufacture, the industry in which use of the single press or the two-course hole would have been an issue. The *Nottingham Review* reports that early in the morning of 21 Febru-ary 1812, several men broke into the home of "Mr. Harvey, West-street, Broad-lane" in Nottingham and "demolished five warp lace-frames, which were em-ployed in making two-course-hole net," and which belonged to him. Evidently, Mr. Harvey had some foreknowledge of an imminent attack, perhaps by this very letter; the *Review* reports that "Mr. H. had two loaded pistols and a blunder-buss in his house."[37] Attacks upon offensive lace frames had occurred earlier, too. Thomis notes that on 12 January 1812 eight frames were broken in Nottingham for making single-press lace.[38]

H. O. 42/119; Russell, "The Luddites" Facsimile B. The versions appear in different hand-writing, but I have not been able to determine which is the original.

❖ ❖ ❖

Mr Harvey

This is to inform you that if you do make any more two course Hole,[39] you
will have all your Frames broken and your Goods too, though you may think

you have made your doom just I shall know how to break your frames, we will not suffer you to win the Trade will die[40] first, if we cant do it just to night we will break them yet, and if we cant break them we can break something better and we will do it too in spite of the Devil

    Remember Nedd Ludd

M16 ❖ 7 February 1812: Letter from "General Lud" to "Unknown
       Stranger," Clifton

In a section of local news including statistics on the numbers of working families on parish relief and information on the trial of William Barnes for breaking frames, the *Nottingham Review* of 7 February 1812 published a letter, purporting to be from "General Ludd," that had enclosed returned items stolen by men who accompanied Luddites on a raid at Clifton. It is not known to whom the letter was addressed or what became of the original.

Nottingham Review, 7 February 1812.[41]

❖ ❖ ❖

LETTER FROM LUDD.—The following is a literal copy of a letter stated to have accompanied the returned articles, which had been stolen at the time when the frames were broken at Clifton.

    Unknown Stranger I have intrusted thees Articles into your Care and I do insist that you will see that they are Restored to their respective oners it is with extream Regrat that I inforn yow hou thay Came into my hans when I came out with my men their weir sum joind us that I Never had ad with me before and it wear these Villinds that plundred but ass we wear goin out of Clifton one of my Men came and told me that he Beleivd that those Men ad got somethinck that they had no Buisiness with I theirfore gave horders that thay should be searchd and what we found on them we left the things at the Lown End and I hope that the oners has got agen we were gust agoen to have hang'd one of the Villends when we weir inforned that the Solders weir at hand and we thort it Right to Retreat.

    N. B. The Men that had the things weir entire strangers to my horders or they Never dworst not have tuch'd one thinck but they have been punished for their vileny for one of them have been hangd for 3 Menet and then Let down

agane I ham a friend of the pore and Distrest and a enemy to the opressers
thron   (signed)   GENERAL LUD

M17 ❖   II February 1812: Advertisement for meeting of framework knitters, by Gravener Henson, Nottingham

There are few extant advertisements for Luddite meetings, perhaps due to
their secretive nature, although a Luddite "ticket" preserved in the Home Office
Papers and reproduced in Thompson's *Making of the English Working Class* might
be an exception, depending on how such tickets were distributed.[42] The encrypted note preserved with its key in H. O. 42/127 (transcribed later) is an even
more obvious exception. At least one advertisement for a peaceful meeting of
Nottingham stockingers has been preserved. The advertisement was circulated
during a period of relative calm, as Home Office Agent Robert Baker noted in a
letter to the Home Office from Nottingham on 13 February 1812: "The total ces-
sation of framebreaking for some days past still happily continues." Such lawful
advertisements tended to appear during periods of calm. In contrast, Luddite letters and proclamations were circulated during periods of unrest, suggesting that
the two discourses (Luddite and lawful) alternated in occurrence. I include this
peaceful advertisement not only for comparison against Luddite texts but also to
entertain the authorial possibilities implied by the alternation of discourses.

H. O. 42/120, an enclosure in a letter from Baker and Conant to the Home Office, 16 February 1812. It is also reproduced in Thomis, *Nottinghamshire* 41.

❖ ❖ ❖

To the
FRAMEWORK KNITTERS
of
NOTTINGHAM, THE COUNTY THEREOF
and the
TOWNS AND VILLAGES ADJACENT
666

The troubled State to which the above Places are reduced, by the pressure of
the Times and the operations of the Frame-Breakers, having at length excited

the Attention of the Legislature; and as many Members thereof have expressed a desire to obtain every possible Information as to the probably Cause of these Disturbances, it has been thought prudent by many of the Workmen, that they, and their Fellow-Workmen at large, should contribute all their power toward furnishing such Information.

Accordingly a few of them held a Select Meeting on Tuesday last, to take the Measure into Consideration; when it was Resolved, that the Workmen in every Town and Village in the Neighbourhood should be solicited to send Two creditable Persons to a Meeting, to be held at the Sign of the Sir Isaac Newton, in Glasshouse-lane, in this Town, on Monday next, at Twelve o'Clock precisely, for the purpose of communicating the best Intelligence in their Power to such Meeting, that such Intelligence may be communicated to Lord Holland, Recorder of the Town, to the Members of the Town, the Members of the County, and Mr. Whitbread.[43]

G. HENSON
Secretary to the Meeting

Nottingham, Feb. 11, 1812

M18 ❖ 13 February 1812: Address "To the Gentlemen Hosiers Concerned in the Manufacturing of Plain Silk Work," Nottingham

Nearly two months after the November 1811 publication of the open letter from the Plain Silk Stocking-Makers, a second newspaper address appeared, conveying disappointment at the failure to persuade a sufficient number of hosiers to accept a proposal for an advance of wages and gratitude to those hosiers who had accepted the proposal.

Nottingham Review, 14 February 1812.

❖   ❖   ❖

TO THE
GENTLEMEN HOSIERS
CONCERNED
IN THE MANUFACTURING OF PLAIN SILK WORK.

GENTLEMEN–Though disappointed in what we conceived to be our REA-

SONABLE REQUEST of an ADVANCE ON OUR PRESENT PRICES, and which to your Honor we have to notice, has not been rejected as unreasonable, but from the present Circumstances of Trade not permitting it, we are compelled to submit to; at the same time we are not convinced the Reason assigned is conclusive, because though the Avenues of Commerce are mostly shut against us, yet in those that are open, we conceive there is not National Competition, but as Persons in our contracted Spheres, and consequent contracted Views, may not be able to perceive the immediate Effects of such an Advance as prayed for, we the more chearfully acquiesce, in hope a Time may speedily arrive that shall be more favorable to our Claims, when we shall not fail again to wait upon you, in confident hope we shall not then wait upon you in vain; for, Gentlemen, we cannot for a Moment relinquish those Claims to an Advance, while the exigencies of the Times so forcibly impel us to urge them.

But we receive with the utmost Gratitude the Signatures of those Gentlemen who have favored us with the Adoption of the Regulations presented to them by the Committee, bearing Date the 22d of January, 1812, and now hope they will adopt those Measures best calculated to carry them into effect, with the least inconvenience to themselves, and to those Workmen immediately subject to the Changes unavoidable to their adoption.

The Committee contemplating those inconveniences, humbly propose, instead of the 14th Instant, the Date agreed to, that the 28th Instant be substituted for the full Establishment of them. A list of the Names of those Gentlemen who have thus favored us, is hereto annexed, and we hope and trust those Gentlemen that have not yet acceded to the Regulations, will, upon mature Deliberation, generously afford us their Names.

The Names of the Gentlemen who have signed for the Adoption of the Regulations above referred to:-

Messrs. Brocksopp & Parker	Wm. Eyre
Wm. Chamberlin	J. Beardmore & Sons
Hall, Northage & Hardwick	G. & S. Nicholls
Child, Cosens & Co.	Thomas Kelk
Hancock & Wakefield	G. & J. Ray
T. Galloway	John Harris
Holmes, Edenborough & Stenson	Abijah Bond
T. Richards	Barwick & Christian

G. & J. Mills

G. Pickering

Wm. Meats & Sons

Wm. Thorne

Thos. Jackson

Richard Ragg

Scorer & Acomb

Pope & Co.

T. Dufty & Sons

James & Neale

Allen & Phillips

R. & T. Frost & Co.

Dove, Gill & Co.

Morley, Wilson & Morley

Joshua Smith

H. & J. Cocks & Co.

Samuel Barlow

Radford & Stones

Strahan, Theaker & Co.

Edmund Wright & Co.

Samuel Clark

George Collishaw

George Hovey

Turner & Smith

G. L. Cocks & Son

Kewney & Richardson

Thomas Jerram

Brough, Cape & Robinson

Renshaw & Wood

Geo. Gibson & Son

Braithwaite & Sons[44]

Several Houses refused their Signatures, but pledged their Word for the Adoption of the Regulations, if they became general. Some also refused, that are now manufacturing according to the Statements. Answers could not be obtained from some Houses, their Principals being residents in London.

Those Gentlemen that shall have the goodness to acceed, subsequent to this Publication, will be pleased to send their names to the Printer, and they shall appear in a future Paper.

From the Committee of Plain Silk Hands,

WILLIAM POCK.

JOHN PRIEST.

JOHN WARD.

THOMAS MARSTON.

JOSEPH MIDDLETON.

WILLIAM MIDDLETON.

WILLIAM CRUMP, Secretary.

Nottingham, February 13th, 1812.

M19 ❖   16 February 1812: Letter from "Joe Firebrand" at "Robin Hoods Cave"
to "Mr. Trevit Biddles Bowler" at Nottingham

Many documents reveal not only specific Luddite complaints but also the
Luddites' values and their identification of the good of the trade with the public
good. This is not quite what Craig Calhoun means when he argues that Luddism,
like other worker movements, "grew directly out of local community roots."[45]
The Company of Framework Knitters was a national entity, with a network span-
ning the Midlands, London, Scotland, and Gloucestershire. Rather than con-
ceptualizing their grievances as growing out of primary community concerns,
the framework knitters insisted that what was good for the trade was good for
the community. The trade itself was primary.

This letter is addressed to specific manufacturers with an invitation that it be
shown to other offending masters. It is among the first of the Nottinghamshire
documents to threaten personal violence, but even the threatened violence is to
be wrought with care not to harm the innocent. (A similar care is displayed in a
21 April 1812 letter addressed to Mr. Garside of Stockport, reproduced later with
other documents from the Manchester region.) The writer also takes care to cast
the threatened arson as a legally justified, even juridical, action, foregrounding
the reconsideration by including both the rejected and the preferred phrasing
("revenge or rather punishment") and locating the threat squarely within the
legal discourse that typifies other Nottinghamshire Luddite proclamations and
letters.

Transcript 1 in Russell, "The Luddites" 59.

❖   ❖   ❖

Robin Hoods Cave,
Feby. 16.
To Mr. Trevit Biddles Bowler and all
others concerned in similar practices.
We are much concerned to find that you and your neighbours Biddles and
Bowler continue to oppose the public good by working those bad articles Sin-
gle Press & 2 Course Warp------
Now do you think that we who have encountered such difficulties & haz-

arded our lives for the good of the Trade are to be opposed & our past efforts made of no effect by your mean obstinacy no it shall not be so you may think that because your frames are secured by the presence of so large a civil & military force you have nothing to <u>fear</u> but can defy us with impunity but you must understand there are more methods of revenge than frame-breaking to be resorted to when that is not practicable![46] <u>for our past labours shall not be in vain.</u> In order that it may not be the case it is thought proper to inform you what will be done to such of you that persist in making the aforementioned Articles.

This information is designed for your good that no Children may perish which if they do blame your own obstinacy not us: as we have at all times manifested a disposition to spare life we wished still to show the same especially where Innocent Blood is concerned. You may think we shall not be able to fire your houses but the means which will be used will be so effectual that the flame will rise to the highest room in the house in a moment, the composition to be used is Spirits of Turpentine Tar & Powdered Gunpowder mixed together a Proper Quantity of this mixture powered in at the bottom of the door & lighted by the application of a bit of Touchpaper will do the business instantly. But there are many other modes of revenge or rather punishment to be inflicted on the obstinate equally injurious to Life which will be used where this is not practicable--to prevent any of which evils take the timely warning as 14 days will be allowed to finish Warps &c., before execution--Mr. Trevit you may get in a mender, go to the Warehouse when others do not & give a charge of secrecy to your men but it will not do for do how you will we shall be sure to get to know how you act in this matter. This warning is intended for all making the same kind of work.

Joe Firebrand[47]
Secretary.

M20 ❖ 17 February 1812: Address "To the Framework-Knitters of the British Empire," Nottingham

Early in 1812, one week after the publication in the *Nottingham Review* of the open letter "To the Gentlemen Hosiers Concerned in the Manufacturing of Plain Silk Hose," the *Review* carried a copy of an address from the United Committee of Framework-Knitters "To the Framework-Knitters of the British Empire." The precise similarity in the nature of demands between this public, aboveboard document and Luddite texts indicates the extent to which Luddism and the United Committee shared much of the same discourse. One notable similarity is that between the open letter's resolution "that the Nobility, the Gentry, the Manufacturers and Tradesmen of the Counties of Nottingham, Derby, and Leicester, be solicited to contribute their Aid to the above" and the lines from "General Ludd's Triumph" requesting that the great lend their aid and advice. This open letter, perhaps more than any other documents except the framework knitters' petition for parliamentary relief, gives a rich exposition of some of the grievances that the Luddite writers usually touch on in a more abbreviated form. It also exemplifies the trade's trend toward nationalizing their concerns.

Nottingham Review, 21 February 1812

❖ ❖ ❖

TO THE FRAMEWORK-KNITTERS
OF
THE BRITISH EMPIRE.

THE United Committee of Framework-Knitters, in conformity with the Resolutions of a General Aggregate Meeting held at Sir Isaac Newton's in this Town, on Monday, February 17th, 1812, consisting of One Hundred and Six Deputies, (Seventy-six of whom were from the Towns and Villages within Sixteen Miles of Nottingham,) beg leave to present to the whole Trade of Framework-Knitters, the following RESOLUTIONS agreed therein:-

RESOLVED-That it is the Opinion of this Meeting, that the War, in which we are so fatally engaged, is the principal Cause of the Calamities with which the Framework-Knitters are so heavily oppressed.

RESOLVED-That for want of the Public being guaranteed by Legislative Protection against the fraudulent and deceptive Arts, practiced by disreputable Manufacturers, the Credit of several Branches of our Trade, hath been almost destroyed; and, that when any Branch of National Manufacture is essentially injured, the Public Revenues must feel a Shock!

RESOLVED-That Cut-up Goods (except Breeches and Waistcoat Pieces) wrought in the Plain or Ribbed Branches of our Trade, are reducing those extensive and valuable Branches to the lowest ebb of Degradation; and, if persisted in, will inevitably throw those lucrative Parts of British Manufacture into the Hands of Foreign Artisans.

R E S O L V E D – That Plain and Ribbed Stockings, or Gloves, *made of whatsoever material*, ought to have their denominative Marks, regulated by the Gauge of the Frame, on which they are wrought, and the Sizes and Qualities by the Number of Jacks, to prevent both the Public and the Workmen from being defrauded.

R E S O L V E D – That every Species of Net, wrought upon any Principle upon a Machine, ought to be paid for by the R A C K or C O U N T, to prevent Impositions, of the most distressing nature, upon the Workmen; which every honorable Manufacturer is ashamed of, and which, in the end, are beneficial to none; *except while these Impositions are a* S E C R E T.

R E S O L V E D – That the making of Single Press Cotton Net, upon Point Frames, or Warp Two-course-hole Net, on Warp Frames, or the making of Net on any Principle of *Single* Cotton Yarn, is considered highly detrimental to the Lace Trade, and dangerous to the future existence of the British Cotton Lace Manufacture; and that is highly desirable, that a Legislative Prohibition should be obtained, against the making of such deceptive Articles. But, if unfortunately, the Legislature should think it improper to prohibit the manufacturing of any Article, however deceptive, yet this Meeting are fully of Opinion, that no kind of Net, wrought with a Machine, should be suffered to be sold without a *Stamp* being affixed on it, denominative of its real Quality, under a penalty proportional to the magnitude of the Offence.

R E S O L V E D – That the practice lately pursued by some Manufacturers of paying their Workmen *in Goods*, is void of every honorable principle, moral, local, political and divine; because, by it, misery the most unbounded is inflicted upon those unfortunate Workmen and their pining Families, who are subject to its baneful operations: many of them having been filched of their hard Earnings, full 50 per Cent, by this vile and unlawful practice.

R E S O L V E D – That Parliament be applied to, as soon as possible, to obtain a Bill for a Redress of the above Grievances; and to establish the Propositions contained in the foregoing Resolutions.

R E S O L V E D – That a Committee of Seven Persons be appointed to draw up a Statement of Grievances of every respective Branch of our Trade; and to carry the foregoing Resolutions into effect.

R E S O L V E D – That the whole Trade in the United Empire be solicited to communicate every Information in their power, and to send Subscriptions to the Sir Isaac Newton, Glasshouse Lane, Nottingham, to enable the said Committee to carry the above Resolutions into execution.

RESOLVED-That the Nobility, the Gentry, the Manufacturers and Tradesmen of the Counties of Nottingham, Derby, and Leicester, be solicited to contribute their Aid to the above.

RESOLVED-That these foregoing Resolutions be inserted to the Nottingham and London Papers.

(Signed, by Order of the Committee,)

JOSEPH HERBERT, Chairman.

GRAVENER HENSON, Secretary.

WILLIAM PAGE, Treasurer.

The Committee beg leave to recommend the practice of colting to a legal decision on the Law of the 5th Eliz. Cap. 4, Sec. 31, which enacts, That every Master, who shall employ any Workman, in any Craft or Occupation, who has not served an Apprenticeship of Seven Years, shall forfeit Forty Shillings for every Month he employs such Workman.

N. B. *The Committee beg leave to state, that the* PROPRIETOR *of the Nottingham Journal,* HAS REFUSED TO INSERT THESE RESOLUTIONS, *consequently they can only appear in the* NOTTINGHAM REVIEW.

M21 ❖ 19 February 1812: Letter from James Richardson at Nottingham to James Kennedy at Selkirk

Letters sent out of Nottingham in the early months of 1812 indicate some correspondence with textile workers in other parts of Britain. One such letter was intercepted and sent to the Home Office by the sheriff of Selkirkshire. Although the letter makes no threats and is not anonymous, it does reveal attempts by artisans of the stocking trade to foster a network of sympathy, political action, and financial support. Such attempts were construed by the authorities to be part of a large stockinger campaign that included and was epitomized by machine breaking.

H. O. 42/122. It appears as a copy included in correspondence to Beckett from the sheriff of Selkirkshire. The Sheriff begins his own message, "Sir—I am ordered to transmit to you an extract of a letter received from Nottingham." The letter is also reproduced in A. Aspinall, *Early English Trade Unions: Documents from the Home Office Papers in the Public Record Office* (London: Batchworth Press, 1949), 124–25.

❖ ❖ ❖

Mr. James Kennedy, Stocking Maker, Selkirk.

Nottingham, 19 February, 1812

Sir—I am directed by the committee of framework knitters to inform you that on Monday 17th instant there was a meeting of the trade of the Counties of Nottingham and Derby to take into consideration the propriety of petitioning Parliament for a redress of grievances; it was carried that application should be made to Parliament for a Bill for the better regulation of the trade—that a subscription should be entered into to defray the expense, and information and aid should be solicited from the most distant places and that the whole should be solicited to make a common cause, &c., &c. Signed, G. Henson.[48]

It would also appear that they labour under great difficulties by being paid their wages with goods, and by introducing fine cotton much beyond the size, adds considerably to their distress. A general meeting was held here on the 2nd instant. It was resolved to collect 2s. 6d. each for their interest to be raised in three months. We hope that on receiving this letter that you will call a meeting of your brethren within your bounds, and have the goodness to give us an account of your proceedings. Mr. John Aitkin, stocking maker, Kent Street, Gallowgate, is appointed collector. You will please address your letters to him.

I am, Sir, for the Committee,

Your obedient servant,

James Richardson.

Selkirk, 12 March 1812.

The committee appointed by the stocking makers of Selkirk having met, they unanimously adopted the following Resolutions:

1st. That although the evils arising from the general stagnation of the trade of the country has as yet been but little felt by us, yet that we deeply feel for the distress of the great majority of our brethren who have been involved in these calamities, and that we will cordially join in co-operation with the great body of the trade in any measures which they may deem proper to pursue for attempting to remedy the evils under which they labour.

2nd. That for this purpose we agree to enter into a subscription of 2s. 6d. each besides expenses, to [be]⁴⁹ raised in three months, which money is to be placed in the hands of a general collector, and to be at the disposal of a general meeting of the subscribers.

3rd. That we earnestly request the whole of the journeymen in Selkirk and Galashiels to subscribe the above Resolutions and to concur in any other measures which may ultimately be deemed necessary for furthering the common cause.

M22 ❖ 22 February 1812: Letter from "Genl C Ludd" at "Shirewood Camp" to Spencer Perceval at London

Following the creation of the Nottingham Corporation Committee and the increased involvement of the national government in suppressing the risings, including the introduction of a parliamentary bill to make frame breaking a capital offense and the sending of London police magistrates Conant and Baker and more than three thousand soldiers into the area, Nottinghamshire Luddism became more thoroughly political and manifested an awareness of injustice perpetrated on a national rather than merely local scale. This February 1812 letter to Spencer Perceval, then prime minister, exemplifies the new tendency.

H. O. 42/120. It has been reprinted in Malcolm Thomis, *The Luddites: Machine-Breaking in Regency England* (Newton Abbott: David and Charles, 1970), 118, and Thomis, *Nottinghamshire* 43.

❖ ❖ ❖

Spencer Perceval Esq   Shirewood Camp. Feb 22 1812

Sir

The first & most important part of my Duty is [to] inform you & I request [you] do the same to all [your] Colleagues in office, also the Regent; that in consequence of the great sufferings of the Poor &-whose grievances seem not to be taken <u>into the least consideration, by Government.</u> I shall be under the necessity of again calling into action (not to destroy, many more frames) ie. but '----------my brave Sons of Shirewood, who are determind & sworn to be true & faithful avengers of their & Countrys wrongs. I have waited patiently to see if any measure were likely to [be] adopted by Parliamt.

to alleviate distress in any shape whatever; but that hand of conciliation is shut & my poor suffering country is left without a ray of hope: The Bill for Punish.g with death. has only to be viewd. with contempt & opposd. by measure equally strong; & the Gentlemen (who framd. it will have to repent the act: for if one man's life is Sacrificed,! blood for !blood. Should you be calld upon you can [not] say I have not given you notice of de---

I have the honor to be

Genl C Ludd[50]

M23 ❖ March 1812: Letter "From head Quarters Genaral Lud" to George Rowbottom at Beaverlee

Most Luddite letters consist simply of handwritten text, sometimes with elaborate underlines and flourishes. Occasionally, letters contain some hand-drawn seals. This letter addressed "For George Rowbottom of Beaverlee near Eastwood / Nottinghamshire / with speed" is one of the few letters that includes an illustration. The letter appears in facsimile immediately following the transcription.

H. O. 42/122, enclosed with General Hawker's 1 April 1812 report to the Home Office.

❖   ❖   ❖

From head Quarters Genaral Lud
George Rowbottom this is to inform you that their is not a man in the town of arnold bulwell Hucknall nor basford that takes work out unless it is full price full fashion and proper price and size and this is to give you Notice that if you bring or give any more work out without it is full fashion full price and proper size you shall work this frame ⟨a sketch of a gallows appears here⟩ with a rope around your neck so shall all men that bring work out under price and I desire will let your town and country round you know that they may not do the like so fail not at your peril for this frame works all full price and fashion

From head Quarters Genaral Lud 488
George Rowbottom this is to inform you that their is not a man
in the Town of arnold bulwell Hucknall nor basford that takes
work out unless it is full price full fashion and proper price and
size and this is to give you Notice that if you bring or give any
more work out without it is full fashion full price and proper size
you shall work this frame with a rope round your neck
so shall all men that bring work out under price
and I desire will let your town and Country round you
know that they may not do the like so fail not at your perl
for this frame works all full price and fashion

Letter of March 1812 "From head Quarters Genaral Lud" to George Rowbottom at
Beaverlee, H. O. 42/122

M24 ❖ 2 March 1812: Poem by Lord Byron, "An Ode to the Framers of the
Frame Bill," London and Nottingham

The 6 March 1812 issue of the *Nottingham Review* contains three interesting
items of verse. The first is a poem titled "Industry Distressed," which includes a
jab at Ned Ludd. The poem represents not only one volley in the poetry wars that
found a field in the pages of the *Review* but also expresses, from an anti-Luddite
perspective, some of the same grievances of which the Luddites complained.[51]
The same issue of the *Review* also contains "An Abstract of The Frame-Breaking
Prevention Bill, Now Pending In Parliament" and, immediately beneath it, Lord
Byron's "An Ode to the Framers of the Frame Bill," copied from the *Morning
Chronicle*, 2 March 1812, and lacking the author's name. Even though it is not a
Luddite document in the strict sense, I reproduce it because of its topicality and
because Charles Sutton, the *Review* editor, evidently saw it as a significant part

of the larger discourse relevant to Luddism, fit to appear in the same issue as the verse attack on Ned Ludd.

Nottingham Review, 6 March 1812.

❖ ❖ ❖

AN ODE

TO THE FRAMERS OF THE FRAME BILL.

[From the Morning Chronicle.]

Oh! well done Lord El—n! and better done R—er! [52]
    Britannia must prosper with Counsels like yours;
Hawkesbury, Harrowby, helps you to guide her,
    Whose remedy only must kill ere it cures!

Those villains, the Weavers, are all grown refractory,
    Asking some succour for charity's sake;
So hang them in clusters, round each Manufactory,
    That will at once put an end to mistake.*

The rascals, perhaps, may betake them to robbing,
    The dogs to be sure have got nothing to eat–
So if we can hang them for breaking a bobbin,
    'Twill save all the Government's money and meat.

Men are more easily made than Machinery,
    Stockings will fetch higher than lives;
Gibbets on Sherwood will heighten the scenery,
    Shewing how Commerce, how Liberty thrives.

Justice is now in pursuit of the wretches,
    Grenadiers, Volunteers, Bow-Street Police,
Twenty-two regiments, a score of Jack Ketches,
    Three of the Quorum, and two of the Peace.

Some Lords to be sure, would have summon'd the Judges,
    To take their opinion, but that they ne'er shall;
For Liverpool such a concession begrudges,
    So now they're condemned by no Judges at all.

Some folks for certain have thought it was shocking,
    When famine appeals, and when poverty groans;
That life should be valued at less than a stocking,
    And breaking of frames, lead to breaking of bones.

If it should prove so, I trust by this token,
    (And who will refuse to partake in the hope,)
That the ——— of the fools, may be first to be broken,
    Who when ask'd for a *remedy*, sent down a *rope*.

* Lord L——— on Thursday night said, the Riots at Nottingham arose from
a Mistake.

M25 ❖   6 March 1812: Letter from Thomas Latham at Nottingham to the Mayor
         of Tewkesbury

The framework knitters' recognition of the increasing politicization of the
conflict resulted, on the one hand, in the creation of a militantly political Luddite
discourse and, on the other hand, an intensification of efforts to use legal means
to bring grievances to light. Henson's committee is one example of the latter.

This letter, signed by a colleague of Henson, was sent to the mayor of Tewkes-
bury, protesting his decree prohibiting a meeting of framework knitters in that
Gloucestershire town, long a center for the manufacture of cotton hose.[53] It at-
tempts to engage the mayor on legal grounds that he would be likely to embrace.
Although it is not a Luddite letter, its legal language is worth comparing with
Luddite documents that employ a similar language.

Despite the appeal to law, the letter was thought to be threatening enough
that it was forwarded to the Home Office on 9 March 1812.

H. O. 42/122. An original draft of the letter appears in the Nottinghamshire Archives CA
3984, I, 22, and that version has been transcribed in the *Records of the Borough of Nottingham*
(Nottingham: Nottingham City Council, 1952), 8:139–40. Substantively, the versions are
identical.

❖   ❖   ❖

Nottingham 6th March '12

Sir,

The Committee of the United Branches of Framework-knitters at Nott$^{\underline{m}}$ with great surprise rec^d a letter of the 2^d from a person in the Town over which you hold jurisdiction stating that you had prohibited the framework-knitters in your Town from meeting to discuss the nature of their Grievances and to prepare a petition to Parliament thereon. You no doubt had you reasons for so doing; but whether they were sane, or otherwise, is not material because they were both unconstitutional and unjust, as well as extremely dangerous to the liberties of the subject.

Know you not, Sir, that the Act, commonly called the Gagging Act, is long since dead of its own natural Death; Therefore your opinion as a Magistrate is of no avail respecting the holding of a popular meeting. But even were that not the case, is it an act of policy on the part of a Magistrate to prohibit men from meeting in a peacable manner, to state their grievances; when, by preventing them from venting their plaints in a constitutional way, they may be driven to the commission of crimes for the purpose of exercising their <u>vengeance</u>, when they cannot exercise their <u>rights</u>. How different were your conduct on the occasion alluded to, to that shewn by the Magistrates of Hatton Garden, London, on a similar occasion—they, when informed of the desire of the London stocking makers to hold a meeting, immediately afforded the men every facility in their power for the accomplishment of the design—They sent an officer to attend the meeting, and presented the resolutions agreed upon at such meeting to the Secretary of State, along with a copy of the propositions sent from the Nottingham Committee. This was a measure consistent with the wishes of every honest man. Then compare this conduct with your own; and, if you are an Englishman, your punishment will be sentimentally complete.

Sir, you may perhaps conceal this letter from all eyes but your own; but that will avail you nothing; for other means, which you to your own confusion, will hereafter be made accquainted with, will be resorted to, to make its contents public. The men of Nottingham are accquainted with the laws of their Country; and, in common with every honest man, condemn the outrageous conduct of a few misguided individuals in their neighbourhood; and they know, that the proper means to prevent those outrages are for those in authority to act directly contrary to the manner in which you have acted.

Sir, the Nottingham Committee will again call upon their Tewkesbury friends to have a meeting; the postmaster may again open the letter directed to them;[54] and you may again exert an unconstitutional authority; but if you do, legal means will be resorted to, to exhibit your conduct in proper colours to the public.

by order of the Committee,

Thos. Latham secty

Mayor of Tewkesbury
Committee Rooms
Newton's head
Glass house Lane

M26 ❖ 11 March 1812: Poem by "A Poor Stockinger," titled
"Poetry," Nottingham

The poem mentioned previously and reproduced in the note 51, "Industry Distressed," was answered two weeks after its publication in the *Review* by "Poetry" written by "A POOR STOCKINGER." Compared with some of the verses that made their way into the Nottingham papers, this poem is rather atypical, having a consistent meter, quotations from Alexander Pope and Samuel Rutherford, and a thoughtful analysis of the relationship between the wealthy and the working poor.

Nottingham Review, 20 March 1812.

❖ ❖ ❖

Poetry
The Stockinger lately so blest,
His household so comely and gay,
Contentment each night gave him rest,
How cheerful he work'd through the day;
His earnings commanded respect,
To church and to market he went;
The landlord's accounts made correct,
He bow'd on receiving his rent.

But now we are dwelling with woe,
O, could I my fears but surmount;
The consequence who can foreknow?
Or suffering who can recount?
The warehouses still want demand,
The frames lie to rust on each floor;
The workman has "nothing in hand,"[55]
The traddle he cannot tread more.

YE POWERS, who govern events,
Your Orders in Council we feel;
Humanity surely laments,
Who *call'd for the hemp or the steel?*[56]
When INDUSTRY fails of support,
From *home* takes the poor-house in view,
And drove to the *dernier resort,*
Disorders may doubtless ensue.

YE SAGES our *living* to save,
Your joint mediation afford;
The thanks of the PUBLIC you'll have,
Whil'st conscience presides at your board;
Consent, your arrangement may meet,
Success may the soldiers withdraw,
Whil'st angels your kindness shall greet,
For "order was heaven's first law."[57]

YE AUTHORITIES, grant us your care,
O, exercise gently your rod;
Distress on distresses to spare,
Is worthy a KING or a GOD:
Ye BRITONS at large through the land,
REPENT, and your war-whoop give o'er;
That rapine no more may withstand
The peace and content of the poor.

Monopoly upheld by war,

The breath of sweet PEACE will destroy;

The PLENTY shall soon re-appear,

And COMMERCE give labour employ:–

BRITTANIA still Peace can command,

In arts or in arms–great are WE:

Can make all the WORLD understand

That BRITONS ARE BORN TO BE FREE.

Nottingham, March 11, 1812.   A POOR STOCKINGER.

M27 ❖   16 March 1812: Letter signed "your for Genl Ludd" to
"Mr Byrnny," Nottingham

As the Nottingham officials, with the assistance of Conant and Baker, became more effective at apprehending and prosecuting machine breakers, Luddite
writers saw the functions performed by members of juries as a type of collabo-
ration with an enemy. In this undated letter, the foreman of a Nottingham jury is
warned that he has been acting outside of the sanction thought by the Ludds to
be appropriate or dutiful given the community and its trade basis. The letter was
included in correspondence from Sir John Bayley, the judge presiding over the
March 1812 Nottingham assizes. Bayley's 18 March 1812 correspondence includes
two of his own letters, "a note handed up to me by the Gaoler from [convicted
framebreaker William] Carnell, which shews that his spirit appears subdued,"
and the threatening letter. Ironically, Bayley reports that a "Case upon [another]
threatening letter terminated in an Aquittal, upon a variance . . ." (18 March 1812,
H. O. 42/121).[58]

The letter is written in a large script, in wide columns, and with line-ending
dashes. It was forwarded to Secretary Ryder on 17 April 1812 with an enclosed
letter by the Duke of Portland (who evidently received it from Bayley).

H. O. 42/122. The letter has also been reprinted in facsimile in Thomis, *Luddites* 135, and
transcribed in Thomis, *Nottinghamshire* 54.

❖   ❖   ❖

Mr Byrnny[59]
> late foreman of a jury held}
> at Nottingham 16 March-12}[60]

Sir,
> by Genaral Ludds Express <u>Express</u>

Commands I am come to—
worksop to enquire of your Character
towards our cause and I am sory
to say I find it to correspond with
your conduct you latly shewed—
towards us, Remember the
time is fast aproaching when
men of your stamp will be—
brought to Repentance, you may
be called upon soon. Remember—
you are a marked man
> > your for Gen[l] Ludd
> > > a true <u>man</u>[61]

M28 ❖   17 March 1812: Posted paper inscribed to "Mr lud," Chesterfield

Derbyshire, a center for the silk manufacture, did not experience the same degree of industrial violence that the other Midlands counties did; nevertheless, there was machine breaking as well as a small amount of Luddite correspondence. The Home Office Papers contain one of the rare instances of Derbyshire Ludd- ite correspondence, this "Inflammatory paper . . . found in the Market place last Tuesday Night" in Chesterfield. The open letter was forwarded to the Home Office on 20 March 1812 by the mayor of Chesterfield, John Main.

H. O. 42/121.

❖   ❖   ❖

Mr lud,

I Ham going to inform you that there is Six Thousand man Coming to you in Apral and then We Will go and Blow Parlement house up and Blow up all afour hus labrin Peple Cant Stand it No longer, dam all Such Roges as

England governs but Never mind Nead lud When generel nody and is harmy
Comes We Will Soon bring about the greate Revelution then all these greate
mans heads gose of

Hear all Confution menchester and Derby and yourk and Chesterfield Shefild
Nottingham mansfield local is going to fling Doon there harmes[62]

The Nation Will Never Sattel No more till these great heads is Cut of We
Will Nock doon the Presions and the Judge We Will murde whan he is aslepe.

M29 ❖ 8 April 1812: Letter with poem by Thomas Large, Nottingham

A Nottingham stockinger, Thomas Large, seems to have been one of the most
literate and lively of the writers associated with the United Committee of Framework Knitters, and internal evidence from the letters in which his verses appear
suggests that Large knew and might have had some connection to the Luddites,
whom he familiarly and affectionately calls "Sherwood Lads." The letters and
verses can be found in the Framework Knitters' Papers in the Nottinghamshire
Archives. Generally, Large seems to inscribe more of the combination of resentment and humor that readers might expect from active Luddites than from the
other, more sober, more diplomatic operatives of the United Committee, such
as Thomas Latham. Large's 26 April 1812 letter from Nottingham to Gravener
Henson, who was staying with "Mr Fryers, Tailor, London," exemplifies that
combination of resentment and humor, most evident in his remarks comparing
the Framework Knitters to Colonel McMahon, secretary to the prince regent:

> We have received a case upon colting, from our friends at Ashford in Watern,
> Derbyshire which they had from Preston. Considering it might be usefull we
> have got it reprinted with necessary alteration & I stuck up in the most con-
> spicuous parts of the Town & Country and Copy of which we have sent you.
> we are up to the ears in business and papers like poor Col M.Mahon only not
> paid quite so well, unless it is this we are paid in the good wishes of the people
> & the poor soul with the curses after taking their money![63]

Large's humor did not go unnoticed by others who shared his labors. In a 4 May
1812 letter from Leicester to Large in London, Thomas Allsop, the leading voice

of the Committee of Framework Knitters in Leicester, addresses Large as "My dear but funny friend" and commends his "Last Dying Speech and Confession of Colting."[64] Additional evidence that might link Large to the Luddites can be found in a 30 April 1812 letter from Thomas Allsop of the committee at Leicester to Large in Nottingham.[65] Allsop questions the wisdom of the Nottingham assailants (intended murderers) of William Trentham and their timing of the attempt. Allsop's letters can be understood as a register of working-class humor and as evidence of Large's possible connection to the Luddites. The combination of humor, the mention of the attempted murder of Trentham, and the understated disapproval of the *timing* rather than the morality of the attack suggests that writer and recipient were at the least sympathetic to the attackers.

Large's own verses appear in the letters that he wrote during his travels on committee business between Nottingham, Leicester, and London. In some instances, the verses comment upon the letters. The first letter was written to Thomas Latham in Nottingham shortly after Large's arrival in Leicester to solicit interest in the work of the Nottingham committee to petition Parliament.

Nottinghamshire Archives CA 3984, I, 44; *Records of the Borough of Nottingham*, 8:141–42.

❖ ❖ ❖

Thos Latham
Sir Isaac Newtons
Glasshouse Lane
Nottm

April 8 1812   Leicester
Gent

This place is a thousand times Worse, than we expected to find it, there is not half a dozen good fellows in the Town those principally are composed of Sherwood Lads - If i had not been assisted by a fellow prentice, and some of his acquaintence we should never have got a meeting, and even then, I was compelled to pay the cryer, out of my pocket, the meeting did not exeed 100 men—there is 2300 frames in town. With much persuasion we raised a committee, they promise to do their best, and damned all the rest,—They have met this morning, and seem much heartyer in the Business, than Last Night. They can't promise much money, but will do what they can for us. The Committee give us such a bad account of Hinkly, we think it prudent not to throw away time and expence after it, so have Resolved to Return by Sileby, Sison, Mountsorrel &c for we are told, they have £50 Left as a fund, Remaing at the Conclusion of the charter concern.

if we get but £45 of this fifty It will be better than nothing, — we also understand by a person just arrived from Melbourn, they are Surprised at not hearing from us, for the Letters We sent, have not been made public, And they wish to Contribute their mite to ours

> Of all the places e'er my Eyes did see
> Oh! Leicester, Leicester, none e'er equaled thee
> They can't step forward, don't possess the means
> Slaves in every sense, even Beans
> Once their food, and filld the Lads with courage
> Are Substituted by bad water porrage
> Here sock, and sandals, cut from top to Bottom
> I'll bring a sample, for by GOD! I've got 'em

Your fellow labourer and friend

Thos Large.

M30 ❖ [Mid to late] April 1812: Letter from "W Balfour, Captain of Division," at Nottingham to William Trentham at Nottingham

As Hammond and Hammond indicate in *The Skilled Labourer*, very little deadly violence in Nottinghamshire was directed by the Luddites at persons but rather at machines. One important exception, they point out, was the "attempted assassination" of Nottingham hosier William Trentham, in April 1812. Hammond and Hammond speculate that the attempt was an act of "private vengeance."[66]

Hammond and Hammond have been criticized for being "moved by a powerful disposition to push violence to the periphery of trade union history."[67] Such a disposition might have been at work in their speculation on the place of this letter. The distinction between private and group vengeance is, on careful consideration, more difficult to maintain than Hammond and Hammond imagine. Based on relationships between apprentices and freemen and masters, work in the stocking trade was a personal as well as a collective matter, and violations of the traditions of the "moral economy" described so well by Thompson merited both personal and collective senses of injustice. "Joe Firebrand" recognizes the blurred line between (personal) revenge and (collective) punishment in his letter to Mssrs. Trevit, Biddles, Bowler, already transcribed. Furthermore, Hammond and Hammond's distinction assumes a fairly ordinary understanding of collectivity as tending toward labor organization—an assumption deriving, perhaps, from their trade-unionist sympathies. Certainly, Luddism was more organized than earlier spates of machine breaking, but it remained a phenomenon, as Thomis demonstrates, characterized not by a central organizing committee but by a more flexible and variable structure that responded as needed in order to correct violations of the implicit as well as the explicit codes of the moral economy. This threatening letter to Trentham appears to have been written in the ad hoc vein, prior to his attempted murder on 27 April 1812; however, evidence contained in the correspondence between Thomas Large and Thomas Allsop suggests that the attempt was neither unexpected nor ad hoc (see Allsop's 30 April 1812 letter, Nottinghamshire Archives CA 3984, I, 74.)

The letter to Trentham is signed "W Balfour, Captain of Division," an obvious pseudonym, but the nearly unreadable handwriting in the signature and closing differs from the handwriting in the body of the letter. The letter appears to be an original rather than a copy, as no Home Office clerk's writing matches that in the letter.

H. O. 42/120. The letter has been reproduced in J. L. Hammond and Barbara Hammond, *The Skilled Labourer, 1760–1832* (London: Longmans, Green, 1919), 270–71.

❖ ❖ ❖

Sir,

I have received instructions from the Captain from his Head Quarters at Grinds Booth in which he orders me to represent [to] you the conduct of a Person of the name of Haywood who takes chevining[68] from your Warehouse. This woman gives her Girls but half a Crown a Week tho' they chevin six pair of Hose a Day for which they work a great number of Hours the Captain has written himself to a Hosier of Nottin[gham] respecting this Woman and he informs me that the result has been most satisfactory, the Captain desires me to represent to you in the strongest terms his detestation and abhorrence of your conduct if you are privy to this Womans transactions as you must be sensible that no human being capable of work can be maintained with 2/6 a Week.

You must be sensible Sir that these unfortunate Girls are under very strong temptations to turn prostitutes, from their extreme poverty.

The Captain authorises me to say that these People being defenceless he conceives them to be more immediately under his protection as his believes their Wages are the lowest in England He hopes you will endeavour to allevi-ate their misfortunes by giving the employ to each of these Individuals at an equitable Price.

Should you neglect to redress the grievance complain'd of I am commanded by the Captain to acquaint you, and I do hereby acquaint you, that however unwilling yet our Duty to the cause will compells us to attack you on your Property wherever you may be found

For this Purpose the Sections 11= 13= and 14 are put under my command and I shall not fail of doing my Duty to my Captain and my Frend

<u>Sign'd</u>   W. Balfour

<u>Captain of Division</u>

Four oClock in the
Afternoun [illegible]
[illegible]

<u>Patrina</u>[69]

M31 ❖ 24 April 1812: Letter with poem by Thomas Large, Nottingham

After having journeyed to London as part of the committee's delegation peti-tioning for parliamentary relief, Large sent another poetical letter, this time to Thomas Roper in Nottingham. Even more than the "Oh! Leicester" letter, the following letter blends prose and verse, somber resentment, and humor. It also reveals a touch of racism against the Romani store owner who is the subject of the verse. It is rare among texts by Midlands laborers for its use of parenthe-ses; in contrast, documents in the Home Office Papers from Yorkshire and other regions make more frequent use of parentheses.

Manuscript: Nottinghamshire Archives, CA 3984, I, 64. Typescript: *Records of the Borough of Nottingham*, 8:143–44.

❖ ❖ ❖

Thos Roper
Newtons Head
Nottingham

April 24, 1812
Sir

    While we was writing to you the other day Mr Toplas[70] was walking up Fleet street, near Temple bar, and was knocked down by the pole of a coach, as he was crossing the road, the horses trode upon his Breast and Leg—but we hope he will be able to attend to Business this afternoon, tho Henson has been to see how he is, and found him very very poorly, he cannot keep anything on his stomach, at present. In the mean time Henson (while I am writing this to you and to derby and Leicester and Godalming) has gone with two of the London Committee to the Hatten garden Magistrates Latham is gone to John Smith,[71] and we are to have an interview with Mr Benson this afternoon. Mr Toplas thinks he can travel by water, we wish if you think it prudent, for you to have a general meeting of the Trade next Monday—and we will send you all the information we can by that time (Monday night) We have engaged the same Room, where the carpinter committee sat, when they brought on the late Trial on the sistem of colting. We have had an opportunity of speaking to them on the subject, they thought we possesed a fund on a permanent principle to answer any demand, at any time, and if that had been the case, would have Lent us two or three thousand pounds, (for there is £20,000 in the fund belonging that Trade) but When they understood our Trade kept no regular fund to support itself, Instead of Lending us money, Their noses underwent a Mechanical turn upwards, and each saluted the other with a significant stare, Ejaculating Lord bless us ! ! ! what fools ! ! ! they Richly deserve all they put ! and ten times more ! ! ! We always thought stockeners a sett of poor creatures ! Fellows as wanting of spirit, as their pockets are of money, What would out Trade be, if we did not combine to gether? perhaps as poor as you are, at this day, Look at other Trades ! they all combine, (the Spitalfeild weavers exepted, and what a Miserable condition are they in) see the Tailers, shoemakers, Bookbinders, Gold beaters, printers, Bricklayers, Coatmakers, Hatters Curriers, Masons, whitesmiths, none of these trades Receive

Less than 30s/-a week, and from that to five guineas this is all done by combination, without it their Trades would be as bad as yours, even govt. cannot
precent bad articles, if your hands are such fools to make them, these are the
arguments made use of by persons who know nothing of our Trade - how far
they are right I believe you can Judge

heris is a shopman, Romanis cheapside, has got such tales about Ned Ludd,
stuck in is window, and two stocking frames at work close to the shop door
a large drawer full of guineas, half guineas, and seven shilling pieces in the
window, all to attract notice, and he sells the damed'ist Rubbish of Framework
goods we ever saw in our Lives, he's got Long armed Cotton gloves, selvages,
marked to sell at sixpence per pair, single press, cut up, &c, shot down at his
door, And shoveled in, the same as you shovel in coals at Nottm., his window
is also full of songs about the amazing cheapness of his goods considering the
price of Labour &c—

> His mash, he sells for silk, and single press
> For What it should be made, or rather Less,
> And tells the Town, that he alone has gotton
> Brown stockings, made of real india cotton
> But when we Eyed them, soon we did disern
> His india cotton, nought but single yarn
> And others silks, this Roman doth declare
> Are not his weight, by half an ounce a pair
> Tho—what we saw, we viewed the window round
> Would take full twenty pair to weight a pound
> His pantaloons, what he calls double milled
> A pound a pair, with twits, and burs and filld
> And cotton Gloves, Long arms and Seemly fair
> Hang in his window, marked sixpence a pair
> Thus is this Villain, trading in the Trash
> That was the cause of many a dreadful Smash
> We hear he's Likely, soon to be in the fleet
> Pray god almighty send, that we may see it
> Before we Leave this Town, for well we know
> Goods Like his, has filld our Trade with Woe.

you will have the goodness to smiths anser to the circular Letter, and all the things that have been wrote for before, we shall write again to morrow

yours

Thos Large.

Mr. Fryers Tailer No 10 Leigh Street
red Lyon Square London
    Give my Wife 12 shillings Large

M32 ❖ [Late] April 1812: Poem titled "Well Done, Ned Lud," Nottingham or Mansfield

By the spring 1812, even Nottinghamshire Luddism had assumed a militant political flavor, and the Luddite writers took serious interest in national political change. This Nottinghamshire poem reflects the new flavor in Midlands Luddism, which, it has been argued by Thompson and others, eventually concludes with the Pentrich rising and the execution of its leader, the former Luddite captain, Jeremiah Brandreth.

The earliest version of the poem appears on one side of a folded document, which apparently belonged to Charles Sutton. Sutton was the editor of the *Nottingham Review*, the radical newspaper sympathetic to the framework knitters' grievances. The handwriting seems to be Sutton's, based on a comparison with other documents known to have been written by him. Most tellingly, his writing is characterized by the frequent use of elision in a type of shorthand.[72] On the other side, in a different handwriting than the verses, is an address, "Mr Sutton / Review Office / Nottingham," and, on the facing side under a date of 23 April 1812, a list of marriages, deaths, and prices at Mansfield market. At the bottom, in the same hand as the lists and the address, is "Mansfield Apr 16, 1812 L S." Despite efforts to find mention of the poem in Sutton's other writings, there is no indication that the document is anything other than a copy, so authorship is uncertain, and it is clearly the best course to consider the document as anonymously authored.

Nottinghamshire Archives M297. A transcription of the poem is followed by a facsimile on page 131. A different version, from the Home Office Papers (H. O. 42/123), appears in its entirety after this version (M33).

❖ ❖ ❖

Well dn, Ned Lud, your cause is good,
Mk Perceval your aim,
By the late Bill 'tis understood,
'Tis death to break a fram.

With dextrs skll the Hosiers kill,
For they are quite as bad,
To die you must by the late bill,
Go on my bonny lad

You may as well be hangd, for death
As brkng a machine,
So now my lad, your sword unsheath,
And make it sharp and keen.

We're ready nw your cause to join,
Whenever you may call,
To make foul blood run fair and fine,
Of tyrants grt and small.
P.S.   Deface this who dare,
       Shall have tyrants fare,
       For Ned's Every where,
       To both see and hear.

An enemie to Tyrants

M33 ❖ [9] May 1812: Poem titled "Welcome Ned Ludd," Nottingham

Another, later version of the preceding poem contains some material differences. The poem illustrates the difficulties in ascertaining a "correct" version of Luddite texts that were copied by correspondents to the Home Office and by Home Office clerks. Despite its later date and significant variants, this version has been reprinted and commented on frequently—for example, in Thomis, *Luddites* 136, Thomis, *Luddism in Nottinghamshire* 55–56, Sale, *Rebels against the Future* 153, and Bailey, *Luddite Rebellion* 43.

H. O. 42/123. The poem appears in the handwriting of a Home Office clerk.

Well on, Ned Lud, your cause is good,
Make Perceval your aim,
By the late Bill 'tis understood,
'Tis death to break a fram.

With dexterous skill the Hosiers kill,
For they are quite as bad,
To die you must by the late bill,
Go on my bonny lad

You may as well be hang'd for death
As breking a machine,
So now my lad, your sword unsheath
And make it sharp and keen.

We're ready now your cause to join,
Whenever you may call,
To make foul blood run fair and fine,
Of tyrants great and small.

P.S. Deface this who dare,
Shall have tyrants fare,
For Ned's Every where,
To both see and hear.

An enemie to Tyrants.

Poem titled "Well Done, Ned Lud," Nottinghamshire Archives M297

❖   ❖   ❖

This paper was <u>posted up in</u> Nottingham on Saturday Morning

<u>May 9th 1812</u>

Welcome Ned Ludd, your case is good,
   Make Perceval your aim;
For by this Bill, 'tis understood
   Its death to break a Frame—

With dexterous skill, the Hosier's kill
   For they are quite as bad;
And die you must, by the late Bill-
   Go on my bonny lad!—

You might as well be hung for death
   As breaking a machine—
So now my Lad, your sword unsheath
   And make it sharp and keen—

We are ready now your cause to join
   Whenever you may call;
So make foul blood, run clear & fine
   Of <u>Tyrants great and small</u>!—

with Mr Thomas   PS.-   Deface this who dare
⟨Illegible⟩ Courts   They shall have Tyrants fare
SWood Street   For Ned is every where
                                          And can <u>see and</u> hear

---

M34 ❖   29 May 1812: Letter from "N. Ludd" mailed to Henry Wood, Leicester

The most famous incidents of machine breaking in Leicestershire took place at Loughborough in 1816, but as early as 1812 Leicestershire Luddism produced some letters that are not only interesting for the Luddite culture that they depict but also for how they were handled by the recipients. One such letter, received through the mail by Henry Wood of Leicester on 1 June 1812, appears on a reward poster printed in Leicester, 3 June 1812. Like many of the threatening letters from Nottinghamshire, the letter to Wood employs a juridical discourse much as was found in magistrate's warrants. Unlike other threats, this letter purports merely to inform Wood of an irrevocable death sentence and does not offer a chance for him to reform. Perhaps the letter's most interesting feature is the new calendar suggested in the date, "29 May year two" (1812, the second year of the Luddite risings, which possibly imitates the French Revolutionary calendar).

The reward poster was sent to the Home Office. It was also forwarded to the Home Office by Gratian Hart of Leicester, in his 4 June 1812 letter, as a "specimen" of threat passed about in Leicestershire.

H. O. 42/124. The entire reward poster is reproduced in facsimile on page 134.[73]

M35 ❖ Late Spring or Summer 1812: Song titled "Hunting a Loaf," Derbyshire

In his *History of the Machine-Wrought Hosiery and Lace Manufacturers*, William Felkin speculates that the primary causes of Luddism were hunger and misery. He remarks that the winter of 1811–12 heard an incessant cry: "Give us work at any price—half a loaf is better than no bread."[74] Correspondents from all parts of the Luddite regions writing regularly to the Home Office report a doubling or even a tripling in the prices of oatmeal and potatoes (Fletcher letter, 6 May 1812, H. O. 40/1, and Maitland letter of the same date, H. O. 42/123).

"Hunting a Loaf," a Derbyshire ballad from the late spring or summer of 1812, explicitly links Luddism to the economic distress felt by Britons in general, rather than primarily to the clash between labor traditions and new technology. The song is also much more politically charged than most of the Midlands documents that were written before late spring of 1812 (and the assassination of Prime Minister Perceval on 11 May 1812 by John Bellingham, the "Liverpool man" of the song), placing blame for the distress squarely on the government. Even more remarkable for a document originating in the Midlands are the indications within the song of a self-conscious political discourse, one that is not only aware of boundaries of acceptable speech but also deliberate in its attempts to direct that speech along the paths of an audience's sympathies. The writer distinguishes between "sedition" and complaint, appealing more to the image of the (less objectionable) bread riot than to the more narrow (and perhaps less pathetic) notion of defending "the trade." Even the stylistic devices cater to audience expecta-

Four Hundred Guineas Reward.

Mr. Wood received the following Letter on Monday .eve-
ning, the 1st of June, by the Post.

" Henry Wood,

IT having been represented to me that
you are one of those damned miscreants who deligh in distressing and
bringing to povety those poore unhapy and much injured men called
Stocking makers ; now be it known unto you that I have this day issued
orders for your being shot through the body with a Leden Ball on or
before the 20th Day of June, therefore it will be adviseable of you to
settle your worlly affairs and make the best use of your spare time, as
nothing can or shall save you from the Death you so Justly deserve.

I am

a frend to the Poore

N. LUDD.

Ludd Office 29 May year Two "

*The following note was sent on a printed Card to the Warehouse of Ann
Wood, & Sons, on Tuesday morning, the 2nd. instant.*

" Leicester, June 1, 1812.

The Gentlemen Hosiers are requested to take notice that the
Framework-knitters' bill will be read by the Attorney, Mr. Toplis, in
the Exchange, at 3 o'clock in the Afternoon of Wednesday the 3rd. of
June Inst. when its parts will be minutely examined, and the Hosiers
will have a fair opportunity of approving or objecting to it.

By order of the Committee

Of the House of Commons,

T. Allsop. Sec."

A copy of the above has been sent to the Secretary of State, and
also to every Member of Parliament, and a Reward of

TWO HUNDRED GUINEAS

is hereby offered to be paid by Ann Wood & Sons, to any individual
who will give such evidence as shall be the means of convicting the person or persons guilty of sending the above threatening Letter. And if
two or more persons were concerned in writing and sending the said letter, and one of them will impeach his accomplice or accomplices, or give
such secret information as shall lead ultimately to a conviction, he or they
shall receive the like reward, and exertions shall be made to procure the
pardon of the person or persons so impeaching.

The Mayor and Magistrates, having been informed of this
threatening Letter, hereby offer a Reward of TWO HUNDRED GUI-
NEAS to be paid by them, over and above the sum promised by the
House of Ann Wood and Sons.

LEICESTER : June; 3, 1812.

Browne, Printer, Market-place.

Reward poster containing 29 May 1812 letter from "N. Ludd" mailed to Henry Wood,
Leicester, H. O. 42/124

tions. The image of the "big loaf" for a shilling was familiar and commonly used by the disaffected and by reformers as an amalgam of the desire for prosperity and for a political reform that would alleviate economic distresses.[75] The highly wrought internal rhyme forces a pause and thereby segments each line into more manageable, oralized lengths—a technique typical not only of popular songs and hymns but also of some of the schoolbooks of the time.

A printed sheet illustrated with a woodcut in the Broadsheet Collection, Derby Local Studies Library, box 15. It has been reprinted with its tune and a great many emendations in Roy Palmer, *A Touch on the Times* (Harmondsworth: Penguin Education, 1974), 289–90.[76]

❖   ❖   ❖

HUNTING A
LOAF.

GOOD people I pray give ear unto what I say,
And pray do not call it sedition,
For these great men of late they have crack'd my pate,
I'm wounded in a woeful condition.[77]
Fal lal de ral, &c.
For Derby it's true, and Nottingham too,
Poor men to the jail they've been taking,
They say that Ned Ludd as I understood,
A thousand wide frames has been breaking.
Fal lal, &c.
Now is it not bad there's no work to be had,[78]
The poor to be starv'd in their station;
And if they do steal they're strait sent to the jail,
And they're hang'd by the laws of the nation.
Fal lal, &c.
Since this time last year I've been very queer,
And I've had a sad national cross;
I've been up and down, from town unto town,
With a shilling to buy a big loaf.
Fal lal, &c.
The first that I met was Sir Francis Burdett,

He told me he'd been in the Tower;[79]
I told him my mind a big loaf was to find,
He said you must ask them in power.
        Fal lal, &c.

Then I thought it was time to speak to the prime
Master Perceval would take my part,
But a Liverpool man soon ended the plan,
With a pistol he shot through his heart.
        Fal lal, &c.

Then I thought he'd a chance on a rope for to dance,
Some people would think very pretty;
But he lost all his fun thro' the country he'd run,
And he found it in fair London city.
        Fal lal, &c.

Now ending my journey I'll sit down with my friends,
And I'll drink a good health to the poor;
With a glass of good ale I have told you my tale,
And I'll look for a big loaf no more.
        Fal lal, &c.

M36 ❖ 4 June 1812: Letter from "L.." at Nottingham to the prince regent at Carlton House

H. O. 42/124 contains many letters, written during the spring and summer of 1812, that threaten public officials. Several of them are addressed to the prince regent from various parts of the country. Most of the letters express grievances, but even the authors of those letters seem to be aware that their pleas will have little effect on the regent. (The prince regent did have some well-wishers, although much apparent well-wishing to public officials was ironic; see, for example, the July 1812 letter from Daypool (Y17) among the Yorkshire documents.) Almost all of the letters indicate popular disapproval of the regent's style of living, and many of those have religious moral and rhetorical underpinnings: one message consisted of nothing more than a stamp of George III with the biblical passage on the destruction of Sodom and the letters "a" and "n" written large in the margins.

Among the threats is a Luddite letter from Nottingham addressed to "His Royal highness The Prince Regent Carlton House London/ Speed." Despite several grammatical problems, the skillful rhetorical balances in the letter—for example, between God's and Lud's "eres" and between "extravegance" and "love" —are remarkable for a Luddite document. The posited connection between divine and temporal justice typifies, in many ways, the later stages of frustrated Nottinghamshire Luddism; however, the insistence on personal justice (that is, against the regent's person) wrought by the "avenger of blood" demonstrates that the writer still envisions the possibility of action, even though that possibility is rendered in the third person, Lud. The vision certainly is not as bold or optimistic as earlier Luddite visions (such as we find in "General Ludd's Triumph") had been. Instead, the writer treats rebellious violence as a last resort of men "whoes lives are not worth keeping in this wretched period of your Reign." The repetition of "you" and "your" throughout imparts to the letter an accusing tone much more pronounced than in many other letters, drawing attention to the disparity between sovereignty ("your Reign") and failed governance caused by moral slackness ("your Country" juxtaposed against "your extravegance"). That disparity is further punctuated by the closing: "one who wishes well/ To his Country," rather than to His Royal Highness.

H. O. 42/124. It is enclosed by a 4 June 1812 letter from Conant (by way of his colleague, Baker). Conant says that the suspected writer "was laid hold of, and it was discovered that he had loose in the breast of his Coat a sharp pointed knife fixed in a wooden handle apparently new, near a foot long" (H. O. 42/124). No more is said about the writer in series 42, except that Conant judged him to be mad and noted that he laid a book—perhaps a Bible—before the judge at his arraignment.

❖   ❖   ❖

George

The cry of your sins, is gone into the Eres of the Lord of hostes. and the day of repentance will shortly be gone by---.

The cry of your hard and unmoveable heart to the sufferings of your <u>Poor Starving</u> Subjects is gone into the Eres of General Lud—

Four thousand of his bravest Men (whoes lives are not worth keeping in this wretched period of your Reign) have sworn to revenge the wrongs of their countrymen and their own, if you dont stand still, and <u>think</u> and <u>act</u> differantly to what you have done—Was it ever known to your Country, (since you have had the power of acting in its behalf) that you have dropt a sentence, or done a single act which has worn the slightest appearance of Love to your Country—O Shame think of your extravegance. Think of your example—repent before the avenger of Blood put it out of your power—

    Take the advice of one who wishes well

        To his Country

           L..

To The Prince Regiant

    Nott^m 4th June 1812

M37 ❖ 7 June 1812: Letter from "Tho Jones" at Bristol to the prince regent at London

Although the following letter, dated 7 June 1812 from Bristol, does not originate in one of the Luddite regions, it adheres to the pattern of some of the ironic well-wisher letters from the Luddite regions to the regent and other authorities and makes specific reference to the disturbances at Nottingham.[80]

H. O. 42/124. It appears without an enclosing letter among a number of letters threatening the regent and cabinet ministers.

❖ ❖ ❖

To His Royle Highness prince Regent London

                        June 7 1812

You Royle Highness

    I have taking Liberty of writing thies few lines To awear you what may happing to your Person and that in averry short time I am informed by sum of the Rioters in Nottingham that if you donot InDever To make peace with the Countrey and France or indever That Bread Shall Be Cheaper That thay will Blow your Braines out. and what I can learn that thay are In wait for you dayley

    I remain your

    Well whisher

        Tho Jones <u>Cabinet Maker</u>

        Bristol

M38 ❖ 11 June 1812: Letter from "a poor woman" at "Lester" to James Stevenson at Leicester

Enclosed with a 16 June 1812 letter from General Dyott in Lichfield to General Maitland is a 15 June letter from the mayor of Leicester, James Stevenson, to Dyott, expressing the mayor's concern about the spread of machine wrecking into his town. Stevenson's letter contains a transcription of an anonymous letter that he had received, dated 11 June 1812. While the authorities believe the letter to be genuine in its declared intentions, it is possible that the letter follows the rhetorical "good cop" form directed to offending recipients by Luddite writers who attempt to convey a threat without appearing threatening, thereby avoiding the consequences specified in the Black Act; perhaps the best example is the April 1812 letter to Joseph Radcliffe from "Mr Love Good" in the Radcliffe Papers 126/28, transcribed below.

I include all of Stevenson's letter to show the reaction of the authorities.

H. O. 40/1/4.

❖   ❖   ❖

Leicester, June 15th 1812

Sir,

I take the liberty of requesting that you will, if it be possible, increase the force of this Garrison. I understand there are only about 158 Soldiers in the place.

It is not possible, in the compass of letter, to explain to you <u>all</u> the reasons which induce me to apprehend for the safety of the Town. I will state a few, but beg you to give me credit for more. Letters threatening assassination <u>have been sent</u> here to several persons. It is pretty clear that these have been sent by the Committee of Frameworkknitters who have as complete an organization of the whole Body as you could have of a Regiment. The <u>Leicester Chronicle</u> has been for some time employed in familiarizing and justifying assassination. It has advertised a Subscription for Bellingham's Widow. The system of terror is here almost as complete as at Nottingham; and do not forget that the Press is here more devoted to Revolutionists than in any other part of the Kingdom. I received by the Post lately the following letter:

"Sir, excues the libberty of a poor woman but
"I am very sorry to inform you that their is moast
"dreadful work carring on wich they say that things
"is quite in their favor they did not think you
"would have let the Sussix gon but Sir if it is
"in your power you had much better get them to
"return or some more boath for your sake and some
"Hundreads wich is in great danger Sir rewards is of
"no youse I should like to say a great deal but durst
"not as I overheard last night but I beg you will be
"as caushas as possable you can for they are in great
"hopes to have it done in a very short time they say
"<u>know</u>. so I conclued with wishing you all may be well
"for their is too many Luds. Lester 11th June."

The letter wears all the appearance of being the genuine effusion of an honest person of low condition. Since the receipt of this the keeper of the very house in which the Committee of Frameworkknitters meet called privately on the Chief Constable and told him he is very miserable—that there will certainly be dreadful work and soon—that he has overheard some of the Frameworkknitters talk of such things as make him shudder &c, the Chief Constable bid him keep his ears open and inform him from time to time. Now, Sir, with a Committee organized by Nottingham men, holding <u>constant</u> communication with them and having very great correspondence in other places, headed by a clever man who has threatened assassination, and assisted by a Press which justifies it, and which is conducted by a man who has confessed privately that he should like a Revolution, can you suppose that if there be a general rising there is any place where more rigorous measures will take place on the part of the Insurgents than this?

I beg you to consider, Sir, that I can not state to you all that leads me to this apprehension—much is derived from the general character of affairs—but if there be ground for fear <u>any where</u> there is at Leicester. If a blow is struck any where it will be here struck with relentless fury by the heads of the organization. It is a <u>art of Nottingham</u> in its' system. They are jointly soliciting a Bill.[81] Delegates from both places are together in London and others conferring here—continually—There is a perfect identity between them, and here the press is more in their favor than at Nottingham or any where.

You may depend upon it that this Town would be the head quarters of the Insurgents for a considerable district, and it ought, therefore, as I am persuaded you will think, to have a force equal to the importance of it. It spreads over a space larger than Nottingham. Many Inhabitants have expressed their surprize to me that we have so few Troops in the Town. I know your readiness to listen to my requests and I beg to assure you that I am,

Sir,

With much respect,

Your obliged humble

Servant,

Jm^s Stevenson, Mayor

Major Genl Dyott &c

M39 ❖ 16 July 1812: Circular letter from "The C--m---tee"

In a 28 July 1812 letter from Mansfield from one Stevens to Sidmouth comes the following "circular," which Stevens relates to papers from "the Arnold Committee" of framework knitters, the secretary of which is a man named Emerson.[82] Stevens says, too, that "the Luddites were first organized by this Committee" (H. O. 42/125). The circular requests that responses be directed to a London address. At about this time, several stockingers were in London attempting to secure passage of a bill of relief for the trade. It might provide another piece of evidence for communication between the lawful and Luddite factions. The circular is printed in italic type.

H. O. 42/125.

❖ ❖ ❖

Gentlemen,

AS our principal care is and has been, to give you every information, are sorry you should have been so long without, the cause is, have waited in full hopes that it would have been in our power ere this to have brought about a reconciliation at least, a Meeting wi'h Employers, such is the case they appear determined to encumber the Trade with so much expence that it may both destroy our fortitude and finances; Gentlemen are proud to say, such cannot take place, while such liberal exertions flow from Country as well as Town

Friends, yet still from the length of time elapsed in our struggle it requires every man's utmost assistance, and in one very particular are well convinced the Town is partially supplied with goods from the Country, either by direct or indirect means, everything you can with propriety prevent that would injure our cause, will redound not only to the general interest, but to your lasting honour; our Prosecutors are seeking all means, not only disgraceful to themselves, but enough to despoil men's minds to cause them to turn the Trade into other Channels such is hoped men will not be driven to the greatest honour and observance on the part of Journeymen, has through this contest been observed, but the oppressive and abitrary will of Employers will not acknowledge. Gentlemen we must pursue the same steady line of conduct which has marked the past proceeding and doubt not from the general disposition of men and circumstances our cause will ultimately succeed. Gentlemen we rely on you every endeavours and are

Your devoted Servants,

London July 16th, 1812   The C--m---te.

P. S. As soon as read destroy. Some of our Communication has fallen into London Masters hands. Direct as usual, No. 8, King-street, Drury-lane.

M40 ❖ September 1812: Encrypted letter and key, "The Committee"

A 20 September 1812 letter from James Stevens at Mansfield to Lord Sidmouth (H. O. 42/127), discloses the means by which the Luddites' communications with other Luddites were encrypted. Stevens writes,

> Several of the Luddite letters which I am in posession of have been unintelligable until this week owing to the following ingenious plan—Their Letter paper is all cut to one size, and every correspondent is in posession of what the term a Key, a specimen of which I have enclosed—and which being placed upon the letter shews at once what they wish to disclose—The remainder of the letter is a Cloak in case it should fall into the Hands of the Police.

The key that Stevens describes is a piece of paper approximately three inches by five inches with three parallel sections cut out. The four remaining strips hide the "cloaking" lines, leaving only the essential information visible.

H. O. 42/127.

❖ ❖ ❖

Sir,
   The Committee
for the relief of the Poor
meet on Wednesday night at 8 'o'Clock
when the case of the woman who lives
on Bullwell Common—
will be taken into consideration
Bullwell Sep 13th 1812   yours &c

⟨The key, when overlaid, reveals only the following three lines:⟩

The Committee

meet on Wednesday night at 8 'o'Clock

on Bullwell Common—

**M41 ❖ May 1814: Letter from "William Trueman" to John Bullock
at Nottingham**

The difficulty that Nottingham authorities had in acquiring copies of the rules
or constitution of the newly formed "Union Society" of framework knitters
dominates the letters circulating among Coldham, Allsop, and the Home Office
during 1813 and 1814. Hammond and Hammond direct readers to H. O. 42/137
and 42/139 for the society's constitution.[83] It is not possible to be certain whether
the organization of the society indicates a resurgence in Luddism, but the authorities' letters suggest that they believed that there was some sort of workers'
conspiracy to raise wages. Coldham even repeats the suspicion of his confiden-
tial source that John Blackner, writer for the *Nottingham Review*, "was one of the
Principals in the Union Society and that he had been engaged in the management of the Attack made upon [Simon Orgill's] property" (Coldham to Home
Office, 8 May 1814, H. O. 42/139; reproduced in Thomis, *Nottinghamshire* 71).
   There are some clear indications, affirming Coldham's paranoia, of a continuous thread connecting some of the writing and frame breaking that took place in
Nottingham in 1814 to earlier Luddism. One such bit of evidence is a letter de-

manding from John Bullock, a Bellar Gate master whose frames were destroyed on 8 May 1814, a "subscription" payment, which Coldham assumes was intended for the Union Society fund; however, nothing in the letter itself suggests that the writer is acting on behalf of the society. The letter is signed "William True-man Secretary," but the name tells little about the agency of the writer. An 1812 letter addressed to Mr. Byrnny, a Nottingham jury foreman, closes, "your for Genl Ludd/a true man" (H. O. 42/122; see letter previously reproduced). Per-haps variations on "Trueman" were formulaic Luddite closings, although "True-man" was quite a common name among men employed in the stocking trade. Whether the letter was pseudonymous or not, Coldham thought the letter to be threatening enough to pass it along to the Home Office.

H. O. 42/139. The 1814 letter to Bullock is enclosed with Coldham's 10 May 1814 letter to the Home Office. The letter is also reproduced in Thomis, *Nottinghamshire* 77.

❖   ❖   ❖

Sir,

This is to inform you that the masters pay their subscriptions the same as their Journeymen and it is hoped that you will not be remiss to do so as the rest of the masters in the branch —

Yours William Trueman Secretary.

M42 ❖   16 June 1814: Letter from S. Simpson at Nottingham to an unknown recipient at Dumfries

In 1814 many hosiery workers suspected formerly to have been associated with Nottingham Luddism in 1811–12 are mentioned in letters to the Home Office as being members of "Societies" organizing the trade. Although the societies may not be part of Luddism proper, they bear a relation to Luddism in more than a shared membership, perhaps justifying the earlier suspicions of Leicester mayor James Stevenson (see 11 June 1812 letter). As part of a larger movement, the soci-eties continue the projects undertaken by the framework knitters, a course (more resembling a cycle, really) including negotiation, frame breaking, negotiation, parliamentary petition, and combination.

Public officials in the region believed that there was a connection between the societies and Luddism. In a 20 February 1814 letter, Coldham writes to the

Home Office, "I imagine that these Societies have a main relation to and connection with the Frameworkknitters, and are the remnant of the System of Luddism and the body of men who applied last year to Parliament"; the letter appears in H. O. 42/137 and in Thomis, *Nottinghamshire* 58–60. Less than two months later, men broke into Thomas Morley's shop and wrecked five frames owned by or connected to Needham and Nixon, as reported in the Morley Deposition, in H. O. 42/138, which has been reproduced in Thomis, *Nottinghamshire* 60. Coldham suspects that the frame breakers struck at machines owned by Needham and Nixon because "they have been one of the leading Houses, in refusing to advance 2d. a pair to a certain Description of the Workmen who have requested and demanded it of their masters. Their Frames have been broken to intimidate them into a compliance with this demand." The incident is reported in H. O. 42/138, Coldham to Home Office, 7 April 1814, and the letter is reproduced in Thomis, *Nottinghamshire* 62, although Thomis has the date as 1812.

In June 1814 the following letter from one framework knitter in Nottingham to another in Dumfries describing a union of trade societies was acquired by the procurator-fiscal of Dumfries, who passed it to Coldham, still town clerk of Nottingham, who forwarded the letter to the Home Office on 11 August 1814. Coldham's letters from the late summer and early autumn of 1814 indicate an increase not only in attempts at combination but also an increase in ludding. The intercepted letter and a discussion of the labor climate around Nottingham at the time appear in Hammond and Hammond, *Skilled Labourer* 232. I include the letter as evidence of the labor climate in the last half of 1814, just prior to a period of Luddism that began in September of that year.

H. O. 42/140.

❖   ❖   ❖

Nottingham, June 16, 1814.

Sir, — Having seen a letter you have sent to your Brother Timothy explaining the Disposition of the Trade of Dumfries to join their Friends in England in uniting themselves under the Union, I feel it my Duty to give you every Information on the Subject. You will see by the Articles that the intent of the Institution is to unite every branch for the support of each other in times of Distress. The Institution has been found to be very beneficial to every branch, as we have all received a small advance on our work except the Plain Silk Hands, which we are now contending for; We have had 300 hands out of employ for more than six weeks because the Hosiers have not the honour to give a reasonable advance. The Hosiers have formed a powerful Combination against us, but this we have not cared for, we have persevered, and resolved to persever until we accomplish the object in view which we hope is not far distant.

The Union is well-established in Nottingham, Derby and their Counties, and is making very rapid progress throughout Leicestershire, London, Godalming, Tewkesbury and Northamptonshire have all formed themselves, and we have long wished to form an Interest in North Britain in order that the principle may be diffused throughout the North; and we are happy to find that Dumfries is anctious to set the example, and hope when you have formed yourselves you will disseminate the principle through all Scotland, for depend upon it if the Trade are united and true to their own Interest, we shall be able to make our Trade as respectable as any other in the Kingdom and no longer be designated by the application of 'Stracking Stockingers.' According to request I have sent four Articles and sixty Diplomas that you may form yourselves as soon as possible. . . . I hope you will excuse us not writing sooner as we are now so throng, we have scarcely time to attend to anything but the Turn Out.

S. Simpson.

N.B.—Direct for me Newtons Head, Glasshouse Lane, Nottingham.

M43 ❖ 31 August 1814: Letter from "A Priest" to the "Editor of the Nottingham Gazette"

During much of 1814, a running battle took place between Richard Eaton, the Tory editor of the new *Nottingham Gazette*, and Charles Sutton, the radical who published the *Nottingham Review*. Eaton and others (including, it appears, a Mr. Tupman) established the *Gazette* nearly two years earlier in frustration over the political perspectives that grounded the two existing Nottingham papers— the *Review* and the *Nottingham Journal*, which identified itself and which typically is identified as a conservative newspaper. Malcolm Thomis notes Eaton's "hostility to suffering mechanics."[84] The battle between Eaton and Sutton over how best to handle working-class disaffection continued even after the decline of the first period of Midlands Luddism, especially during the late summer of 1814, in series of articles in which Eaton advocated harsh measures. Pseudonymous replies in the *Review* expressed sympathy for the Luddites and other workers in language that ranged from indignant to highly satiric.

One satiric attack consisted of the double letter, transcribed here, that appeared in the *Nottingham Review*, 9 September 1814. The writer obviously is well educated and perhaps not a member of the framework knitting trade at all, but the letter expresses many Midlands Luddite sentiments, including the desire to maintain traditional, useful distinctions in society. (We find the same idea in "General Ludd's Triumph" and other documents that call on the upper classes to fulfill their paternalistic obligations toward the working poor.) Against these traditional notions, we find that the desire to level distinctions was not incompatible with the new commercial conservatism of the gentlemen hosiers in Nottingham. Magistracy and tradition were occasionally seen as impediments to the rise of the large masters. The following letter does, however, move beyond the mainstream of Midlands Luddism in its clearly implied sympathy for political reform and its sense of the national scale of the Luddite rising.

Nottingham Review, 9 September 1814

❖ ❖ ❖

LOST MANUSCRIPT!

To the Editor of the Nottingham Review.

Sir–Walking near the rock-holes in the park, early this morning, I picked up the inclosed manuscript, which, as it was "unwafered and unsealed," I had the curiosity to open; and must confess, that the reading of it had such an effect upon my risible faculties, as for a moment, to drive the morning devotional thoughts from my mind. I found it addressed to the Editor of the Gazette, and having heard that an advertisement had been posted up in different parts of Nottingham, offering a reward for the recovery of a "*Lost Manuscript*," I thought the Editor might have lost it there a night or two before. Reflecting on the oddity of the circumstance, the words *amor merctricor;*[85] *meretrix inusia lues venerea* came forcibly into my head. I determined, however, to take the article to the office; but when I got there, the offered reward was refused, because the author, I was told, had furnished another copy; I therefore send it to you for the perusal of your readers.

Your's, &c.

August 31, 1814.   PETER COMIC.

To the Editor of the Nottingham Gazette.

Sir–Having been a constant reader of your luminous publication, permit me to say, that I have perused the efforts of your transcending genius with extatic pleasure; and have viewed your matchless triumphs over the cold-water Tory and Jacobin factions, that is over the readers of the Journal and Review, with supreme delight. At a period when a Jacobinical war raged around the kingdom, and a not less cruel, and still more dangerous one raged within, which was carried on by mysterious gangs of depredators, called Luddites, at this period you commenced your arduous labours. Your laudable and professed object was, to crush the monster Bonaparte and his myrmydon follower, and all the Luddites, with the magic of your pen; and to convert the cold-water Tories and Jacobins, into ranting true-blue Royalists; whilst the incorrigible Burdett, Whitbread, Brougham, Cochrane, Cobbett, White, Hunt, Drakard, Lovell, Cartwright, Wood, and Waithman, along with John Smith, Lord Rancliffe, the Political Scribe, and the Rev. Editor, you were to muzzle or confine in strong holds. And, worthy Sir, have you not succeeded?– have you not driven Bonaparte to Elba, and his man-eating myrmydons into the mouths of the Cossacks?–have you not proved this wife, the daughter of the Apostolic Emperor, to be a *prostitutum;* and the wife of our immaculate Regent to belong to the Cyprian sisterhood?–nay, have you not driven her into exile, as too dangerous an animal to remain on British soil?–have you not laid every Luddite prostrate at your feet, and made them lick the dust in sorrow and anguish?–have you not driven the cold-water Tories into hiding places, with faces as long as a maypole?–have you not silenced the Burdetts, Whitbreads, Broughams, Cobbetts, Whites, Hunts, Drakards, Lovells, Woods, Waithmans, Smith, Rancliffes, Political Scribes, and Reverend Editors, and driven the troublesome Cochrane into a dungeon–have you not cleared the very *Pig-styes* of their filth, though you got a little *soiled* in the operation?–have you not rendered an essential service to society, by discovering and *practising a new mode of chastisement in Sunday Schools for girls in their teens,* for which a saucy cobler was silly enough to threaten you with the vengeance of this lap stone and strap?–have you not almost ruined the Review, by reducing its sale to *Fifteen* Hundred; while you have *advanced* the *sale* of your self-instructing paper to *three hundred,* besides what you generously give away?–and I need not say how fully and satisfactorily you have proved that the Review has been the occasion of the premature death of all those unfortunate men who have been hung at York, as well as of the rebellion in Ireland, for to the REVIEW may be attributed all that disaffection which now manifests itself; and there can be no doubt that you will be able to prove, that the differences between this country and America, have been owing to the filth of the Review; and were you properly to trace cause and effect, there can be no question but every moral and political evil would be found to have arisen from this source.

But my principal object for troubling you with this letter, is to inform you, that it is in the contemplation of the two Houses of Parliament, at the commencement of their next Session, to vote public thanks to you for the many and extraordinary services you have rendered this country and the world at large, by your not less extraordinary publication, and, I have heard it whispered too, in the higher circles, that the Regent intends devoting ten thousand pounds out of his *savings*, to the erecting a statue to commemorate your virtues in Westminster Abbey, for having driven away his wife.

There are some evil disposed persons that say, that you were the cause of frame-breaking, by suggesting and putting in practice, a plan for reducing the workmen's prices, in your capacity as a hosier, in 1811.–This, I hope, is all sheer gammon and malice; otherwise the blood of a Horsefall, a Trentham, and the seventeen men hung at York, with a long catalogue of other crimes, you will have to expiate, either in this world, or the next. There are persons, likewise, who maintain that you wish to level all distinctions in society, and to create a national convulsion, by driving the working class in acts of desperation for want of food, hoping thereby to become a Robespierre or a Marat. But this insinuation, also, I hope, you will be able to refute, or it shall be attempted to be done by

Your humble servant,

A PRIEST.

M44 ❖ 5 October 1814: Letter from "General Ludd" to "the Editor of the Nottingham Review"

In the *Nottingham Gazette*, 16 September 1814, Eaton had suggested that the authorities offer a large reward of five thousand pounds for information leading to the detection of Luddites. The suggestion was attacked in a 20 September

1814 letter from Southwell, signed "Vindex," printed in the *Nottingham Review*, 7 October 1814:

> But what will Englishmen feel when the dark veil of hypocrisy is torn off, and the half-hidden detestable object presented in full view? that a fellow renowned for his hostility towards the honest artizan, has, with the most unblushing impudence, proposed a scheme for giving a bribe sufficient to cause a man to desert his native land, and to maintain him in a foreign clime: — this he would offer to any person who possessed enough depravity of heart to accuse any other person of the crime of Framebreaking.

In the *Nottingham Review*, 14 October 1814, a letter signed "General Ludd" appeared, partly in response to the *Gazette* proposal. L. Allsopp of Nottingham reported the occurrence to Lord Sidmouth in a letter dated 18 October 1814 (H. O. 42/141). In the 21 October 1814 *Review*, the editor and publisher, Charles Sutton, printed an expression of regret:

> The Proprietor of the NOTTINGHAM REVIEW, is exceedingly sorry to find that an article which appeared in his last Number has given disgust to some of his friends, who have conceived it as having a tendency to encourage the spirit of insubordination and outrage, which has been so long prevalent in this neighbourhood, and which no man laments more than himself. He will not multiply words upon the subject. He knows his own intentions, and he knows that nothing could possibly be further from his thoughts, either in that article or in any other, which at any time may have appeared in the Review.

Speculation that Sutton had some association with Luddism could be fueled by the facts that Sutton sympathized with the motives of the disaffected framework knitters and that a version of a seditious Luddite song, "Well Done, Ned Ludd," appeared on a sheet of paper in Sutton's possession and in his handwriting before the song was posted in Nottingham on a handbill that was later sent to the Home Office. It is quite clear from the letters that appear in the *Review* that Sutton carried on a running battle with the editor of and contributors to the *Nottingham Gazette*, a battle centered on the treatment of the framework knitters.

Nottingham Review, 14 October 1814

❖   ❖   ❖

GENERAL LUDD

To the Editor of the Nottingham Review

Sir—I take the liberty of dropping you a few lines to inform you of the good fortune of one of my sons, who is come to very high honor. You must know that some time ago, owing to a little imprudent conduct, my eldest son, Ned, decamped, and enlisted into his Majesty's service, and as he was notorious for *heroism* and *honorable* enterprize, he was entrusted with a commission to exercise his prowess against the Americans, and I am happy to say he has acquitted himself in a way which will establish his fame to generations yet unborn.[86]

I assure you, Mr. Editor, I scarcely know how to keep my feeling within bounds, for while all our former and united efforts in breaking frames, &c, were commented upon with some severity, and in a way which cast an odium upon my character and that of my family, I now find the scales are turned, and our enemies are converted into friends; they sing a new tune to an old song, and the mighty deeds of my son are trumpeted forth in every loyal paper in the kingdom. My son is not now confined to the breaking a few frames, having the sanction of government, he can now not only wield his great hammer to break printing presses and types, but he has a license to set fire to places and property which he deems obnoxious, and now and then even a little *private pillage* is winked at. Even the Gazette Editor at Mr. Tupman's who was formerly one of my greatest enemies, and threatened to pursue both me and my family to the uttermost, is now in my favor, and is become a patron, and an admirer of my son, on account of his atchievments in Washington. There is one thing though in the conduct of this Gentleman which has created me some little uneasiness; a few weeks ago he strongly recommended to the magistrates to offer a very large reward, to any person who would disclose our secret system of operation in this neighbourhood: he went so far as to say 5000*l.* ought to be offered; enough he said to enable the informer to live independent in another country, intimating such a character would not be considered as a proper person for the society of this country, and therefore he would emigrate to seek other associates. I hope it is not true that this notorious Editor has any secrets to disclose about me and my family, and that he is waiting for this large reward to be offered, that he may avail himself of such an opportunity of making his fortune, and fleeing his country. Now, I really think, as my son is become truly loyal, and is working for his country's good, and all under the sanction of the Crown, and as his atchievements have been of the first rate, "old grievances ought not to be repeated;" though, bye the bye, I am of opinion that all which I and my son have done in Nottingham and neighbourhood, is not half so bad as what my son has done in America; but then you now he has supreme orders, from indisputable authority, for his operations in America, and that makes all the difference.

I am, Sir, your obedient servant,

GENERAL LUDD.

Ludd Hall, October 5, 1814.

M45 ❖ 17 October 1814: Letter from "Ned Lud" at Basford to William Beer at Derby

Luddite letters following the period of most intense activity (1811–12) are not well represented in the Home Office Papers, even though authorities and Home Office correspondents refer to threatening letters sent by Luddites in 1814 and 1816. One letter from the later periods of Midlands Luddism was enclosed in a 25 October 1814 letter from E. Ward at Derby to Lord Sidmouth. Ward says that the letter, which bore a Derby postmark, was "received by Wm. Beer, the officer commanding at the Depot yesterday evening about six o'clock" (Ward to Sidmouth, 25 October 1814, H. O. 42/141).

H. O. 42/141.

❖   ❖   ❖

Mr Bare
Depot
Derby

Sir,
We want som bal Cartrig an Sum Harms, You may expect us very soon
Ned Lud

Basford
Oct. 17—1814

M46 ❖ 12 June 1816: Letter from "Edward Ludd" at Hinckley to "Needham and Bray and Company" at Hinckley

By 1816 Midlands Luddism had shifted to Leicestershire. A 14 June 1816 letter from J. Dyke and G. Mettam at Hinckley, Leicestershire, to the Home Office encloses a copy of a threatening letter "sent to the firm of Messrs Needham & Bray Hosiers in Hinckley" (Dyke and Mettam to Home Office, H. O. 42/151). The location of Luddite activity might have shifted, but the discourse of Midlands Luddism remained much the same as in the late months of 1811. In this case, not only is the practice of abating wages just as objectionable as it was in Nottinghamshire in 1811, but also the letter to Needham and Bray follows a familiar pattern of ascribing guilt to the offending recipient for a particular offensive employment practice and then offering the offender the opportunity to amend or "turn off."

H. O. 42/151. The copy of the Luddite letter follows the Dyke and Mettam letter.

❖ ❖ ❖

To Needham and Bray & Co

I learn you hare[87] about to Bate your hands of their Prizes[88] this Week and by that you hare guilty of death—and you may both—repare for that change as you will not be suffered to live much longer if you purceed, sooner turn off.—

From me

Edward

Ludd

Hinckley June 12th.—

M47 ❖ 10 March 1817: Letter from Thomas Savidge in Leicester County Gaol to his wife

The 28 June 1816 Luddite raid on John Heathcoat's lace factory at Loughborough was the last great Luddite attack. Sixteen Luddites, led by James Towle, a framework knitter from Basford, destroyed almost all of the more than fifty lace frames inside the factory. More than one hundred Luddite sympathizers kept a watch out for the authorities and prevented interference with the destruction within the factory. One watchman, John Asher, was shot and wounded. James Towle was arrested, tried at Leicester, and executed at Leicester Gaol on 20 November 1816. He confessed his own guilt for the raid but did not name any of his accomplices. In January 1817 John Blackburn, a knitter from Nottingham who had been involved in the Loughborough raid, was arrested for poaching on Lord Middleton's estate. In order to secure immunity from prosecution, Blackburn named several Luddites who participated in the Loughborough. Six of those were convicted and executed on 17 April 1817. They included Thomas Savidge, John Amos, John Crowder, Joshua Mitchell, William Towle, and William Withers, whose letters appear hereafter.[89]

After the execution of the Loughborough Luddites, *Nottingham Review* editor Charles Sutton published a brief account of the execution of some of the executed men and their letters. In his introduction to the account and letters, Sutton notes that after conviction the Luddites "betook themselves to serious reflection, and to the use of those means best calculated to prepare them for their awful exit. In this great work they were assisted by the Chaplain, and others, who laboured to impress deeply on their minds, the necessity of true repentance."[90] The letters that they wrote to family members from Leicester Gaol are marked by the reflection that Sutton mentions.

Despite their reflection, all of the writers of the letters persist in denying that they committed the crime of which they were convicted—namely, the attempted murder of John Asher, the watchguard at Heathcott's factory. Nevertheless, most confess to having participated in the Loughborough raid. That might seem to indicate that the men's letters are authentic and that they were not distorted or fabricated by the chaplain of Leicester Gaol, who probably would have presented to the world only the customary full confession, expression of regret, and warning to others not to fall into the company of wicked men.

The first letter in the collection is a letter from Thomas Savidge, a thirty-six-year-old framework knitter, to his wife. ("Savidge" is Sutton's spelling; he is called "Savage" in histories and other documents.) Savidge's place in this volume is not clear. Although he participated in the Loughborough raid, shortly after his conviction he offered to provide samples of treasonable correspondence between Major John Cartwright, Sir Charles Burdett, and Gravener Henson. Should a volume of Luddite confessions and the information of spies and informers ever be conceived, Savidge's letters probably deserve a place in such a volume.

Sutton does not reveal how the personal letters of the convicted men came into his hands. Opening letters of prisoners was practiced at other gaols, such as York Castle and Chester Castle, but copies of the letters went no further than the Home Office Secretary.

Charles Sutton, *Some Particulars of the Conduct and of the Execution of Savidge and Others* . . . (Nottingham: Sutton and Son, 1817), 4.

❖ ❖ ❖

Leicester County Gaol,

March 10, 1817.

My dear Wife,

I write these few lines to you, hoping they will find you in good health, and my dear children. I am as well as can be expected in my situation; tell my dear father he must do every thing in his power for me; I have had no attorney to see me at present; what I have got to say will be to my attorney; so no more at present from your loving and affectionate husband,

THOMAS SAVIDGE.

M48 ❖   2 April 1817: Letter to E. Ward, Derby

Perhaps the very last Luddite letter is one of those most suggestive of a connection between Luddism and the more political movements, such as the Pentridge rising of June 1817. In April 1817, shortly after the previous month's march into Derbyshire of the few remaining Blanketeers to make it beyond Leek in Staffordshire, a threatening letter bearing a London postmark and dated 2 April 1817 was sent to the town clerk of Derby. The letter was forwarded to Sidmouth on 8 April 1817 by the mayor of Derby, who wrote, "I consider it my duty to communicate to your Lordship, the contents of a Letter which has been lately addressed to Mr Ward, the Town-Clerk of Derby, from which it appears that a desperate attempt is to be made by the Luddites, during the present month, in some quarter" (Hope to Sidmouth, H. O. 40/5/2). The lateness of the document and its appearance at the door of a Derby town clerk (Derby had never been the site of much Luddism) suggest that Luddism might have served as a discourse of power appropriated by the writer of the letter, who might not have been a frame breaker. (One wonders where the spy Oliver was at the time that the letter was written.)

H. O. 40/5/2.

❖ ❖ ❖

Mr E Ward
Town Clerk
Derby
Private

Stir not from Derby till the 22 April or else your life will suffer for your rashness as the Luddites will lay wait for you. but after the 22 the last die will be cast and either the Luddites or the Military will have the Command—despise not this advice but keep this letter secret.

April 2

M49 ❖ 6 April 1817: Letter from William Towle at Leicester County Gaol to his father

William Towle, also known as Rodney, was the brother of James Towle, the leader of the Luddite raided on Heathcoat's factory at Loughborough. James Towle was executed on 20 November 1816 for shooting at John Asher, Heathcoat's watchman, and confessed his own guilt but refused to name his accomplices. William Towle was convicted upon the evidence of John Blackburn and William Burton and was executed on 17 April 1817, along with Thomas Savidge and four others.

William Towle's letter to his father resounds of penitence and caution to his brother. Towle's letter precedes a letter in a similarly cautionary vein, written by Reverend E. T. Vaughan to Towle's brother, but there is no firm evidence that Vaughan wrote Towle's letter or assisted him in its composition.

Charles Sutton, *Four Additional Letters* . . . (Nottingham: Sutton and Son, 1817), 1.

❖ ❖ ❖

TO W. TOWLE'S FATHER.

DEAR HONORED FATHER,

I write these few lines in hopes they will find you, my dear sisters and brother in good health, as for myself, I am as well as I can expect in my awful situation. O that I had kept better company. My dear brother I hope you will take warning by my untimely end, and attend the sabbath day, had I done so this would not have been my fate—Could it have been so as my life could have been spared, I would pay the duty I owe to my God. The Rev. Mr. Mitchell, of Leicester, attends me and my fellow prisoners and prays with us every day, that worthy Gentleman has made a deep impression on my mind, and I hope with true repentance through the merits of our blessed Saviour to enter into everlasting life. O in a few days I shall be no more. Farewell, farewell, adieu, adieu, for ever in this world!

I remain your unfortunate Son,

W. TOWLE.

Condemned Cell, April 6, 1817.

M50 ❖ 7 April 1817: Letter from Thomas Savidge at Leicester County Gaol to his father

In a letter written ten days before the Leicester executions, Savidge denies engaging in any bloodshed, particularly in the attempted murder of Nottingham hosier William Trentham in April 1812. From a juridical perspective, Savidge's denial is immaterial because he could have hanged for frame breaking under the 1812 act of Parliament and for burglary under earlier statutes. From another perspective, Savidge's letter is important because it indicates the Midlands Luddites' preferences for nonviolent frame breaking—that is, riot that avoids bloodshed.

Sutton, *Some Particulars* 4–5.

❖   ❖   ❖

Leicester County Gaol,

April 7, 1817.

Dear honoured Father,

I have just had my son with me, who has informed me of a circumstance which has hurt my mind, to think that I should be thought guilty of such a crime. Mitchell I may call a stranger to me, as I did not know him at the time Mr. Trentham was shot; and I declare, as a dying man, that I do not know who shot him, nor ever did. I am as innocent of the crime as a child unborn; and this I solemnly declare, that I never embrued my hands in the blood of my fellow-creature, nor ever thought of committing such an act. I never was a procurator to the Luddites in my life, and if I am so judged, I am judged wrongfully. The men who were along with me, I had no acquaintance with at all. I acknowledge being at Loughborough, and had the truth been spoken, it would not have appeared so bad against me.

I remain your affectionate son,

THOMAS SAVIDGE.

Condemned Cell.

M51 ❖ 8 April 1817: Letter from Thomas Savidge in Leicester County Gaol to his wife and children

Sutton, *Some Particulars* 5–6.

❖ ❖ ❖

Leicester County Prison

My dear Wife and Children,

I beg and pray of you, when you peruse these few lines, that they will be some consolation to you, though I know not how to find words to express myself to you. Let me intreat your not to lay my unfortunate end too close to your heart, though I am sensible of your true affection for me; but let me press this on your mind, consider that there are six dear children, besides being pregnant again ! ! O let me intreat you again, my dear wife, don't give way to fretting, for the sake of my dear children. I need not say any thing more to you, consider that I know your good heart; I need not tell you that duty you have to perform; you know the duty of a wife and a mother, that you will bring them up in a right way; this I do assure you, my heart is at rest about that. Dear wife, let these few words comfort your heart. O what disgrace I have brought upon my family. Pardon, pardon me for that distress I have brought on you; I know I have robbed a virtuous wife of every comfort in this world, but I know you will forgive me. I have one consolation impressed on my mind, that with true repentance, through the merits of our blessed Saviour, I shall enter to eternal life, where I hope to meet you and my dear children. My dear wife, my fate is hard; but I assure you I am preparing my soul to meet that God I have so offended. Dear wife, I feel much composed to meet my fate. Give my love to your father and mother, your brothers and sisters, my love to all my friends and relations. I have wrote a letter to my dear father, which I hope he will let you see. My desire is to be fetched home to my father's house, unless you would desire I should be taken to you; but you have seen my friend before you receive my letter. My desire is to be laid where you and my dear children shall lie together; this is the desire of your loving and affectionate, but dying husband. I shall now conclude;---may God give you strength, and support you through all your trouble. I pray to God to give you health so as to enable you to see my dear children brought up. Farewel! Farewel! my dear wife and children, farewel! Adieu!

I remain your affectionate but unfortunate husband,

THOMAS SAVIDGE.

Condemned Cell, Tuesday, April 8th, about three o'clock in the afternoon.

M52 ❖ **8 April 1817: Letter from Joshua Mitchell at Leicester County Gaol to his brother**

Another of the Loughborough Luddites executed at Leicester was an unmarried framework knitter, twenty-year-old John Mitchell. Mitchell assumes in his letter a greater tone of remorse than the other Loughborough convicts do, even though the phrasing of all the letters is quite similar.

Sutton, *Some Particulars* 9.

❖   ❖   ❖

Leicester County Gaol

My dear Brother,

I received your kind and welcome letter. I am sensible of my awful situation: had I took your advice, and followed your good example, this would not have been my fate. I have just seen Mr. Burton, and he says the Rev. Mr. Hall is out of town; there are three clergymen attend us every day, preparing our souls for that awful sentence which the laws of our country has inflicted upon us. Dear brother, give my humble and hearty thanks to Mr. Alderman Barber and the Rev. Mr. Jarman, for their kind offer. Dear brother, I have one consolation imprest upon my mind, with true repentance, through the merits of our blessed Saviour Jesus Christ, I shall enter eternal life. Dear brother, I hope your will remain a comforter to my dear mother, and God will reward you. Dear brother, I should like to see you, and my dear sisters Elizabeth and Melicent, and John Spears, and any of my relations that has a great desire to see me. Dear brother, I expect I shall leave this vain world next Monday, in hopes of finding eternal life through the merits of our Lord and Saviour Jesus Christ. Dear brother, I hope you will forgive me my trespasses against you, and still remain praying for your unworthy brother,

JOSHUA MITCHELL.

N. B. I have heard that my dear mother wishes to see me; I think it would be more than she could bear. Dear brother, I would have you tell her, there is my two dear young brothers to bring up, and she must think of them; but I shall leave it to you; dear brother, there is one consolation that we shall meet again in heaven, with true repentance, through our Lord and Saviour Jesus Christ.

Condemned Cell, Tuesday,
April 8th, 1817.

M53 ❖ 8 April 1817: Letter from William Withers at Leicester County Gaol to his wife

William Withers, a thirty-three-year-old husband and father of one, like most of the Loughborough convicts, repented his actions and association with the Luddites but denied being guilty of the crime for which he hanged.

Sutton, *Some Particulars* 11–12.

❖ ❖ ❖

Leicester County Gaol

My Dear Wife,

These are the last few lines you will ever receive from your loving and affectionate, but dying husband: pardon me for the distress I have brought upon you, and my dear child. O how I reflect upon myself, to think I had no better conduct. Oh! pardon me for the distress I have brought upon you, but I know your good heart; you will forgive me. My dear, let me intreat you not to fret after me. I hope, when it shall please the Lord to call you from hence, we shall meet together in heaven, to part no more. Most of my time is spent in prayer, and I hope, with true repentance, through the merits of our blessed Savior, to enter into eternal life in Jesus Christ. I cannot die without making one remark to you, it was nothing but distress that ever induced me to be at Loughborough; I now repent, but, alas! it is too late. I received your letter and my mother's at one time. I forgive my enemies, though you are truly sensible that Blackborne has been the ruin of me; I bear him no malice, I have freely forgiven him.---There are Clergymen attend us, and are very kind to us; they take great pains to prepare our souls for that awful moment when I must forfeit my life to the laws of my country. My dear wife, my fate is very hard, for I am going to die for a crime I never committed, nor intended. O my poor dear mother, and my brothers and sisters, I know the Lord will protect you all for ever. My dear friends will look at my dearest wife and sweetest child, for if I had taken the advice of my dear wife, I should not have been in this awful situation; but I assure you I am preparing my soul to meet my God on that fatal day in which I am doomed to die.---Dear wife, I have one remark to make; John Blackborne swore several things against me that I never did; and I solemnly declare, as a dying man, that I never was in the factory, till all the frames were destroyed. Dear wife, I should like to see as many of my friends as can make it convenient to come. Give my love and duty to my poor, dear mother; and I hope I shall meet her, and all my friends and relations in heaven. I hope my tender mother will excuse me answering her letter, as the principal part of my time is employed in preparing, by prayer, to meet the Lord my God. Farewel, my friends! Farewel! Adieu!—I remain your loving and affectionate, but unfortunate husband,

WILLIAM WITHERS.

Condemned Cell, April 8th, 1817,
    11 o'clock in the morning.
    This is my Confession.

M54 ❖ 10 April 1817: Letter from John Amos at Leicester County Gaol to
his wife

John Amos's letter to his wife seven days prior to his execution echoes Thomas
Savidge's letter to his wife two days earlier. The reasons for the similarities between these and other Loughborough Luddites' letters are not clear. Perhaps the
prisoners received assistance from the chaplain in compositional as well as spiri-
tual matters, or perhaps they lifted passages from one of the convicts, or perhaps
they collaborated in writing the letters. Amos, like Savidge and Withers, denies
committing the crime for which he later hanged. This common feature suggests
that the chaplain, whose job it typically was to elicit a complete confession and
acceptance of the judicial determinations, might not have been consulted.

Amos's denial continued to the moment of his death. An account in the 19
April 1817 *Leicester Chronicle* recalls that Amos addressed the crowd that had gathered to watch the hanging: "Friends and Fellow-Countrymen—You now see six
young men going to suffer for a crime they are not guilty of . . . for the man who
committed the crime will soon be at large. I would have you take warning by our
fate, and be careful what company you keep.—Farewel!"[91] Amos was thirty years
old at the time of death and was the father of five children.

Sutton, *Some Particulars* 6–8.

❖ ❖ ❖

Leicester County Gaol

Dear Wife,

I write these few lines to you, hoping they will find you in good health, as
they leave me in good health, considering the awful situation I am placed in,
bless the Lord for it.—Oh what disgrace I have brought on my family. O my
dear wife, pardon me for the distress which I have brought on you and my dear
children. O pray forgive me; I know I robbed a virtuous wife of every comfort in this world. My dear wife and children, and my dear father and mother,
is all that is dear in this world. I know not how to find words to express myself; but my dear wife, I know your heart, I know you'll forgive me when you
read these few lines from a dying husband, who speaks the sentiments of his
heart; you know it was nothing but distress that induced me to go to Lough-

borough; O, I now entreat, but, alas! it is too late; but I have one consolation impressed on my mind, that with true repentance, through the merits of our Lord Jesus Christ, I shall enter into eternal life. Most of my time is spent in prayer to God, to forgive my sins: I am sensible of my awful situation, without true repentance I cannot be saved. There are nine of us who are likely to forfeit our lives to the offended laws of our country. My dear wife, my fate is very hard, for I am going to die for a crime which I never committed. I shall make only one observation on the man that swore against me: Burton swore that I was with him at the Peach Tree, in Nottingham, on the morning the frames were broken at night; I do solemnly declare, as a dying man, that I never was in the public house with that man in all my life, nor do I remember that I ever saw him in all my life until I saw him at Squire Mundy's. O my poor dear father and mother, and my dear sister, I hope the Lord will protect you; and I hope, dear friends, you will always look upon my dear wife and five poor dear children, for if I had taken the advice of my wife, I should not have been placed in this awful situation; bu I assure you, I am preparing my soul to meet my God on that fatal day which I am doomed to die. My dear wife, don't give way to fretting, for the sake of my dear children: I need not say any more to you on this subject, for I know your good heart, you will bring them up in the right way. Let me assure you my mind is at rest. Dear wife, let these few lines comfort you. I expect in a few days to meet the fate which the laws of my country will inflict upon me. Give my love to my father and mother, and my dear sister, and all my relations and friends; I hope we shall all meet in heaven. Farewel my friends! farewel! adieu!

I remain,

Your affectionate and unfortunate husband,

JOHN AMOS.

N. B. I should wish my body to be interred in Nottingham, if my friends can fetch me.

From the Condemned Cell,

April 10, 1817.

This is my Confession.

M55 ❖ [Before 17] April 1817: Verses titled "The Last Gift of John Amos."

Immediately following Amos's letter is a poem, titled "The Last Gift of John Amos" and addressed to his five children. The syntax, rhyme, and mixture of metrical regularities and irregularities are typical of much Luddite and working-class verse. Although the poem does not appear to imitate Methodist hymns, Amos was quite familiar with hymns and might have been influenced by them, particularly in matters of diction. The *Leicester Chronicle*, 19 April 1817, recounts Amos's leading the convicts and crowd in a John Wesley hymn, just prior to execution:

How sad our state by nature is!
Our sin, how deep it stains;
And SATAN binds our captive souls
Fast in his slavish chains.

But there's a voice of Sovereign Grace
Sounds from the sacred word;
Oh! ye despairing sinners come,
And trust upon the Lord.

O may we hear th' Almighty call,
And run to this relief!
We would believe thy promise Lord;
O help our unbelief!

To the blest fountain of thy blood,
Teach us, O Lord, to fly!
There may we wash our spotted souls
From sins of deepest dye!

Stretch out thine arm, victorious King,
Our reigning sins subdue;
Drive the old dragon from his seat,
And form our souls anew.

Poor, guilty, weak, and helpless worms,
On thy kind arm we fall;
Be thou our strength our righteousness,
Our JESUS and our all![92]

Sutton, *Some Particulars* 8. The poem immediately follows Amos's letter to his wife.

❖   ❖   ❖

THE LAST GIFT OF JOHN AMOS,
TO HIS DEAR CHILDREN.

Oh! my dear children, when this you see,
Pray serve your God, and think on me!
I'm torn from you, to an untimely end,
But on the Lord I do depend!
To serve him truly is my delight,
And to find mercy in his sight.
I hope, dear children, you will do the same,

And when you read this, think of his name,
And serve him truly in his sight,
He is our Saviour and delight;
I hope in heaven to meet you there,
Then death's alarms we need not fear.
Farewel, vain world, I have done with you;
I have a better world in view!
To meet my Saviour, Christ our Lord,
Who better joys can me afford!

The above was written in the Testament, which had been given to him, by the Rev. Mr. Mitchell, of Leicester.

M56 ❖   17 April 1817: Letter from John Crowder at Leicester County Gaol to his wife

John Crowder was, at age forty, the oldest of the executed Loughborough Luddites. A Nottingham stocking knitter, he was the father of five children. The tone of Crowder's letter is especially bitter, and his grievances against the informers Blackburn and Burton are not softened by any professions of his own guilt at having participated in the attack.

In some other documents and histories, the name is rendered "Crowther."

Sutton, *Some Particulars* 10.

❖ ❖ ❖

New Bridewell, Leicester, 8 o'clock, on the morning of our execution.

O my dearest and best of Wives,

When you receive this, I shall be no more in this world. But I die happy, in the hope of a blessed Saviour. O what a comfortable thing it is to serve the Lord. I still think my sentence very cruel and unjust, I may say murderous, for Blackborne owned upon the trial he was the man that shot Asher, for which we suffer for aiding and abetting. I was never in the factory at all; I was an outside sentinel, forty or fifty yards from the factory at the time Asher was shot, therefore I could not be assisting in the shooting of Asher, for I did not know he was shot until we had got several miles from Loughborough, on our return home. Blackborne and Burton swore that all the outside sentinels had pistols, which was false, for I had none until it was nearly over, and that which I had then was not loaded, for I threw stones at first.

My dearest wife, I most earnestly wish I had taken your advice, I should not have come to this end. I feel quite calm and in good spirits. O trust in the Lord, for he can strengthen us in the time of trouble: O trust in a blessed Saviour, for he will give us rest. I could wish for John Rawson, John Roberts, and John Roper, to be my bearers; dear wife, choose the other three thyself.

Pray remember my love to my mother and relations; remember my respects to my neighbours, shopmates, and all inquiring friends. For ever adieu! Adieu! I hope, dear wife, to meet you and my dear children and mother in heaven.

JOHN CROWDER.

Northwestern

THE LUDDITE DOCUMENTS from the Northwest come from Manchester and its environs, including Stockport, Macclesfield, Rochdale, Wigan, Bolton, and other cotton towns. A couple of texts originated in Liverpool and Flintshire, Wales. No Luddite texts that I have found came out of the other growing cotton centers of Preston and Blackburn. Most of the texts are threatening letters, addresses, and copies of oaths forwarded to the Home Office by Manchester magistrate Revered William Hay, Stockport solicitor John Lloyd, and Bolton magistrate Colonel R. A. Fletcher. Not even the many spies who worked for Colonel Fletcher seem to have found (or fabricated) Luddite writings. They did, however, report a great many variations on oaths that were occasionally described in the authorities' letters as "horrid" and "sanguinary" but which actually seem to have been fairly standard among disaffected groups of the time. Most of the texts are preserved in the Home Office Papers in the Public Record Office, Kew; only a few appear in regional collections.

Northwestern Luddism was not as tidy as its Midlands predecessor—that is, it crossed boundaries between machine breaking, food rioting, and agitation for political reform more easily and frequently than Midlands Luddism did. For this reason, I have included in this section texts that may appear to be less related to Luddism than the framework knitters' committee papers that I included in the section on Midlands Luddism. The texts give a sense of the discursive culture into which Luddism was imported. Other texts from the culture, the Luddite oaths, are widely available, of suspicious origin, and share most features. For these reasons, I have chosen not to reproduce them here.

NI ❖ February 1812: Letter to Mr. Kirkby, Ancoats

Most scholarly treatments of Luddism in the cotton districts concentrate on the weavers, the most active Luddites in the region of Manchester and Stockport. Letters complaining of hiring practices in the spinning trade, however, indicate that labor dissatisfaction in the region was not limited to the weavers. Generally, spinners did not suffer to the same degree as other artisans in the textile trades, largely because even the depressed weaving and knitting trades required tremendous quantities of yarn and thread.[1] Furthermore, the changes in spinning—from outwork performed mostly by women to factory work performed by men—were accompanied by an increase in wage rates. Such circumstances caused the spinners, especially the mule spinners, to be considered an elite among textile workers. Certainly, the cotton spinners did not participate in Luddite riots in the same numbers as weavers did, but they nevertheless had clear grievances about employment practices, primarily related to gender and wages.

Early in 1812 the owners of spinning mills received letters addressing their practices of hiring women to replace more expensive male workers. A copy of one such letter was forwarded to the Home Office by David Holt, who says in his enclosing correspondence that the threatening letter had been received by "Porters." The copy that Holt sent indicates that the largest Manchester spinning concern, McConnel, Kennedy and Company, also received the same threat. This letter contrasts greatly in tone with the other letters of complaint to McConnel and Kennedy that follow.

The letter is undated but was enclosed in Holt's 22 February 1812 letter from Chorlton.

H. O. 42/120.

❖ ❖ ❖

Mr Kirkby
Cotton Master at
　　Candis his factory
　　　Ancoats
Sir,
　　We begin with the Language of the Prophets of old, in saying, that your

Destruction is at Hand, and why? because we the Cotton Spinners of this Town, have been the means of raising you from the Dunghill, to Independency; & now you with others, have employed so many of the Female Sex, that we, and our little ones, are starving for want of Bread; and if you are determined to persevere, you may expect something destructive immediately —

So we conclude with a Reform or Death

The same has also been rec^d by

Mr Pollard

" —Ja^s Kennedy

" —McConnoll & Co

N2 ❖ 8 April 1812: Poster titled "Now or Never," Manchester

Even though Luddite meetings are reported as having taken place on Lancashire moors in December 1811, and power looms in Stockport were attacked in February and March 1812, as late as 25 March 1812, Manchester boroughreeve Richard Wood, in a letter undersigned by two constables, was able to report perfect tranquillity in that vicinity:

> We have observed with great regret in the London newspapers reports of serious disturbances among the Weavers & Mechanics in this town and neighbourhood, which we are happy to be enabled to contradict. There is no foundation for such reports, on the contrary, it is with pleasure we bear testimony to the exemplary patience with which the working Classes have borne the pressure of the present times.[2]

In less than two weeks after Wood's report, Luddism erupted in the cotton districts of Lancashire and Cheshire and continued throughout the spring. Machine breaking around Manchester often coincided with food riots and other political unrest. Thompson remarks that "when Luddism came to Lancashire it did not move into a vacuum. There were already, in Manchester and the larger centres, artisan unions, secret committees of the weavers, and some old and new groups of Paineite Radicals, with an ebullient Irish fringe."[3] Indeed, it is difficult to distinguish the various motivations. Perhaps this difficulty defines the special character of Lancashire Luddism and may explain why no major historical work has concentrated solely on Luddism in that vicinity, where attacks on steam looms, food riots, and political reform blend almost seamlessly into each other.

One of the first episodes that the authorities associated with Luddism in Manchester was also tied to political reform—the riot at the Manchester Exchange. A loyalist meeting to be held at the exchange had been called by 154 persons, described by Manchester magistrate William Hay as "the respectable committee of Gentlemen, who have sat in this town in aid of & for the information of the civil power." A group of reformers, led by a wealthy Unitarian named Ottiwell Wood, opposed the meeting and published broadside addresses asking the public to attend the loyalist meeting to voice its support for political reform. John Lloyd reports to Undersecretary Beckett that "many quires" of the handbill were confiscated from the main distributor in Stockport.[4] Anticipating possible violence, the boroughreeve, Richard Wood, withdrew his permission to hold the meeting at the exchange, citing the inadequacy of the building's stairs.

In the Home Office Papers, immediately following John Lloyd's examinations of the informers Whitehead, Taylor, and Yarwood, is the printed broadsheet address reproduced here. Hay, in an April 1812 letter, said that he believed the broadsheets to have been commissioned by Ottiwell Wood, whom he describes as a "young man" not directly involved in ludding but sympathetic to the protests of the weavers. The printer, J. Plant, is occasionally described as "seditious" in Hay's other letters in H. O. 40/1. The slogan, "Now or Never," was carried about on a banner in a "rough parade" in Manchester on 8 April 1812 (which also saw the prince regent burned in effigy). Sale introduces the slogan with the adjective "enigmatic"; however, perusal of Hay's letter and its enclosure reduces the enigmatic character of the slogan.[5] Regardless of whether it is enigmatic or not, the slogan became popular even outside of Manchester, as its appearance on a handwritten poster addressed to "Croppers" in the West Riding during the second week of April testifies.[6]

The address itself is undated, and Hay provides no date for it; however, it would have been written during the week before the Manchester Exchange riot, 8 April 1812.

H. O. 40/1/1. A Home Office clerk's copy appears in H. O. 40/1/5. There is also a copy in the Manchester Central Reference Library, Local Studies Division, Manchester.

❖   ❖   ❖

NOW
OR NEVER!

Those Inhabitants who do not wish for an Increase of Taxes and Poor Rates—An Advance in the Price of Provisions—A Scarcity of Work, and a Reduction of Wages, will not fail to go to the Meeting on Wednesday Morning next, at the Exchange, and

Oppose the 154 Persons

Who have called you together; and you will then do right to express your Detestation of the Conduct of those Men who have brought this Country to its present distressed State, and are entailing Misery on Thousands of its industrious Mechanics.

Speak your Minds now!

Before it is too late; let not the Prince and the People be deceived, as to your real Sentiments. Speak and act boldly and firmly, but above all, be PEACEABLE.

Reprinted by J. Plant, Manchester.

N3 ❖ 19 April 1812: Letter from "General Justice" to Thomas Garside, Stockport

On 14 April 1812, near the beginning of a week of riots in Stockport and its environs, John Goodair's power-loom mill at Edgeley was destroyed in a Luddite attack. A Stockport mill owner, Thomas Garside, was caught in the attack, but his life was spared by the timely commands of one of the Luddite leaders. The following letter to Garside arises from the context of that attack.[7] The letter is distinguished by its emphasis on duty; only a couple of Midlands letters mention the word. The conflict between duty and justice perhaps necessitates this letter's informing Garside that his mill is offensive but cannot yet be fired without harming innocent "Industrious masters" located in proximity to it.

The letter appears in two places. The first is the original manuscript; the second, a copy by John Lloyd, is more legible than the original. I rely heavily upon

Lloyd's copy for making sense of words that are blurred in the original. It seems likely that this is the "16 April 1812" letter threatening steams looms mentioned by Frank Darvall.[8]

H. O. 40/1/1.

❖ ❖ ❖

Stockport
21 April 1812
Mr. Garside

April 19th

Sir

We think it our Duty to inform you that We was Intent upon Seting fire to your factory on Account of those Dressing Machines that was and still are Within it. But We Consider that it would Be very Injurious to those Industrious Masters that Occupy the Different parts of it therefore in justice to humanity We think it our Bounin Duty to give you this Notice that is if you doo not Cause those Dressing Machines to be Removed Within the Bounds of Seven Days from the above Date your factory and all that it Contains Will and Shall Surely Be Sit on fire Remember We have given you fare Warning and if your factory is Burn[d], it is your own falt: it is Not our Desire to doo you the Least Injury But We are fully Determind to Destroy Both Dressing Machines and Steam Looms Let Who Will be the Owners We Neither Regard those that keeps them Nor the Army for We Will Conquer Both or Die in the Conflict Remember, We have given you Both time and Warning and if you pay no attention you Must abide by the Consiquence

41   Sign[d] General Justice[9]

N4 ❖ 23 April 1812: Letter from "Thousands, upon thousands" to "Mess McConnal & Kennady," Manchester

As I mention earlier, historians of the Luddite risings have not paid much attention to Luddism among the cotton spinners. Wages were not depressed to the same degree as the weavers' were, and demand for yarn continued through the period. Nevertheless, there seems to have been more Luddite expression among the Lancashire cotton spinners than scholars previously have thought. A 23 April

1812 letter bearing a Manchester postmark and addressed to the McConnel and Kennedy Company, the largest Manchester spinning concern, is one of a couple of texts that utilize Luddite discourse in treating a question of gender and employment—specifically, the hiring of women for spinning work formerly performed by men. It is also unusual for the deference shown to the addressees; indeed, the threat is not even directed at McConnel and Kennedy but rather at the women employees and the factory overseers. In its tone and style, it contrasts with the earlier February 1812 letters to Mr. Kirkby, and to McConnel and Kennedy. By several accounts (the previously mentioned letter to Kirkby excepted), McConnel and Kennedy were conscientious employers, a fact that might explain the absence of malice shown toward them in this letter. One piece of evidence of their generosity toward employees is a 23 December 1812 letter of complaint from Philips and Lee, proprietors of the Salford Cotton Mills. Philips and Lee ask that, in the future, McConnel and Kennedy refrain from giving New Year's gifts to employees: "We find our Business considerably affected by the pernicious tendency of the custom, and shall ourselves, from this time, decline the practice of it" (McConnel and Kennedy Papers 2/1/18/4).

McConnel, Kennedy and Company Papers 2/1/18/1, John Rylands Library, Deansgate.

❖ ❖ ❖

Mess McConnal & Kennady
Cotton Spinners
Manchester

April 1812
Gentlemen
This is to aquaint you that wee are determined to a man to put a stop[10] to the Eregularities that is going on in the spinning branch, gent^m, we wish to Speake with respect to you because you have all ways Conducted your Selves [to your spinners] with that sevility[11] and kindness which is a strong mark of your good Sence and humain harts and Cold wish to Serve you to the best of our power We only wish to have a liveing for our selvs and families with hard working for wpe wish for peace and quietness but we can Not nor will not bare owre distress any Longer our poor helpless Children have Hundreds of time's cryed unto us for bre[d]ds but a lass we had none to give them and we think it quiet inconsistent with Our duty as men as husbands and as fathers

to Suffer our Selves to be ruined[12] Any longer by a set of vagabond Strum-
pets and them Jibbet deserveing Raskals that is looking Over them, we will
lud them to thare Satisfaction we have laid out a plan for them and will not
rest till we have A Complished it we nither Care for (bona____e Con____bles
nor the whole pack of [the] poor grind ing[13] Curse.[14] We will die by the sword
sooner than die as we do)

    We sincearly hope Gentlemen that you will discharge the biches and take
men in to your Employ a gain or they must take what they get

We are Gentlemen

Your truly devoted

Servants thousands

Up on, thousands

N5 ❖ 26 April 1812: Letter from "Falstaff" to Fire Office Agents, Wigan

Arson was the most common method of destroying power looms and dressing machines in Lancashire and Cheshire. A Lancashire letter dated 26 April 1812
and addressed to a fire insurer in Wigan treats the economic distresses of workers
in that Lancashire spinning town, concentrating, as many Luddite letters do, on
the means of destroying the obnoxious machines. Like the letter to McConnel
and Kennedy, the letter makes an oblique threat against the power-loom owners.
The writer recognizes not only a larger financial system connecting the power-
loom owners with their insurers but also the possibility of fulfilling a reciprocated
potential in destroying by fire the steam looms that oppress and displace weavers
by the use fire to produce steam.

Copy in H. O. 40/2/3, Part 1. The copy does not seem to have been made by a Home Office
clerk.

❖ ❖ ❖

Sirs,

    I am ordered by General Ludds Command in Chief of the Army of Bread
Seekers &c &c &c

    That shou'd you have any of the Persons Insured in your office not to Insure
them anymore (for the sake of your Employers) who keeps winding machines
or any other such like things in their Employment (For as it has pleased provi-

dence to bless the British Isle with abundance of Fire it ill behoves Gen^m of Pro^y to make use of it to take away the Work of the Poor and therefore their Bread, and if such work continue to be done in Wigan and in the same way the same providence has given the said General and his followers an Heart to make use of the same means to find Work as such Vile Persons has taken to take the Work from them (i. e. Fire) as it is thought better a few die than all Perish — The G^l has perfect information of all in Wigan and viewed the premises this day in Person before his men set to work, Mesrs Pe - s - n Da - - l Me - - lg Pin - - - g - - n B - a - - y^{15} &c &c will be looked to in a short time if continue in said way of Robbing the Poor of their Bread.

Given at Head Quarters at Westhoughton

This 26th Day of April 1812

Signed Falstaff Sec^y

(Circular)

Direction

    To Fire Office Agents

    Wigan —

N6 ❖ 26 April 1812: Posted notice "To Whitefield Luddites"

On the same Sunday that "Falstaff" wrote to the Fire Office Agents, a handbill appeared in Prestwich calling on Luddites from the nearby Whitefield area to join "the Northern National Army." Like the Nottinghamshire document sent from Mansfield by James Stevens to Lord Sidmouth along with a key to decipher it (H. O. 42/127, reproduced earlier), this Lancashire notice also is said to have a key. In the letter in which he had transcribed the brief notice, Hay describes the circumstances surrounding it: "We are informed that the Head Quarters of those who direct the revolutionary proceedings are at Manchester. The Confederacy is called The Northern National Army. . . . A notice was yesterday stuck up on paper on the Hearse House in Prestwich Church Yard. In words - it was directed 'To Whitefield Luddites' — and in figures 1. 2. 3. . . . By some key which a respectable man was in possession of, the figures were decyphered. . . ." Unfortunately, William Hay says very little that sheds light on the key, those persons who might have possessed it, or the reasons that a solicitation and call to arms would be encrypted. Hay does not speculate on the significance of the seditious handbill's being posted in a churchyard on a Sunday.

The Whitefield notice and the existence of a key complicate my thesis that Luddism provided a scheme by which the distressed populations of the Manchester area employed certain discourses and, in the process of employing those discourses, constituted themselves as a community. The existence of a key entails the prior existence of a discursive community whose members possess the key and agree that certain communications will be encrypted. The complication inheres in the fact that no other documents reveal the discursive community among the Whitefield or Prestwich Luddites. Perhaps because so many questions were not answered by Hay's letter, few scholars have attended to the notice. Malcolm Thomis ignores the key altogether and makes little of the "Northern National Army": "There is no ground for connecting this with machine breaking, except the fact that the framers of the notice chose to use the term currently in vogue, and there is no entry made by the 'Northern National Army' into the Luddite story at any other point."[16]

H. O. 42/122. The notice was transcribed in Hay's letter to Ryder, 27 April 1812.

❖ ❖ ❖

To Whitefield Luddites—
You are hereby required to be ready on the shortest notice to join our army. fail not at your peril. Amen.

N7 ❖ Late April 1812: Posted address "To the inhabitants of this Town," Macclesfield

A handwritten address from Macclesfield, undated but evidently written in late April 1812, was forwarded to Francis Freeling, postal surveyor for the Post Office, by T. W. Jones of Macclesfield on 9 May 1812. Jones's enclosing letter details the context in which the address was composed:

On Wednesday morning last a Paper was found stuck up in a part of this Town of an Inflammatory Nature threatening the lives of the Witnesses who gave evidence before the Magistrates agst the three Rioters Committed to Chester Gaol for Rioting at Macclesfield on on Monday 13 April last past adding that

Mr Chas Wood was the Cause of the disturbance (which is not strictly true) by Discharging his Men it contains 9 Articles on mode of destruction, & grievances—adding that Knives and Razors in the ends of Sticks would be made use of as Weapons of destruction agst those who'd dare to give further evidence to the Conviction of the Rioters and a further desire that the Prince Regant would change Ministers—the whole of which appears to have been writ by some very illeterate Person & the whole of which I deem too insignificant to notice. (H. O. 42/123)

H. O. 42/123.

❖ ❖ ❖

To the inhabitants of this Town i under Stan the newspapers informs you that General Lud is taken prisoner but i can contrdict that Satement for i have Just recievd a Leter from him Which he informs that he as Taken a fresh plan which is this no 1 Plan That the Shall be a List of those persons which is worst Against the poor in evry Town and Vilage No 2 And that evry Poor Person whill Get blunder b[u]shes Guns pistols axes forks ~~riors~~ rasors knives No 3 that you Devide youselvs ~~And by And~~ 3 by 3 And two And ind in Any rioting to Stick ther horses in the neck No 4 And if any one is taken that man that Swears against him must Be way Laid if it is for one or two years of weks or months And Shot by the Law that we have made No 5 that i Shall take the Command in Person in a Short time my Self when you have Got ready No 6 [I] understand by you you have had 3 men Sent to Chester who was no way Concer[n]ed in rioting bu never mind that i will come over after the Trial And if the Come to Any harm i whill Put you in A way to Send them And All Such for Sworn Deivls to hell No 7 that it is Agreedon to Shoot All masters that Puls Down wages or invents things to hurt the Poor No 8 that if Price of wales whill not Change is ministers he Shall Lose his head No 9 that we whill All be Good Subjects if the whil let us have work to keep our por Starving hungry naked Cheldren And we Desire that you whill Let Mr Devenport know that A hungry below whill not be keept Down by the Sword And Chales wood that he as Been the Cause of a riot in macclesfield with Droping poor mens wages And Saying that water Should Be as Dear as milk And Speaking Against the School | And i have to Contradict A Statement which i read with Great indignation Concerning Stubbs in the macclesfield Courier which was to this efect that Stubbs was one of the most Daring amongst them All he might well for I never Saw A man Cut And knocked in sutch a maner in All my Life now I was behind that man All The way And i heard him [to ask] Several persons to Give over flinging And the Person that flung that Stone was betwixt him And me he made A bod resistance we alow And he was right for so doing for the knocked him Down he Got A stone up for to fling but head not time he was right to Stand in is hown Defence now if that [man] Comes to harm besides is imprisoment Shall be Sto Broadhurst Tunstal Servant woman Shall be Shot One time or another what must that poor man think to be towrn from his Family for nothing Left & wife And 7 Small Children

thanks to Eaton [an] Daintry for the Goodness on the 13 of Aprall

---

N8 ❖ 30 April 1812: Letter ("A") to Mr. Simpson, Manchester

On 1 May 1812 William Hay forwarded to Home Office Secretary Richard Ryder two anonymous threatening letters, each of which is overtly political in its own way. The letters followed several Luddite actions during a turbulent April—riots at the Manchester Exchange, food riots in Manchester and several of the surrounding towns, and attacks on mills in Manchester, Stockport, Middleton, and Westhoughton. Describing the two letters to Secretary Ryder, Hay writes,

I have the honor to enclose a letter received I believe this morning by M^r. Simpson a young gentleman of property, who is the proprietor of considerable Cotton Works, & who has much to his honor taken an active part as a Special Constable in patroling &c That letter is marked A - upon recollection it appeared to be written in the same hand as one received yesterday or the day before by M^r. Milne. M^r. Milne is a Coroner for part of the Hundred of Salford, is Clerk to some of the Magistrates at Manchester, & of course has much business both at the Assizes & Sessions. That may explain some of the allusions in the letter marked B - but the writer has made a mistake for the Coroners inquest that met on the men who fell at Middleton was not in the district of M^r. Milne, but of the other Coroner. (Hay to Ryder, 1 May 1812, H. O. 40/1/1)

The first enclosed letter, marked "A" and addressed to the Mr. Simpson described in Hay's enclosing letter, was signed "Eliza Ludd." It is the only Luddite document purporting to have been written by a woman. The letter's exercise in comparative political science is quite curious. The writer is careful to separate, in a manner reminiscent of Edmund Burke, "ministerial tyranny" from British "spirit" and is also careful to couch the threat of rebellion in patriotic, pro-British, and implicitly anti-Gallic terms. Like many Manchester documents, the letter expresses the writer's opposition to the wars. The language of the letter is every bit as interesting as its political theory. It swings from gracefully executed allocution and acrolect ("cannot such an action be accomplish'd here") to a working-class dialect ("his" for "is," and inconsistently applied at that).

The first letter bears a very faint date in a clerk's hand, which appears to be "April 30^h."

H. O. 40/1/1 (copied in H. O. 40/1/5). The letter is enclosed in Hay's correspondence along with the letter to Mr. Milne and a printed broadsheet, titled "Second Letter / Fellow Weavers," opposing the Luddites.

❖ ❖ ❖

Sir,

Doubtless you are well acquainted with the Political History of America, if so you must confess that, it was ministerial tyranny that gave rise to that glorious spirit in which the British Colonies obtain'd their independance by force of arms, at a period, when we was ten times as strong as now!—if bands of husbandmen could do this, in spite of all the force our government was then able to employ - cannot such an action be accomplish'd here, now the military strength of the country is so reduced—Consider Sir, what a few troops there is at present in England,—remember that none can be call'd home; because that would relinquishing the little we have gain'd to the fury of the enemy— little indeed to have coss'd so much money and such torrents of blood, yes British blood!————let me persuad you to quit your present post, lay by your sword, and become a friend to the oppress'd—for curs'd his the man that even lifts a straw against the sacred cause of Liberty.

Eliza Ludd—

Manchester

N9 ❖ 30 April 1812: Letter ("B") to Nathaniel Milne, Salford

The second letter, labeled "B," seeks, like the Midlands letter to "Mr. Byrnny," the Nottingham jury foreman, to intervene in the juridical process. Nathaniel

Milne, Salford coroner and clerk to the Manchester magistrates, received the letter shortly after the returning of a verdict of "justifiable homicide" in a case involving Daniel Burton, owner of a steam-operated power-loom mill. Burton's power looms had displaced many weavers and reduced wages since their installation two years earlier. Several Luddites were killed in an April 1812 attack on Burton's Middleton mill.

The Middleton attack, the largest in the Manchester area, was a particularly bloody event. Following a 19 April meeting on a Lancashire moor, at which General Ludd was represented by an effigy that was later carried into the attack, perhaps more than two thousand people gathered around Burton's mill in the early afternoon of 20 April. Burton ordered his hands to fire upon the crowd, which had begun to throw stones at the mill. In the musket discharges of the first day, four or five people were killed and eighteen wounded. The next day, 21 April, seeking vengeance, Luddites and their sympathizers raided a militia depot in Oldham and carried weapons back to Middleton. After the crowd attacked outbuildings and burned the home of Burton's son, Emmanuel, and the homes of workers loyal to Burton, a troop of Scots Greys attacked the crowd, killing at least another five people (*Leeds Mercury*, 25 April 1812; *Manchester Mercury*, 28 April 1812; W. Chippindale to Col. Ralph Fletcher, 23 April 1812 letter, H. O. 40/1/1; Darvall, *Popular Disturbances* 99; Thomis, *Luddites* 110; Sale, *Rebels against the Future* 136–40). The coroner's verdict, just days after the failed attack on Rawfolds and the similar verdict in that case, prompted the letter to Milne, the Salford coroner, who seems to have been an erroneous target of Luddite vengeance, as the enclosing letter from William Hay points out.

H. O. 40/1/1 (and is copied in H. O. 40/1/5). It is enclosed with the letter signed "Eliza Ludd."

❖ ❖ ❖

Sir,

This would be an error that our very blood could not expiate, if these lines were stuff'd with nothing but mere malice and injustice; for conscious we are you must at first think so: but if you will take a little advice from a few friends, you will then immediately become an apostate to your principles—The Fable of, "The Plague amongst the Beasts"[17] - is well worth a coroner's reading— Had some poor man murder'd two or three rich ones in cool blood, Nat. Milnes would then have buss'd in the ears a "Packed Jury" loaded with contagion, these Words, "Willfull murder"–instead of "Justifiable homicide": but know thou cursed insinuator, if Burton's infamous action was "justifiable", the laws of Tyrants are reasons' dictates—Beware, Beware! - a month's bathing in the Stygian Lake would not wash this sanguinary deed from our minds; it but augments the heritable cause, that stirs us up to indignation–

Milnes if you really are not a Friend to the great Oppressors, forgive us this–but if you are–"the rest remains behind"—

Ludd finis est.

N10 ❖ 5 May 1812: Letter from Holywell, Flintshire, to Mr. Douglas and others at Manchester

On 6 May 1812 William Hay forwarded copies of three Luddite documents from northern Wales. One of the documents is a copy of a letter received on 5 May 1812 by "Mr. Douglas & some others" living "at or near Manchester." It is postmarked at Holywell, Flintshire, the site of a "very extensive cotton works" called "the Holywell Twist Company" owned by a partnership of Manchester clothiers, "Douglas & some others," living in Manchester and keeping a warehouse there. In his accompanying correspondence, Hay observes that the wages at Holywell were as high as at Manchester and that there had been no complaint about wages by the "Welch" work force until the appearance of the letters. None of the documents makes clear whether the Holywell Twist Company was a spinning concern, as the name "Twist" would imply. If so, then perhaps the spinning trade might have been more involved in Luddism than previously believed.

This anonymous letter is rare in that it contains some lines of verse (as does the subsequent letter) but is typical for its numerical claims of wider popular support. The miners and colliers of the region actually did participate in machine wrecking on occasion.[18] The letter does, however, follow a typical Luddite pattern of detailing distress, threatening destruction on more than one level, and pointing to other Luddite attacks as cautionary examples. Like many other letters from the Northwest, it manifests the writer's awareness of economic matters beyond the simple disbursement of higher wages. The writer actually confronts capitalist motives ("You had better be content with a moderate profit"), though without slipping entirely into the language of class resentment.

H. O. 40/1/1. It was enclosed within a letter from William Robert Hay to Richard Ryder, sent on 6 May 1812 from the Manchester Police Office.

❖ ❖ ❖

S^r. If you do not advance the wages of all your workmen at Holywell, you shall have all your mills burnt to the ground immediately. it is harder upon many of us here than upon those who receive parish relief. we are starving by inches by reason of our small wages & provisions so high. You had better be content with a moderate profit, than have your mills destroyed. You know how it is with Burton & Goodier & many others, it will be the same with you in a few days, if you do not advance all hands.[19] All the Miners and Colliers are ready to join us. 3000 men can be collected in a few hours

> The poor cry aloud for bread
> Prince Regent shall lose his head
> And all the rich who oppress the poor
> In a little time shal be no more

Take care you be not in the number of the oppressors. we cannot wait but a very few days, we are ready for blood or bread, anything is better than starving by inches.

NII ❖ 5 May 1812: Letter to Mr. G. Platt, Holywell, Flintshire

Hay's 6 May 1812 report to the Home Office contains other documents sent by the same post and accompanying the Holywell letter to Douglas on 5 May 1812. The second document is a copy, sent to Douglas, of a letter "addressed to Mr. G. Platt, who is one of the Principal servants at the before mentiond mill." Hay notes that "All the papers &c are in the same handwriting." Regarding the verses at the end of the letter, Hay informs the Home Office that "a copy of these lines in the same handwriting was taken from the window shutters of Mr. Jones Junr. last week." Hay does not specify whether Mr. Jones lived in Holywell or Manchester.

H. O. 40/1/1.

❖ ❖ ❖

Sir,

We can not live with the wages we have. unless all hands are advanced the mills shall be burned to the ground immediately. the miners & colliers are all ready to join. 3000 men may be called to join us in a very short time. We can also send for Bolton & Middleton mob to come. We have proper direction to some of the leaders. letters have been received therefrom leatly. We are all read for blood or bread. anything is better than starving by inches as we do, rely upon it.

> The poor cry aloud for bread
> Prince Regent shall lose his head
> And all the rich who oppress the poor
> In a little time shall be no more
> With deep regret, I write these things,
> They'll come to pass in spite of kings.

N12 ❖ 5 May 1812: Handbill posted up at Holywell, Flintshire

The final document forwarded to Secretary Ryder in Hay's 6 May 1812 letter is "a copy of a Hand Bill taken from the wall of a house in Chapel Street Holywell." Hay added to the end of his letter, "Sr Thos Mostyn has notice of the handbill." The primary grievance of the writer of the letter is the increase in food prices caused by a tripling of farmers' rents by local landowners in Flintshire. Hay indicates that the handbill is written in the same hand as the previous two documents from Holywell. Common authorship would suggest that Luddite writing in Holywell, like Manchester, blends a number of discourses—wage complaints, opposition to machinery, distress caused by high food prices, and frustration at the government.

H. O. 40/1/1.

❖ ❖ ❖

Come brave boys, & make ready your arms, pikes & pitchforks to upset the rich tyrants of the land who grind the face of the poor, such as S^r. Thos Mostyn, Sir Pyerce, Pennant and many others too numerous to mention, have tribled the rents of the farmers, the poor are the sufferers.

N13 ❖ 6 May 1812: Letter from "Thomas Paine" to Richard Wood, Manchester

Some of the reformers in the Manchester area were eager to draw a distinction between themselves and the Luddites. In his 11 May 1812 correspondence to Secretary Ryder at the Home Office, Hay enclosed a copy of a letter addressed to "Richard Wood / Boroughreeve / Manchester" with a Lancaster postmark. The writer refers to the 8 April loyalist meeting at the Manchester Exchange, described earlier in the headnote for the handbill titled "Now or Never." Wood had withdrawn his permission to hold the meeting at the exchange, arguing that the anticipated crowds would have been too much for the building's stairs.

Richard Wood was adamantly opposed to political and economic reform and had said that Luddism was a part of "an insurrection against society . . . and of this the Luddites were clearly guilty."[20] By the standards of both the Luddites and the reform movement, Wood and the committee members who engaged in restoring civic order by suppressing riots against machines and high food prices surely deserved punishment. Although the letter disavows "connection with machine breakers," its expressed aims are similar, if not identical, to those of the weavers engaged in Luddism in the Manchester region.

Paineite influences upon Luddism were significant in Lancashire and Yorkshire. John Baines, a hatter from Halifax and one of the leading figures in Luddism in the Huddersfield vicinity, is occasionally described as an old "Tom Painer."[21] Furthermore, Paine's works were read widely among the weaver groups who began to organize opposition to machinery in late eighteenth-century Lancashire.

Interestingly, the use of the term "Hampdenites" foreshadows the growth of Hampden clubs; such clubs, A. Temple Patterson has demonstrated, were intertwined with Luddism.[22]

H. O. 40/1/1.

❖ ❖ ❖

Lancaster 6 May 1812

Richard Wood

You have been the cause of much bloodshed; you convened the people and did not meet them: you are therefore marked for punishment. Your childish excuse of Stairs! You might have adjourned to the Square called St Anns or to a field. The fact is; that there is a regular, general, progressive organisation of the people going forward. They may be called Hamdenites, Sidneyites, or Paineites. it has fallen to my lot to unite many thousands. WE for I speake in the name of multitudes. I say we deny and disavow all, or any connection with machine breakers, burners of factories, extorters of money, plunderers of private property or assasans. We know that every machine for the abridgment of human labour is a blessing to the great family of which we are a part. We mean to begin at the Source of our grievances as it is of no use to petition, We mean to demand & command a redress of our grievances. We have both the will & the power. What? must the industrious artisans or the humble cultivators of the soil, be always robb'ed of the rewards of their labours? must they be forever doom'd to behold their helpless infants unfed, uncloathed, untaught. in short deprived of every comfort that makes existance worth holding? must they see the Vultures of Oppressions legally robbing them to pay Sinecures, make loans, to other nations virtual fleets & armies: To give extravagant establishments to all the branches of what are called the Royal Family, when other paupers are obliged to exist on 3 or 4 shillings p week? no not long. Tell Mr Ottiwell Wood, that his character character has travelled farther than his feet, that he is much esteemed & respected by our Society & if ever we have an opportunity we will reward him, request him to accept our best wishes for all his families Happiness & Comfort.

We mentioned you as being marked for punishment but as [we Beleive] you had no evil intention you rather erred for want of fortitude & experience than disrespect for the people; therefor your punishment shall be very easy it shall be light.

There appeared among the 154 names to you requisition Some Honest Lawyers of which We have taken p_a_r_t_i_c_u_l_a_r = n_o_t_i_c_e. honest useful upright Men. They shall be rewarded, Yes they deserve a recompence in proportion to their utility!

For Hampdenites

Thomas Paine

N14 ❖ 11 May 1812: Letter to the prince regent at London

The following letter addressed to the prince regent appears in the Home Office Papers located among other threatening letters and correspondence from the
Manchester region. The relationship of the writer to Luddism is unclear, but it
is safe to say that the writer is sympathetic to the Luddites' aims and approves
their methods. Sympathy aside, ascertaining the geographical origin of the letter is difficult because it appears with an indeterminate postmark and without
any enclosing correspondence. Evidence of a Manchester origin consists of the
writer's calling the prince regent's attention to "poor men that are in gaol," a
reference to those persons awaiting trial at the May assizes in Chester and Lancashire. There are, however, complicating features in the letter, one of which is
the mention of breaking frames. As one would expect, no documents from the
Manchester vicinity refer to the objects of Luddite violence in that region as
"frames." In May 1812 there was a small contingent of Nottingham framework
knitters in London petitioning Parliament for regulations advantageous to the
trade, and at least one of them—Thomas Large—might have been capable of
writing such a letter. Nevertheless, because of the allusion to the Chester and
Lancaster assizes and because much of the other correspondence in this section
of H. O. 42/123 originates in the Northwest, I include the letter in this section.

H. O. 42/123.

❖   ❖   ❖

HRH The Prince Regent
Carlton House
London

Sir,
    Although the Hand of justice is a little impaded by your unreasonable un-
just and <u>unfeeling</u> Officer's in the Manufacture=ing Towns yet perhaps your
attention may soon be called another way The poor men that are in gaol (for
endeavouring to obtain a bit of bread to supply the craveings of nature) and
destin'd (perhaps) to <u>Hang</u> Yet if there be not an order Issued Immediately
for their release and some provision made for their Starving family's there is a

Most Powerful and Annimated body of Men in London who are determined to <u>Crush</u> the <u>Bones</u> of their Oppressor's as their Father's and Brother's did the Frames

The Slighted English Servants

N15 ❖ [12 May] 1812: Letter from "Luddites" at Manchester to Richard Ryder at London

Following William Hay's 14 May 1812 letter to the Home Office is a letter addressed "The Right Hon. Richd Ryder/ 30 Great George Street/London." Although dated 13 April 1812, the date makes no sense, given the reference to Perceval's death ("you may Prepaire to go to the Divel to Bee Secraterry for Mr Perceval theire"). A date of 12 May, the day after Perceval's assassination, would be more likely. Furthermore, although the letter appears without enclosing correspondence, it is found among letters from May 1812. The reference to Perceval's death and the dates of surrounding letters are reasons enough, I believe, to conclude that the date is either the result of an error by the writer or a Home Office copying clerk's mistake.

H. O. 42/123.

❖ ❖ ❖

Honorable
   Sir/
      Every frame Breaking act you Make an amendment to only serves to shorten your Days Theirfore you may Prepaire to go to the Divel to Bee Secraterry for Mr Perceval theire for there are fire[23] Ships Making to saile by land as well as by Warter that will not faile[24] to Destroy all the Obnoctious in the both Houses as you have been at a great Deal of pains to Destroy Chiefe part of the Country it is know your turn to fall The Remedy for you is Shor Destruction Without Detection—prepaire for thy Departure and Recomend the same to thy friends your Hbl sert &c
Manchester april 13th 1812}   Luddites

N16 ❖ 23 May 1812: Letter from "Ned Ludd" to Nicholas Vansittart at London

The new chancellor of the exchequer in the Lord Liverpool administration, Nicholas Vansittart, had not been long in office before he received the following letter from Manchester. Vansittart was no friend of the textile workers. In 1802, as a member of Parliament, he had introduced a petition from a number of large clothiers seeking repeal of old statutes fixing apprenticeships (5 Elizabeth, cap. 4) and the number of looms that could be kept by one master (2 & 3 Philip and Mary, cap. 11). The process that he initiated led eventually to the repeal in 1809 of parts of the code that had protected woolen weavers for centuries.[25] Strangely enough, in June 1812 Vansittart supported some of the regulations petitioned for by the United Committee of Framework Knitters, and he actually wrote into the bill the clause prohibiting payment in goods.[26] The bill, of course, never passed.

The letter appears without an enclosing letter.

H. O. 42/123.

❖ ❖ ❖

Mr Vansittart

Sir,

As you have now accepted the place of Chancellor of the Exchequer I hope you will learn Wisdom from the fate of your predecessor,[27] for if you be determined to persevere in the iniquities & oppress the poor as he did depend upon it you will share the same fate but I trust the Justness of his death have a proper effect upon your conduct & ⟨so⟩ you will do all that lays in your power to amend & note the injuries he has done otherwise you must take the consequences—I just give you this Gentle hint if you dont profit by it it will be your own fault or you will be watchd narrowly if an immideate amendment be not made for the poor you may expect to hear from me again shortly

yours truly

Ned Ludd

May 23 1812

N17 ❖ 27 May 1812: Letter from "Iulius - <u>Lt. de Luddites</u>" to "Revd W. Blacow" at Liverpool

Near the end of May 1812, Reverend W. Blacow of St. Marks Church in Liverpool sent to the Home Office a copy of a Luddite letter that he had received and a seditious posting. Blacow reports in his enclosing letter that the threatening letter had been sent to him by the two-penny post some days shortly after a sermon in which he professed his support of the government and denounced the Luddites and others among the disaffected. Little is known of any Luddite activity in Liverpool, but there were disturbances in the vicinity, and the connection of the port of Liverpool to Manchester's cotton manufacture might perhaps suggest some communication between the workers in the two cities. Without the certainty of any actual connection, it is nevertheless possible to read the letter as part of the more politically comprehensive idea of Luddism that typifies the writings from Lancashire.

H. O. 42/123. The letter is enclosed by Blacow's 27 May 1812 letter. The threatening letter is a copy; Blacow's verifications are reproduced at the bottom of the letter.[28]

❖ ❖ ❖

<u>Duke Street</u>

<u>Sir</u>

It was with the greatest indignation and regret that I sat still, last Sunday, to hear thee profane, the holy temple of the Lord with impious falsehood on the subject of hellborn Percivall.. According to the opinions of our most eminent divines, no man has any right to obtrude his own political opinions from the pulpit to any congregation, and much less to back them with falsities - had it been in any other place than the church my Pistol would have soon silenced thy blasphemy.-however beware tho' thou art spared for a time yet when that time arrives, not even the Prince of Wickedness whom thou prays for, shall afford thee protection: thou art weighed in the balance and art found wanting, and this is the call of a christian for thee to repent; I do understand thou hast long been a disgrace to the holy order of Christianity.-and a most wily hypocrite, taking care to secure to thyself the places of two better men.-therefore art thou worthy of dying with thy depraved master George the Prince whose body shall be sacrifised to the manes of the brave and patriotic Bellingham and all those who have talk'd against him must repent and drop tears of their hearts blood--for I will overturn, overturn,-overturn,-this is decreed,-

I am thine and his

eternal enemy

Iulius - <u>Lt. de Luddites</u>[29]

Rev<u>d</u> W. Blacow

S<u>t</u> Marks-

The above is a true Copy of the original Letter of which the same purports to be a copy the same having been carefully compared and examined with the original by me.

In Faith and Testimony whereof I have
hereunto subscribed my name and affixed my
Seal as a public notary this 27th May 1812.
<u>Arch</u>d Keightley[30] Public Notary Liverpool

N18 ❖ 30 May 1812: Letter from "L[?] Teoxperorator" at Manchester

Among the letters sent to the prince regent from Lancashire during the spring of 1812 is one bearing a 30 May 1812 postmark. The writer's concerns are the economic distresses caused by high food prices and the adverse effects on trade of the Orders in Council. The signature is difficult to read. The "L" is certain, but is followed by one or two unclear letters. The longer word could be "Teoxperoster" or "Teoxperorator." I have been unable to determine the significance of the signature, except to note that "perorator" is one who makes highly formal speeches.

Like many threats to the regent, the letter was placed directly into the Home Office Papers without enclosing correspondence.

H. O. 42/123.

❖ ❖ ❖

Sir,

If you do not look into the affairs of the Country and rescind the orders in council and make bread Cheap & dismiss your present ministers you may expect the same fate as Percival we are a long suffering people--look at the affairs at Nottingham Manchester - Chester - Liverpool the people are [in] a starveing State you may try to stop them rioting—you may introduce foreign soldiers--can they govern a starving people Take this hint - and reform

Your obedient servent

L⟨illegible⟩ Teoxperorator

I am not a Lunatic

N19 ❖ 13 June 1812: Posted "Notice" signed "Guilty Death," Chow Bent

In a 13 June 1812 letter to Major General Acland, preserved in H. O. 40/2/2, Major Hankin writes, "Inclosed I have sent two Anonymous Papers the one stuck up this morning at Chow Bent & the other brought from Wigan, they may or may not be of consequence. I have thought it right to forward them for your inspection." The papers to which Hankin refers are not included in the same box with his letter. Rather, copies of two documents, grouped together, appear in H. O. 40/2/4. The "Notice" here is marked as coming from Chow Bent. The other paper grouped with the "Notice" is a "Constitution," precisely similar to that included in Hay's letter from the Manchester Police Station; however, nothing except the proximity to the "Notice" testifies to its being the other paper referred to by Hankin.

The Home Office copy includes this footnote: "The above is the constables name this was posted up the morning they were to suffer June 13th 1812 at *Chow bent*."

H. O. 40/2/4.

❖　❖　❖

NOTICE

Hereby given if these men be hanged Warburton &c may wake for fear for Death will Soon apeear for Damnation Shall Seize upon your Bodies and Destruction shall fall upon Effects and your Families Shall Com to Poverty and be Disdined for ever, he that reads this let It Remain and Let the Country Judge there misdemainer

GUILTY DEATH

N20 ❖ [Late] June 1812: Address posted in the neighborhood of Bolton

Perhaps the following address was the second anonymous paper accompanying Hankin's 13 June 1812 report to Acland, in H. O. 40/2/2. This address was not grouped with the "Notice" or with Hankin's letter. Unlike the "Notice," this address says nothing about the trials of Luddite prisoners but concentrates only on food prices.

This address appears to be a copy.

H. O. 40/2/2.

❖ ❖ ❖

"No watch & ward or soldiers, &c and constables can put a stopt to us - but the prices of bread and meal must fall or the regent - The general will watch the shops"
Wigan Saturday

N21 ❖ Summer 1812: Letters to and from Lancaster Castle prisoners

This collection contains copies and extracts of a number of letters sent to and written by Luddite prisoners who had been committed to Lancaster Castle. Most of them were accused of administering unlawful oaths. Their letters were opened, copied, and forwarded to the Home Office in August 1812.

H. O. 42/129.

❖ ❖ ❖

To Simon Simons, Crown Side, Lancaster Castle, post paid.
Manchester June 29th, 1812.
Dear Friend,
I take the opportunity of writing a few Lines to you hoping they will find you in good Health and Spirits as your Confinement will admit of. You desired me to see my and your Friends, to send you a small sum of money to help you out while you remained in that solitary Confinement. I have done all that lay in my power for the support of you all. There is a subscription raised to carry

on the Petitions to the Prince Regent and to the House of Commons and for the relief and support of you and your Families and to make an able Defence for you. There is another Committee formed to carry on the whole Business whether M^r. N. will or not. I suppoe if he can find them and another Fleming you will have Lancaster Castle filled with petitioners and your Friends. There is four Counsel detaint for you all. Dear Friend, your Wife and Child is well in good Health and gives their kindest Love for you. Your Wife has received from the Spinners 8^s/- the one week and 10^s/- the other, and by you get this Letter there will be 10^s/- for you. There is two pounds sent for you and Washington, Thornaly and Woolling to be divided amongst you four whilst the Committee is properly arranged. Dear Friend you asked me to see Thomas Nevin, which I have done, and he said that he was very sorry for you and he would see some of your Friends, but I have not seen him since. I shewed him the Letter so I cannot give you an account of what he has done for you, but by the time you writer to me again I shall be able to see him, and if he does any thing for you I shall [-ard] the same to you without fail. so Dear Friend, I have given you the particulars as they now stand, for I will give Flattery no Countenance, shew Ignorance no Favor, afford Ambition no Encouragement, and Pride Folly and Corruption with their hateful Train of Consequences will at once disappear, which has preyed like the deadly Locust upon the Vitals of the Country–has devoured the poor Man's Means and swallowed up the hard Earnings of honest Labor–which has blasted the Bud of Liberty and with its deadly Poison would destroy the sacred Root. Give my best respects to all of them and it is my earnest Wish that God may soon release out of the Hands of bad men–so adieu John Marshall.–Please to direct for me near Mr Shaws and Balers Factory, higher Ardwick. You are desired to remember William Washington's Wife to him.

30^h June 1812. Extract of a Letter from Charles Smith, a prisoner, to James Smith of Great Encoats Street Manchester. "I have an ardent desire for peace without which the happiness, nay even the comforts of the poor Inhabitants of these Kingdoms is irrecoverable, and I am firmly convinced with Thousands of intelligent men that we have no opportunity of obtaining and perpetuating that Blessing without a full radical complete reform in the House of Commons, such a reform as shall make that House feel with and participate in the Happiness or adversity of the people."

N22 ❖ 1810s: Song titled "The Hand-loom Weavers' Lament," Lancashire

The recurrent theme of "old prices" in "General Ludd's Triumph" and other Luddite writings does not originate solely with the risings of 1811 but can be traced back to at least two sources. It was inherited from previous textile workers and developed just prior to Nottinghamshire Luddism among the weavers of Lancashire, who earlier, in 1792, had taken violent action against the new Cartwright steam looms in Manchester. In the face of increasing mechanization, wages (following prices) fell; in Bolton, average weekly earnings declined from twenty-five shillings in 1800 to fourteen in 1811.[31] Such circumstances gave rise to the "Lament" and its wishing after "old prices."

The "Lament" provides an excellent example of the difficulty of dating popular verses. Palmer dates the "Lament" as nearly contemporary with "John o' Grinfield," although much of the decrease in wages came in the years of distress following 1807, especially on the heels of the American Non-Intercourse Act and the expansion and collapse in trade with South America, pointing to the possibility that the song may have been composed initially in 1807 or after but during the period of the wars against the French.[32] If this date is accurate, then the song might have evolved through the period of the Luddite risings, eventually being emended, by the addition or revision of the sixth stanza, after the exile and death of Napoleon. Such emendation and variation of songs was not at all unusual, as the "John o' Grinfield" series of songs bears witness. Such emendation would also explain the contradictory evidence for dating within the song itself ("When the wars are at an end," indicating a date before 1815, versus "Now Bonyparty's dead and gone," suggesting a date of 1821 or after).

The song is unusual in that it has an identified author, John Grimshaw. Sung to the tune of "A Hunting We Will Go," it remained a favorite among the factory workers of the North through the years of Luddism, but more significant is the fact that the themes and phrases from its early versions gave birth to new songs, among them the "Triumph."

John Harland and T. T. Wilkinson's *Ballads and Songs of Lancashire: Ancient and Modern*, 3rd ed. (London: Heywood, 1882), 193–95. A version that is missing the sixth stanza is in the Broadsheets Collection, Derby Local Studies Library, box 15.

❖ ❖ ❖

You gentlemen and tradesmen, that ride about at will,
Look down on these poor people; it's enough to make you crill;
Look down on these poor people, as you ride up and down,
I think there is a God above will bring your pride quite down.

Chorus
You tyrants of England, your race may soon be run,
You may be brought unto account for what you've sorely done.

You pull down our wages, shamefully to tell;
You go into the markets, and say you cannot sell;
And when that we do ask you when these bad times will mend,
You quickly give an answer, "When the wars are at an end."

When we look on our poor children, it grieves our hearts full sore,
Their clothing it is worn to rags, while we can get no more,
With little in their bellies, they to work must go,
Whilst yours do dress as manky as monkeys in a show.

You go to church on Sundays, I'm sure it's nought but pride,
There can be no religion where humanity's thrown aside;
If there be a place in heaven, as there is in the Exchange,
Our poor souls must not come near there; like lost sheep they must range.

With the choicest of strong dainties your tables overspread,
With good ale and strong brandy, to make your faces red;
You call'd a set of visitors—it is your whole delight—
And you lay your heads together to make our faces white.

You say that Bonyparty he's been the spoil of all,
And that we have got reason to pray for his downfall;
Now Bonyparty's dead and gone, and it is plainly shown
That we have bigger tyrants in Boneys of our own.

And now, my lads, for to conclude, it's time to make an end;
Let's see if we can form a plan that these bad times may mend;
Then give us our old prices, as we have had before,
And we can live in happiness, and rub off the old score.

N23 ❖ May 1816: Handbill poem titled "The Death of Calico Jack"

One of the final documents from the Manchester region that was forwarded to the Home Office by authorities who feared it to be part of a resurgence of Luddism is a printed handbill in a comic vein, "The Death of Calico Jack; or the Weavers Downfall." The handbill does not use the name "Ludd" or convey any direct threats to individuals, but its printing coincided with John Lloyd's 13 May 1816 report to Undersecretary Beckett at the Home Office that "Ludditism" had returned. It also fits into the shifting of artisan discontent in the region from an active anger to a satirizing despair. From the internal evidence, it appears that "The Weavers Downfall" might have been composed by a minister (perhaps dissenting) or, less likely, by a schoolteacher (a profession not infrequently taken up by some literate weavers who had been crippled or plagued by ill health).

The handbill was forwarded along with a weavers' petition to Sidmouth at the Home Office by Reverend Charles Prescott of Stockport as evidence of a resurgence of Luddism (21 May 1816, H. O. 42/150). Another copy, printed by "Rogerson, Printer, Blackburn," was sent to the Home Office by Colonel Fletcher of Bolton (27 May 1816, H. O. 42/151). The first version is reproduced here.

H. O. 42/150.

❖   ❖   ❖

The Death of Calico Jack; or the
WEAVERS DOWNFALL.

Bad markets . . . . Several tradesmen threatened with arrest, Oh! the effects of high living. Curse upon lewd women, and fie upon the foreign Company, they under sell us. For what reason? They have their goods made from good wool, we have ours from waste. They have their yarn spun for little or nothing, so have we. The merchants enjoy the juice of the grape, but we will be content with a little malt liquour. Oh! St. David's Day, be thou like the days of Job . . . . let no sun shine upon it . . . . and let it be blotted out from the other days of the year, and let every spinner and weaver of cotton tremble at the remembrance thereof, and let love and friendship be united and dated from this day, and handed down to the latest posterity. But find us the man whose foundation is not shaken at such unprecedented proceeding Quere, is this the way they mean to go to heaven? if so, God enlighten their dark understandings.

Sunday. The prayer of the congregation are desired for the cotton trade and let all the people say, Amen.

Tuesday. Dissected and examined by numbers of Anathamptists, and the Cotton Trade found to be wilfully murdered by persons well known, viz. absolutely choaked with waste.

Wednesday. The town in general disordered. The right honourable and most ignoble Lord Strut, chief president of the company of starve beggars, seduced by some means his fellow creatures to shut up their warehouses, workshops, &c. till such times trade mends or work for whatever they please to give them. Agreed nem con.

Thursday. The spinners and weavers agreed to weather out the storm, and support themselves by other means.

Saturday. Wages paid, shops shut, & a general fast & mouring proclaimed.

Sunday. The spinners and weavers agreed, let us eat and drink to-day, for to-morrow we die; and like the widow of Zarepah, die with a full stomach, flattering themselves they will not be the worse received in Heaven.

Monday. The Military arrived, some say to quell a riot, sed fulsum est, take nothing from nothing, and nothing remains: and every day since, the town has been rigidly strict in abserving Mourning and fasting, (particularly the poor distressed Spinners and weavers)[33] and will for a long time.

Go to, ye great men, mourn and weep, for the time cometh when you must balance not only with your Merchants, but with one who will not take light gold, bad bills, nor blank securities—'tis hard for a Camel to go through the eye of a needle—when you die, which you certainly think you never must—you will not be asked how much money you possessed here.

The Funeral will be solemnized; the Trade interred in Oliver Cromwell's Grave, near Lancashire Bridge, on Saturday by ten o'Clock
The Processiou[34] as follows: Evil to him who thinks on Evil, doodle doodle doo.

⟨The next several lines appear in a smaller typescript and are divided into two columns on the handbill, with the left-hand column appearing first.⟩

To be extended full length upon the bottom of a Coach or Chariot of some exalted Weaver or Barber, covered with a plaid Paul, to be 8 bearers.

Major General Short Tongue
The Right Honorable Admiral Shifter,
Colonel Black Sam, and Captain Stewmug,
The Honorable Colonel Plowshare,
Captain Snuff,
And Brigadiers Shuffle and Cut, Esqrs.

To be drawn by thirty broken Tradesmen, in

⟨The right-hand column begins.⟩

Second Mourning,

The distressed Spinners with scarfs and cock-
ados of Waste Cotton, two and two.
Badgers, Butchers, Shopkeepers, Hucksters, and
Ale-sellers, in full mourning, two and two.

Carding Engine, Jenny makers, and Loom makers, Spinners and Weavers, Wives
and Children, two and two in ragged be-gowns, and old Shoes on. The Perpetrators of this Murder to be tarr'd and feathered.

⟨In the same size of type as the text appearing in the columns, the following text
appears without columns.⟩

A Funeral Sermon will be preached at the Tabernacle, from Isaiah xxiv. 10. 11.
"The City of Confusion is broke down, Every House is shut up, that no Man
come in. There is a cry for Wine in the Streets, All joy is darkened, and the mirth
of the land is gone." Aspinall. tvn

Yorkshire DOCUMENTS

YORKSHIRE LUDDISM evidently began with the 19 January 1812 firing of a large Oatlands cloth-finishing mill owned by Oates, Woods, and Smithson. In their letter to the Home Office, the owners write that the fire was deliberately set to destroy finishing machines—gig mills and shearing frames—that they had only recently installed.[1] Through the first half of 1812, croppers—the shearmen whose job was to dress woolen cloth by manually shearing its nap, thereby making a smoother article—continued to attack shops and large mills around Leeds and Huddersfield where owners were using machinery to reduce wages and bring under one roof the various processes involved in the manufacture of woolen cloth.

The ludding croppers of Yorkshire's West Riding did not produce as many proclamations, open letters, or documents employing a legal style of discourse as did the Midlands framework knitters. They did not write as many documents that professed an affiliation with the parliamentary reform movement, indicated an awareness of a larger economic reality, or aimed at constituting a collectivity where one did not exist previously, as did many writers from Manchester and its environs. Rather, we find that the Yorkshire Luddites wrote many threatening letters, some of them Jacobinical in tone, and that the writers of those letters quickly recognized the complicity between manufacturers and local officials. Their writing shifted from threats against the owners of shearing frames and gig mills to threats against the authorities who counteracted what the Luddites believed to be a righteous cause. Besides their being more overtly, though locally, political, the Yorkshire letters are also more personally violent than the Midlands and Manchester varieties. Even when the language turns toward the political, it frequently retains a language of vengeance and moral indignation.

Most of the West Riding Luddite documents are found in the Home Office Papers and the Papers of Sir Joseph Radcliffe, the Huddersfield magistrate most active in quelling Luddism in that region. Several documents, particularly songs, can be found in works by local historians and in works of historical fiction written during the last half of the 1800s. Those works draw upon local lore and oral reports of persons alive during the risings. Their authenticity has been called into question by twentieth-century scholars, but most of the songs found in such works seem to be consistent in style and content with others collected during the period of Luddism.

YI ❖ Pre-1812: Song titled "Horsfall's Mill," Huddersfield vicinity

Frank Peel's works of oral and local history for the region around Huddersfield preserve a few songs that were sung or composed during the Luddite machine breaking in that region. One of those songs celebrates the destruction by fire of the dressing machines (both shearing frames and gig mills) at William Horsfall's Ottiwells Mill in 1803. Horsfall and his father were among the most recalcitrant of mill owners in the vicinity of Huddersfield and were aggressive in their introduction of dressing machines to the region's woolen manufacture.[2] Horsfall is perhaps most famous in his connection to one of the Huddersfield Luddites, George Mellor. In one confrontation prior to the attack on Rawfolds Mill, Horsfall struck Mellor across the face with a riding whip as Mellor comforted a poor woman whose infant had starved. Weeks later, Horsfall was shot to death on Marsden Road after leaving the Warren House Inn. Mellor and two Luddites were found guilty and hanged for the crime.[3]

"Horsfall's Mill" might have been composed earlier, in 1803, during the Yorkshire croppers' resistance to the use of shearing frames and gig mills in the first years of the nineteenth century; nevertheless, it was sung during the Luddite risings and perhaps serves as the basis for a later, nearly identical Luddite song, "Forster's Mill." Lesley Kipling, the person probably most familiar with Luddite texts related to the region of Huddersfield, speculates that "Horsfall's Mill" might have been composed sometime after the "Forster's Mill" song.[4]

Frank Peel, *Spen Valley: Past and Present* (Heckmondwike: Senior and Company, 1893) 258–59. It has been reproduced in Roy Palmer, *The Sound of History: Songs and Social Comment* (Oxford: Oxford University Press, 1988), 5.[5]

❖ ❖ ❖

Come all you croppers, stout and bold,
Let your faith grow stronger still,
These cropping lads in the County of York,
Broke the shears at Horsfall's Mill.
The broke the shears and the windows too,
Set fire to the tazzling mill;
They formed themselves all in a line,
Like soldiers at the drill.

The wind it blew, and the sparks they flew,
And awoke the town full soon.
People got up in the middle of the night,
And they ran by the light of the moon;
When these lads around the mill did stand,
And they all did vow and swear,
Neither blanket nor can, nor any such thing,
Should be of service there.

Y2 ❖ February 1812: Song titled "The Cropper's Song," Huddersfield

Whereas Nottinghamshire Luddism comprised primarily workers in the hose and lace trades, West Riding machine breaking was organized around the croppers, the highly skilled artisans who finished woolen cloth using handheld shears, four feet in length and weighing from forty to fifty pounds, to cut the nap from the cloth. The croppers were held in high regard, not only among themselves, but also by the working families in the textile communities. The following song in praise of the croppers is attributed by Frank Peel to John Walker, who sang it at a meeting of Huddersfield and Liversedge croppers at the Shears Inn, Hightown, in February 1812, not long before they ventured forth to Hartshead Moor, where they destroyed shearing frames being transported by wagon to William Cartwright's factory, Rawfolds Mill.[6]

The song is remarkably apolitical (that is, regarding national politics) for West Riding Luddism. Its apolitical character reflects the primarily local concern of the various movements in their early phases, a cross-cultural phenomenon that has been analyzed by E. J. Hobsbawm in *Primitive Rebels* as "social banditry" or "Robin-Hoodism."[7]

Frank Peel, *The Risings of the Luddites*, 3rd ed. (Brighouse: J. Hartler, 1895), 47–48, and Peel, *Spen Valley: Past and Present* 242. The song has also been reproduced by Roy Palmer, with his typical small variations in punctuation as well as some concatenation of lines which Peel left apart, in *The Sound of History* (Oxford: Oxford University Press, 1988), 105–6.[8]

❖ ❖ ❖

"The Cropper's Song"

Come, cropper lads of high renown,
Who love to drink good ale that's brown,
And strike each haughty tyrant down,
    With hatchet, pike, and gun!
Oh, the cropper lads for me,
The gallant lads for me,
Who with lusty stroke,
The shear frames broke,
The cropper lads for me!

What though the specials[9] still advance,
And soldiers nightly round us prance;
The cropper lads still lead the dance,
    With hatchet, pike, and gun!
Oh, the cropper lads for me,
The gallant lads for me,
Who with lusty stroke
The shear frames broke,
The cropper lads for me!

And night by[10] night when all is still
And the moon is hid behind the hill,
We forward march to do our will
    With hatchet, pike, and gun!

Oh, the cropper lads for me,
The gallant lads for me,
Who with lusty stroke
The shear frames broke,
The cropper lads for me!

Great Enoch still shall lead the van.
Stop him who dare! stop him who can!
Press forward every gallant man
    With hatchet, pike, and gun!
Oh, the cropper lads for me,
The gallant lads for me,
Who with lusty stroke
The shear frames broke,
The cropper lads for me!

Y3 ❖ [February or March] Early 1812: Song titled "T' Three Cropper Lads o' Honley"

On 16 October 1880 a serialized story written exclusively for *The Huddersfield Weekly News* began its run. The story, *Daisy Baines, The Luddite's Daughter* (sometimes titled *Daisy Baines, A Sad Story of Sad Times*), contains accounts of most of the major Luddite events in the West Riding. Like works by Peel and Sykes, *Daisy Baines* draws a great deal upon local history and the reported memories of person who lived during the time.

The following song, "T' Three Cropper Lads o' Honley," appears in the story. The author of *Daisy Baines* claims that William Hall and a number of other croppers sang the song in a public house at Honley shortly after the murder of William Horsfall: "'Horsman's shot! Three cheers for t' croppers; three cheers for t' Luds. I'll sing t' Croppers' National Anthem. All join t' chorus.' Hall then sang the following song to a rollicking tune, the men joining in the rowdy chorus. . . ."[11] Lesley Kipling notes that the song "refers to the old legend that croppers, having died and gone to Hell, were so unruly that the Devil sent them back."[12] "Gairner," in the first line, is the West Riding dialect pronunciation of "Garner." There was a John Garner who had a cropping shop in Honley, which was attacked by Luddites on 11 March 1812.[13] For these reasons, the song is included in this collection.

Daisy Baines, serialized in *Huddersfield Weekly News*, 22 January 1881.

❖ ❖ ❖

T' Three Cropper Lads o' Honley.

T' three Honley lads o' Gairner shop—
    Sim, Rube, an' Squentin Jimmy,
Ne'er cared a slart for coffee slop
    If they could ha' some Timmy;
They cropp'd, an' swet, an' swigg'd ther ale,
Wi' gullets like a Greenland whale,
An' seldom did owt else but sail
I' Timmy—boout o' t' Tuesdays.

        Hurrai! my lads fill up to t' brim!
        An' drink whol booath yer leets ur dim
        To Squentin Jimmy, Rube an' Sim,
        T' three cropper lads o' Honley.

One day theas cooanies wagg'd to t' Thong,
    As jolly as three hatters,
To rant an' rooar i' ale an' song,
    An' other scram'lin' matters;
But as they paddled wom at neet
Daan t' Jagger Loin, they lost ther feet,
An rooagish Rube an' Sim did leet
At top o' Squentin Jimmy.
        Chorus—Hurrai! &c.

They snarted, grooan'd, then cuddled up
    Lawke suckin' pigs together,
An' wished 'at they'd a drop to sup
    Fro' th' Upperthong or t' Nether.
An' sooin ther breeathin laad an' deep,
Wi' naah an' then a grunt i' th' heap,
Denooated they wor gooin to sleep,

Sim, Rube, and Squentin Jimmy.
>   Chorus—Hurrai! &c.

An' whol they snooz'd, fro' th' Owdfild Rigg,
>   Just like a rocket rooarin,
Owd Nick aleetin', donced a jig
>   Araand t' three doydies snooarin',
An' sayin', 'I have ye naah,' he took
His watch-keigh fro' his pocket-book,
An' blew sich blasts at in a snook
Two div'ls coom like leetnin'.
>   Chorus—Hurrai! &c.

Th' two flew away wi' Rube an' Sim,
>   An' Satan tackled Jimmy,
As he wor th' heaviest lump o' limb,
>   An' allus drank t' mooast Timmy.
An' in a twink theas chums i' hell
Wor wakken'd wi' a stawflin' smell;
An' wheer they wor they couldn't tell
'Mang lost o' rostin' taties.
>   Chorus—Hurrai! &c.

T' three skenn'd araand, all blazin' shawn'd,
>   Yet ivv'ry think look'd glaamy,
An' they wor twitched an' short o' waund,
>   Tho' th' haas wor flaysum raamy.
'A quairt o' ale!' then Rube did blate,
>   Div'ls, grinnin, crush'd ther rost potate,
But nivver itched a peg to wait
>   O' Sim, an' Rube, an' Jimmy.
>   Chorus—Hurrai! &c.

Ther dander rooas, ther blooid did boil,
>   n' mad wi' burnin' throttles,
They baanced abaat an' pois'd raand th' hoil
>   Chairs, stooils, an' pots, an' bottles;
Whol t' blackest fiend i' hell turned whawte,

An' promis'd ' em if they'd be quawte,
He'd try to get—at leeast he'd wrawte—
To Lookud for sum Timmy.
   Chorus—Hurrai! &c.

They'd nother leeav, nor do na wark,
  At fawrin', shooilin', wheelin',
They sed, as long as they'd a spark
  'At couldn't get sum keelin'.
They play'd owd Harry wi' Owd Nick,
An' made his caancillors as sick,
'At they wor wanted off quick, slick,
To Heaven, or else to Honley.
   Chorus—Hurrai! &c.

At last th' Owd Lad his Cabinet
  Call'd up, for its opinion
Ha's best an' sooinest he could get
  T' three aat o' his dominion.
An', what seem'd lawkliest not to fail,
I wor agreed to cooin a tale
At just th' aatsawde a looad o' ale
Wor stannin' thear for haasin'.
   Chorus—Hurrai! &c.

T' wor done, an' bang to t' doorhoil rush'd,
Sim, Rube, an' Squentin Jimmy;
An' one another push'd an' crush'd
  To get t' first seet o' Timmy.
But sooin as they'd smell'd th' air they fell
Daan fast asleep, an' wi' a yell
T' div'ls switched 'em back ageean fro' hell
To t' Jagger Loin i' Honley.
   Chorus—Hurrai! &c.

T' three thowt they'd had abaat a week
  Teetooa i' limbo smartin';

But when they'd wakken'd, t' factory reek
  T' same morn wor nobbut startin'.
Yet all sware ooaths befoore the'd goon
To t' pleck ageean to suffer soon,
They'd see it damn'd fro' top to toon —
An' t' div'ls didn't want ' em.
  Chorus — Hurrai! &c.

Naah lads, as long as yo can sing,
  An' tak yer share o' Timmy,
Let t' Cooach an' th' Horses' kitchen ring
  O' Sim, an' Rube, an' Jimmy;
For nivver did three lads befoore
Soon best Owd Nick o' his own flooar'
An' hadn't he ' lawd ' em sat o' t' doore,
They'd sooin ha' smash'd his kingdom.
  Chorus — Hurrai! &c.

Y4 ❖ [March] 1812: Address "To all Croppers, Weavers &c & Public at Large," Leeds

The papers of the Leeds woolen manufacturer Benjamin Gott, one of the largest of the clothiers and factory owners in the Yorkshire woolen industry, contain two letters that reinforce a reader's sense of the consciously political character of West Riding Luddite writing after several weeks of attacks on factories and shearing frames. By the spring of 1812, the West Riding Luddites had comprehended the complicity between the government and the factory industrialists. Although the language violently reflected the comprehension of national complicity, the circumstances of address and delivery remained local, even in this call for mobilization, which addresses the textile workers of the region. Surprising as it may seem, given the pride the croppers had for their trade and their special place in the process of woolen manufacture, the croppers welcomed into the Luddite ranks woolen weavers and members of other trades in the region. For example, John Booth, the friend of the executed Huddersfield cropper George Mellor, was a saddler's apprentice in the Huddersfield region.

Both letters appear in the same handwriting on a single sheet, apparently Gott's transcriptions. It is unclear whether the two letters came into Gott's hands at the same time. The dates suggest that they may have, although each letter greets a different audience. The date "Before 9 March" apparently is Gott's addition.

Leeds University Manuscripts 193, Gott Papers, vol. 3, 106 (first letter). The two letters are also copied, with several emendations, in W. B. Crump, *Leeds Woollen Industry* (Leeds: Thoresby Society, 1931), 229, where they are labeled 75a and 75b, referring to an older cataloging system for the Gott Papers.

❖   ❖   ❖

Before 9 March.

To all Croppers, Weavers &c & Public at Large

Generous Countrymen.

You are requested to come forward with Arms and help the Redressers to redress their Wrongs and shake off the hateful Yoke of a Silly Old Man, and his Son more silly and their Rogueish Ministers, all Nobles and Tyrants must be brought down. Come let us follow the Noble Example of the brave Citizens of Paris who in the Sight of 30,000 Tyrant Redcoats brought A Tyrant to the Ground. by so doing you will be best aiming at your own Interest. Above 40,000 Heroes are ready to break out, to crush the old Goverment[14] & establish a new one.

Apply to General Ludd Commander
of the Army of Redressers.

Y5   ❖   9 or 10 March 1812: Letter from "Ned Ludd Clerk" addressed "To Mr Smith Shearing Frame Holder at Hill End Yorkshire," Hill End near Leeds

The second Luddite letter in the Gott Papers is addressed to a "Mr. Smith." To my knowledge, no one has precisely identified "Mr. Smith." Only two miles west of Leeds is a locale called Hill End, very near Gotts Park, but no other documents that I have found place a clothier named Smith in that area. Darvall identifies him as a resident of Huddersfield.[15] Thomis mentions one "Mr. Smith, of Snowgatehead, near Holmfirth"—more than twelve miles from Gott's location at Leeds and nearly six miles from Huddersfield—who "had all his dressing-frames and shears broken" on 5 April 1812.[16] The timing of the letter, only a month before the attack near Holmfirth, suggests that Gott's Mr. Smith and Thomis's might be the same.

Like many Yorkshire documents, the letter is militantly political, almost Jacobin (but for some millenarian expressions and the nationalistic observations about the "Hanover Tyrants"). It is also remarkable for its exceedingly democratic tenor, for the democratic process it describes, and for the variety of discourse that it reveals to exist even in one region. In contrast, the General Ludd of the 11 May 1812 letter to "Mr. Edward Ludd" (Radcliffe Papers 126/46) appears at times to be much more authoritarian than the General portrayed in this letter, who writes at the request of his men rather than authorizing a "Peter Plush, Secretary" to write for him. The letter to Mr. Smith would imply that Ludd's men identify an injustice and represent it to the General, who conveys the grievance to the offending Mr. Smith and, absent Smith's compliance, delegates responsibility for redress to a lieutenant. The "Commander of the Army of Redressers" is also aware of proportionality as a rhetorical tactic, as the choice of the word "Redressers" implies. The Luddites will respond with degrees of severity that are tied directly to Smith's actions. From a rhetorical standpoint, the letter is also interesting for its implications to framing Luddism (as opposed to other outbreaks of machine breaking) as a discursive phenomenon: General Ludd is an author who gives utterance to the complaints of a collective body.

Leeds University Manuscripts 193, Gott Papers, vol. 3, 106. It, too, can be found with several emendations in Crump, *Leeds Woollen Industry* 220–30 (labeled 75b), and in H. O. 40/1/1.

❖ ❖ ❖

To Mʳ Smith Shearing Frame Holder at Hill End Yorkshire.

Sir

Information has just been given in that you are a holder of those detestable Shearing Frames, and I was desired by my Men to write to you and give you fair Warning to pull them down, and for that purpose I desire you will now understand I am now writing to you. you will take Notice that if they are not taken down by the end of next Week, I will detach one of my Lieutenants with at least 300 Men to destroy them and furthermore take Notice that if you give us the Trouble of coming so far we will increase your misfortune by burning your Buildings down to Ashes and if you have Impudence to fire upon any of my Men, they have orders to murder you, & burn all your Housing, you will have the Goodness to your Neighbours to inform them that the same fate awaits them if their Frames are not speedily taken down as I understand their are several in your Neighbourhood, Frame holders. And as the Views and Intentions of me and my Men have been much misrepresented[17] I will take this opportunity of stating them, which I desire you will let all your Brethren in Sin know of. I would have the Merchants, Master Dressers, the Goverment[18] & the public to know that the Grievances of such a Number of Men are not to be made sport of for by the last Returns there were 2782 Sworn Heroes bound in a Bond of Necessity either to redress their Grievances or gloriously perish in the Attempt in the Army of Huddersfield alone, nearly double sworn Men in Leeds.

By the latest Letters from our Correspondents we learn that the Manufacturers in the following Places are going to rise and join us in redressing their Wrongs Viz. Machester, Wakefield Halifax, Bradford, Sheffield, Oldham, Rochdale and all the Cotton Country where the brave M[r] Hanson[19] will lead them on to Victory. the Weavers in Glasgow and many parts of Scotland will join us the Papists in Ireland are rising to a so that they are likely to find the Soldiers something else to do than Idle in Huddersfield and then Woe be to the places now guarded by them for we have come to the easier Way of burning them to Ashes which will most assuredly be their Fate either sooner or later. The immediate Cause of us beginning when we did was that Rascally letter of the Prince Regents to Lords Grey & Grenville, which left us no hopes of any Change for the better, by his falling in with that Damn'd set of Rogues, Percival & C[o] to whom we attribute all the Miseries of our Country. But we hope for assistance from the French Emperor in shaking off the Yoke of the Rottenest, Wickedest and most Tyranious Government that ever existed; then down come the Hanover Tyrants, and all our Tyrants from the greatest to the smallest. and we will be governed by a just Republic, and may the Almighty hasten those happy Times is the Wish and Prayer of Millions in this Land, but we won't only pray but we will fight, the Redcoats shall know that when the proper time comes We will never lay down our Arms. The House of Commons passes an Act to put down all Machinery hurtful to Commonality,[20] and repeal that to hang Frame Breakers. But We. We petition no more that won't do fighting must.

Signed by the General of the Army of

Redressers

Ned Ludd Clerk

Redressers for ever Amen,

You may make this Public

March 9th or 10th

Y6 ❖ [Before 15] March 1812: Letter to Frank Vickerman, Taylor Hill

near Huddersfield

The first large-scale Luddite operation in the West Riding was the 15 March 1812 attack on the guarded cloth-finishing shop of Frank Vickerman, a Taylor Hill wool manufacturer. The raid, which was an especially daring and violent affair, destroyed several of Vickerman's shearing frames. The raid was preceded by a threatening letter, thrown into Vickerman's premises a couple of nights earlier. Vickerman had been a member of the Committee of Merchants and Manufacturers, established 23 February 1812 at Huddersfield to organize troops and coordinate the activities of the Watch and Ward to suppress Luddite activities. After assembling in Pricking Wood, the Luddites hit Vickerman's shop before nine o'clock in the evening, destroying ten frames, thirty shears, woven wool cloth, a clock, and every window pane in the shop building.[21]

H. O. 42/121. The threatening letter is enclosed with the letter from magistrate Joseph Radcliffe to the Home Office, 17 March 1812, reporting some of the details of the raid.

❖ ❖ ❖

We give you Notice when the Shers is all Broken the Spinners shall be the next if they be not taken down vick man tayler hill he has had is Garde but we will pull all down som Night and kill him that Nave and Roag.[22]

Y7 ❖ 20 March 1812: Letter from "Soliciter to General Ludd" to "Mr Ratcliffe"

at "Millsbridge"

One of the officials responsible for quelling the disturbances around Huddersfield, Milnsbridge magistrate Joseph Radcliffe, compiled a large collection of letters pertaining to West Riding Luddism. The letters threatening Radcliffe him-self are among the most interesting and numerous. The following letter seems to have been the first Luddite threat received by Radcliffe; no threatening letters bearing an earlier date appear in his collection. It is one of the most legible of the Luddite texts and contains a rare Luddite footnote. The readable script en-hances the tone of formality otherwise evident in the civil opening and closing, as well as in the legalistic discourse. Not reproduced in the transcription here is the flourish with which the writer underlines "March-20th 1812" and "Soliciter to General Ludd." The legal style of the letter is not typical of most Huddersfield documents. It is interesting that this Yorkshire letter, atypical for its legalisms, incorporates a rhetorical appeal to Nottingham, where Luddite texts abounded in legalisms. Nottingham holds a certain fascination for the Luddite writers in the Huddersfield area.[23] It frequently is the basis of a rhetorical appeal, vaguely temporal and numerical in its nature, harkening back to a recent past with a tra-ditional grounding and speaking with a single, unified voice against the use of particular machines. Although the handwriting appears to be the same on both sides of the letter, the style changes. The second side is rougher, less literate, with some misspellings—"coutinance" and "Genearal." The second side seems to have been added in haste; the letters are not so finely drawn as on the first side and the lines are more cramped.

Radcliffe Papers 126/27, West Yorkshire Archives Service, Leeds. Facsimiles of each side of the letter follow on pages 214 and 215.

❖ ❖ ❖

⟨Side 1⟩

For Mr Ratcliffe Esq
Millsbridge[24]
Genl Ludd's Solicitor March 20 1812

Jos Ratcliffe
    Sir
        Take notice that a Declaration was this Day filed against you in Ludd^s Court at Nottingham, and unless you remain* neutral judgment will immedi-ately be sign^d against you for Default, I shall thence summon a Jury for an Inquiry of Damages take out Execution against both your Body and House,

and then you may Expect General Ludd, and his well organised Army to Levy it with all Destruction possible

And I am Sir your-

Nottingham

March-20th 1812   Soliciter to General Ludd

*PS you have Sir rather taken an active part against the General but you are quiet and may remain so if you chuse (and your Brother Justices also) for him, but if you Either convict a [one], or coutinance the other Side as you have Done (or any of you), you may Expect your House in Flames and, your-self in Ashes in a few Days from your next move, for our Court is not Govern^d by Terms[25] But Equity

⟨Side 2⟩

NB, In shewing the General the other Side for Inspection He orders me to inform you the Cloth Dressers in the Huddersfield District as spent Seven Thousand Pounds in petition Government to put Laws in force to stop the Shearing Frames and Gig Mills to no purpose so they are trying this method now, and he is inform^d how you are affraid it will be carried on to another purpose but you need not be apprehensive of that, for as soon as ye Obnoxious machienery is Stop^d or Distroy^d the Genearal and his Brave Army will be Disband^d, and Return to their Employment, like other Liege Subjects

---

Y8 ❖ 8 April 1812: Letter from Leeds signed "I ham for lud and the poor" to "Mr Joseph Ratcliff, Milnsbridg"

Previous commentators, relying upon a cataloger's erroneous description, have assumed that this letter was sent by "the poor," congratulating Joseph Radcliffe on his efforts to suppress the Luddites; however, reading the letter as congratulatory would be a mistake, caused by misreading the nearly illegible second half of the letter, wherein a clear threat is couched in the ironic language of congratulation.

Josh. Ratcliffe

Sir,

Take notice that a Declaration was this Day filed against you in Ludds Court at Nottingham, And unless you remain* neutral Judgment will Immediately be Sign- against you for Default, I shall thence Summon a Jury for an Inquiry of Damages take out Execution against Both your Body and House, And then you may Expect General Ludd, And his well Organise Army to Levy it - with all Destruction possible

And I am Sir your

Soliciter to General Ludd

Nottingham -
March - 20 1812

* PS you have Sir rather taken an Active part against the General but - you are quiet And may Remain so if you Chuse (And your Brother Justices also) for him, but if you Either Conviat, or Continance the other Side as you have Done (or any of you), you may Expect your House in Flames and, your- Self in Ashes in a few Days from your next move, for our Court is not Govern: leg Terms but Equity

Letter of 20 March 1812 from "Soliciter to General Ludd" to "Mr Ratcliffe" at "Millsbridge," Radcliffe Papers 126/27, side 1

The fact that the letter is full of misspellings, grammatical errors, omissions, and insertions explains some of the confusion. Indeed, as is the case with many Luddite texts, the handwriting is bad but is made worse by bleeding through from the other side of a transcription of a Luddite oath, in a hand belonging neither to the writer of the note nor to Radcliffe.

nts. In shewing the General the other Side for Inspection He orders me to inform you how the Cloth Dressers in the Huddersfield District as spent Seven Thousand Pounds in Petition Government to put the Laws in force to Stop the Shearing Frames and Gig Mills to no porpose so they are trying this method now, and he is inform'd how you are affraid it will be Carried on to another purpose but you need not be apprehensive - of that, for as Soon as ye Obnoxious machinery is Stop or Distroy. the General and his Brave army will be disband'd, and Return to their Employment, like other Liege Subjects

Letter of 20 March 1812 from "Soliciter to General Ludd" to "Mr Ratcliffe" at "Millsbridge," Radcliffe Papers 126/27, side 2

The date the note was received is added at the bottom in Radcliffe's own hand —12 April 1812.

Radcliffe Papers 126/1.

❖   ❖   ❖

Mʳ Joseph Ratcliff
Esquier Milns bridg
 Near Hudersfield

Leeds 8 April

Sir,

I ham verrey Happey to Hear of your acktivety in taking of those people
Caulled luds for they Have been verrey troubbles Some of late you are verrey
acktive just ass as theare are maney more sutch like Skindevils at present making mutch to do about nothing but striving to take poor people labor from
them i think the medalon soon to be given to sutch villons as you is a ledon
ball with powder that will not dist jest soner and beter

I ham for lud and
the poor.

Y9 ❖ [Early] April 1812: Letter from "Mr Love Good" to Joseph Radcliffe at
Milnsbridge near Huddersfield

Two letters from the early spring of 1812 "indict" Thomas Atkinson, a mill
owner and brother-in-law of the Rawfolds mill owner, William Cartwright. The
first letter, which opens with the words "This comes from a friend" and which
is signed "Mr. Love Good," is an example of the Luddite writers' use of rhetorical duplicity. Aside from satisfying a writer's possible desire for rhetorical
variety, the purposes for such a tactic are unclear. Perhaps by conveying a threat
indirectly, through "report," the author's actions might not be classified among
those prohibited under the eighteenth-century Black Act statutes and their judicial interpretations that made sending anonymous threats a capital felony. In
any event, the tactic here is transparent, and the "friend's" warning conveys few
particulars and no useful information. Another purpose might be to convey to
Radcliffe an understanding of some reasonableness and discrimination on the
part of the Luddites—that is, to demonstrate that their rage is selective rather
than indiscriminate. Such a purpose would be important given the bad press
that the Luddites had been receiving in the *Leeds Mercury*, which called them
"depredators" and portrayed them as indiscriminate destroyers of shops and private property.

Because the letter does not mention the attack on Rawfolds Mill, it is likely to have been composed before the raid.

Radcliffe Papers 126/28.

❖ ❖ ❖

Mr
Radcliffe Esq
  Mills Bridge
  near Huddersfield

Mr Radcliffe Dear Sir

This comes from a friend

I found my Self to be and got into the Seckrets of the Ludites and knowing the dredfull plots that is going forwards I Send this to you there is dredfull Praprations goen forwards for Great Destruction

It is reported you back Thos Atkinson it was ordered a wile a go for your place and Bradley Mill to be burnt one Night But I pled it of with great to do

When that Time comes foot nor Horses will be of any use there will be a Great Destruction You must not compell Watching & Warding You must side with the Luds if you Live

I should a spook[26] personley to you But durst Not

If this was known it is deth to me

From Mr Love Good

April 1812

Y10 ❖ [After 9] April 1812: Song titled "Forster's Mill," Huddersfield vicinity

Portions of two other Yorkshire songs have also been preserved by Peel, the products of his interviews with persons who recalled the Luddite risings. Peel's transcription of an oral recollection of the song may explain his rendering the name as "Forster's mill" rather than "Foster's." The event at "Forster's mill" refers to the 9 April 1812 attack on Joseph Foster's house and mill at Horbury, seven miles from Huddersfield.[27] Peel notes that the verse was "composed after the destruction of the mill between Horbury and Ossett," an attack that drew hundreds of Luddites from several West Riding communities.

With the exception of song narratives of dejection, including "Hunting a Loaf," the song is the closest approach to narrative in Luddite balladry. No date is given, but the song could have been composed immediately following the raid, because the form of the "Horsfall's Mill" song, which it clearly imitates, was already available. The narrative qualities might be understood as the croppers' attempts to write for themselves a narrative in which their agency would lead to a desirable end.[28]

Peel's version of the song is untitled. I have given the title as "Forster's Mill" rather than "Foster's Mill" because it might be the case that Peel's spelling (which he retained through three editions of his book) preserves more accurately the sounds or perhaps even the spelling of Foster's name among the people of the region at the time.

Peel, *The Risings of the Luddites* 120.[29]

❖   ❖   ❖

Come all ye croppers stout and bold,
    Let your faith grow stronger still,
Oh, the cropper lads in the county of York
    Broke the shears at Forster's mill.
            The wind it blew,
            The sparks they flew,
    Which alarmed the town full soon
And out of bed poor people did creep
And ran by the light of the moon;
Around and around they all did stand,
    And solemnly did swear,
Neither bucket, nor kit nor any such thing
    Should be of assistance there.

Y11 ❖ [Before 18] April 1812: Proclamation to "Croppers"

Yorkshire's West Riding produced few posted proclamations. The dearth of proclamations coincides with the highly personal nature of the conflict between the croppers and the owners of the shearing frames. Nevertheless, one such proclamation appears in the Home Office Papers, enclosed with a letter from General Grey to the Home Office, dated 18 April 1812. Grey remarks that he sends the proclamation in consequence of the 12 April 1812 attack on Rawfolds Mill. It is printed large in letters consisting of double lines. The slogan, "Now or Never," appears also in a broadside posted at Manchester in early April 1812 (H. O. 40/1/1, 40/1/5, reproduced above). The Manchester placard is connected to a larger disaffection, one that encompasses both Luddism and political reform and involves larger organized demonstrations, than is usually thought to be characteristic of West Riding Luddism in early 1812.

H. O. 42/122.

❖ ❖ ❖

Croppers

To harms

Inocent Blood

Crys For

Vengance

Now or Never

Y12 ❖ 19 April 1812: Two letters from "John and Martin Middleton" at Houghton and "G. D."

Letters from people who apparently were not engaged in machine wrecking but who nevertheless sympathized with the Luddites illustrate popular attitudes toward the Yorkshire Luddites prior to the murder of William Horsfall. Radcliffe kept two such letters intercepted from the mail. Radcliffe describes the first letter as a "copy of a letter put in the Post Office at Dobcross." The second letter, from "G D," describes a clash between the Luddites and the Army, but the events described seem to be those associated with the failed Luddite attack on William Cartwright's Rawfolds Mill, 11 April 1812, in the defense of which soldiers participated.[30] The "son of a Church parons" would be John Booth, the saddlemaker's apprentice who was shot in the leg during the attack and died later. Immediately after recounting the Rawfolds attack and asking for more particulars, "G. D." extends a curious offer, perhaps to any persons involved in attacks who would need to leave the region to escape detection: "and hif there is any person that ar obliged to come away I have procured a seat of work for them."

Radcliffe Papers 126/32.

❖ ❖ ❖

Houghton April 19th 1812

Dear Brothers & Sisters

We take the oportunity of answering your letter which you sent by your friend & we are glad to hear that you are all well which these lines have us all at present. Bless God for it. We are glad to hear that you have gained the Victory which your friend related to us which He did the last night & today which we was very glad to listen to him & receiv^d him as a friend from you which we believe He is. & we have enjoyed ourselves over a pot or two of Beer. & he read Mr Luds Song. We shall relate no particulars for we sopose you have in of[31] papers & we can give you no satisfactory account And we will leave you to judge about it———

Yr father & mother gives thier Cind love to you all & we shall all be very glad to see you at the time you have proposed which is all at present from your loving Brothers

John and Martin Middleton

Frien I called at Tideswell as you ordered me for to call on your brother but he was not there which I was determined to find him which I have found your father & mother & all together but it was with much Ado I went to Litton & slep all night & was recieved as a friend with Bingham & Bramwell there as an engagement been betwixt the Luds & the Army which the Luds was defeated which was oing to Halifax Luds not coming up as they was apointed There was 16 men stormed the plaise which they had two Cilled there wounded man was carried of and none of them as been taken since which the two men was buried on Thursday last at Hudersfield which the Corps was put in a Dark room with six mold candles which the friends of the Luds followed them every man in morning with a with aprom edged with Black which the minister refused to Burie them but the Luds insisted on them being Buried in the Church which are to have a grand stone he lived fore and twenty hours after he was taken he was the son of a Church parons which many visited him but He refused to invulge anything I have but sent you all the particulars I have and I hope you will write to me by return of post & send me all the particulars and hif there is any person that ar obliged to come away I have procured a seat of work for them you will please to ax Wiliam pasomell were I may find the wife making in Manchester please to direct for Edward Good over Mill Saddleworth nine Manchester Yorkshire

Which you will not put any name
on the letter at all

And put a Cross on the bottom of the letter as I shall see your brothers on Whitson Sunday so no more from yr well wishing friend

G D——

Y13 ❖ 27 April 1812: Letter from "A. B." to Joseph Radcliffe, Milnsbridge near Huddersfield

Another April 1812 letter, from "A. B." to Radcliffe, mentions Thomas Atkinson, along with William Horsfall, as a target for Luddite wrath. The mingling of legal language ("tribunal" and "judge") with religious notions of divine judgment and retribution distinguishes this letter from much Luddite discourse in other regions. The religious language in the letter is vague in its orientation. It could be generically Anglican or evangelical. Methodism and other dissenting movements were particularly strong in the West Riding, as Frank Peel, Eric Hobsbawm, and J. A. Hargreaves have demonstrated.[32] Joanna Southcott, the millenarian prophet, had her greatest following in the West Riding. Despite the vagueness, the threat of civil war juxtaposed with Scripture calls to mind the political and religious strife of the seventeenth century. In contrast, Midlands documents occasionally threatened civic riot but rarely, if ever, implied civil war or interpreted the conflict along religious lines. The writer evidently believes Radcliffe to be susceptible to the influence of a Christian discourse—to such an extent that the writer makes no threats at all against Radcliffe but rather seeks his help in a righteous cause.

Reid speculates that the letter was written by George Mellor.[33] Certainly, the militantly political flavor of the document would have been agreeable to Mellor, and his behavior prior to his January 1812 execution at York suggests that he may have been influenced by one of the Methodist or evangelical movements.[34] Compare Mellor's letter from York Castle, transcribed below. Also, the letter is dated one day before the murder of William Horsfall, for which Mellor was convicted and hanged.[35]

The signature, "A. B.," might seem to be the most insignificant part of the letter, but from the perspective of an intertextual study it is one of the more interesting features. "A. B." was a typical nominal in the Luddite oaths reported by spies and informers ("I A B—on my own voluntary will and accord, do declare and solemnly swear. . . . ")[36] The use of the nominal here lends credence to the spies' and informers' reports of oathing in the northern counties and hints at a connection between those who administered oaths and those who wrote letters and addresses.

Radcliffe Papers 126/38.

❖ ❖ ❖

April 27th 1812

Sir,

I thought it my duty as a Friend, to address you with a few lines upon the Perrilous situation of this Country; as you are the principle Magistrate for this District, they look to you, and only you, for some Redress; If this Machinery is suffer'd to go on it will probable terminate with a Civil War, which I could wish to be avoided, there fore as you are not intrested by Machinery and the Spirit of the People appears so resolute in the Cause, that if some measures be not adopted and immediately, it will be attended with great Distruction, and particular those who are our greatest Persecutors. With respect to this Watch and Ward Act, you are not aware of the additional, Oppression you are bringing upon your Tenants, and other Occupiers of Lands, and all for the sake of two Individuals in this District, which I am not afraid to subscribe their names, Mr Thˢ Atkinson, & Mr Wᵐ Horsfall, who will soon be number'd with the dead, and summoned before the awfull Tribunal, and that God who will Judge every Man according to the Deeds done in the Body. And Jesus knew their thoughts and said unto them, every Kingdom divided against itself is brought to desolation; and every city or house divided against itself, shall not stand.

A. B.

Y14 ❖ 1 May 1812: Letter from "Peter Plush" purporting to write from Nottingham to "Mr Edward Ludd" at Huddersfield

E. P. Thompson points out in his essay, "The Crime of Anonymity," that there were usually two audiences for anonymous threatening letters. One audience comprised rich employers or social superiors, and the other audience consisted of fellow workers or social equals. In both cases, the letters adopt a collective pronoun, "we."[37] The following letter, demonstrative of the political and militant tendencies of the writing associated with Yorkshire Luddism, is unique in that the writer and recipient (both already eponymous and, thereby in the Luddite rhetorical schema, collective) constitute a larger "we."

The address and salutation are confusing. The letter is addressed to "Mr Edward Ludd Market Place Huddersfield." Below the address is the salutation, "To General Ludd/Juner." To the right of the salutation is the town of origin, Nottingham. Thompson speculates that the letter may have been written by "a freelance Nottinghamshire Luddite . . . intended more to alarm the authorities than to communicate with Yorkshire Luddites."[38] There does seem to have been some communication between Midlands and northern Luddites. In a 21 November 1811 letter to the Home Office preserved in H. O. 42/117, Colonel Ralph Fletcher reports from Bolton that one "Williamson" of Nottingham met artisans in Manchester. Frank Peel mentions a visit to croppers in the Spen Valley by a man named George Weightman, whom Peel describes, using the same language as the authorities and spies, as a "delegate" from Nottingham.[39] Additionally, one piece of internal evidence in support of Thompson's speculation is that the writer makes no mention of the murder of William Horsfall, three days prior to the date of this letter. A writer in the West Riding certainly would have heard of the murder and, given the mention made of other events, undoubtedly would have included congratulations. A writer from Nottingham might not have heard of the murder by 1 May. Finally, the letter shares some of the characteristics of the rhetorically duplicitous "friend" letters sent to authorities: it conveys little real information, except for the news about "dispatching a few individuals by pistel shot," and it professes Luddite potency.

Nevertheless, it would be wise to consider the possibility that the letter was intended for an internal audience. For an audience of machine breakers, the letter might serve much the same function as "The Cropper's Song," sung by John Walker during a Feburary 1812 meeting at the Shears Inn. The self-congratulatory tone of the letter from Ludd to Ludd supports this possibility. Furthermore, no external address or postmark is evident, indicating that it might not have been sent through the mail or that it was intended to have been intercepted at the Post Office.

Radcliffe Papers 126/46.[40]

❖ ❖ ❖

Mr Edward Ludd Market Place Huddersfield
To General Ludd   Nottingham
Juner   May 1 1812

By order of Genral Ludd sener the levetinent colonel and every rank of oficers in the generales servece in the town and county of Nottingham

I am reqested to expres the hye sence of honer We entertan of the meritoreous movment you and your forses have so gallantly mad in the neborood of Hudersfield to secure the rites of our poor starving fellow creturs—

I am also desired to say that We lamment with extrem regret the fate of the two brave boys who galantly spilt theire blood in a ladeble case at Rawfolds— They further learn with pleser that a noble attempt was mad about a mil from Huddersfield tho without suckses to destroy the Hytown <u>machenry man</u>[41]

The Generl futher autherises me to say that he trusts to the attachment of his subjects for the avenging of the death of the two brav youths who fell at the sege of Rawfolds—He also wishes me to state that tho his troops hear are not at present making any ostensable movments here that it is not for want of force as the orgenisation is just as strong as in Yorkshire but that they are at present only devising the best means for a grand attack and that at present they are dispatching a few individuals by pistel shot on of which fel last nite—[42]

I am futher otherised to say that it is the opinion of our general and men that as long as that blackgard, drunken whoreing fellow called Prince Regent and his servants have any thing to do with government that nothing but distres will befole us there foot stooles. I am further desired to say that it is expected that you will remember that you are mad of the same stuf as Gorg Gwelps[43] Juner and corn and wine are sent for you as wel as him

Peter Plush
Secretery to Genl Ludd

Y15 ❖ 15 May 1812: Letter from "I-G" at Leeds to Benjamin Gott at Leeds

A third letter in the Gott Papers raises questions not only about authorship but also Luddite rhetorical tactics. A 15 May 1812 letter appears in the Gott collection immediately following the letter to Mr. Smith. It is addressed to Mr. Gott from "I-G," who identifies himself as Gott's "Gardin angell" and "well wisher" and warns Gott of a Luddite conspiracy against his life.

Other Luddite letters notifying large masters of a judgment against them use threatening, sanguinary language, but most of those letters do not provide much evidence of rhetorical sophistication sufficient to execute the "well wisher" trope very effectively. Many such letters lapse too quickly into the genuine threatening voice, but this letter withholds the genuine voice and reveals the writer's true sympathies in only a couple of ways. First, the letter conveys the fact of a threat with no real or useful information. No Luddites are named or placed in jeopardy by the information that the author communicates.[44] Second, the ambiguous abuse of the Luddites, calling them "Tigars," actually praises them and portrays them as deserving to be feared. Finally, the letter is interspersed with limiting qualifications as to how effective the writer's efforts to protect Gott might be, thereby accomplishing a Luddite intention to smite their oppressors with fear. This last feature distinguishes the "I-G" from "Mr Love Good's" April 1812 letter to Joseph Radcliffe, quoted earlier. "Love Good" claims to have been successful in dissuading his colleagues from attacking Radcliffe. The absence of such claims in the letter to Gott diminishes the likelihood that the writer wishes to convey the reasonableness of the group.

Leeds University Manuscripts 193, Gott Papers, vol. 3, 106. The letter appears in Crump's *Leeds Woollen Industry* 230–31 (labeled 76).

❖ ❖ ❖

I-G to Benjamin Gott,   Leeds, 15th May, 1812.
Sir.

No doubt you are Informd as to the proceedins of the Ludites But feariful you Should Not to the Extent is the Caws of My Trublin you thus = a friend of Mine ad it from a Man that was Theair and on Sunday Night at Rounda wood to the Number of 400 thay theair Decreed the Death of 2 and with

Great Diffecalty He Extorted from the Man that you was one = Be Carful of your Self for a few Weeks = alter your usal walks to your Busness = I will Giv you all the Information In My power Be of Good Currige But Be Carful = I Mentioned it to two of My friends who know your worth to the Town and world In general as well as Myself you do Not know Me But I will Be your Gardin angell as far as My abilities Go—rest Satisfide that if I Can find out the Tigar^s that is apointed for that Infernall Job you Shall ave a Good account of them or Him. God Bless and preserve you through these difficalt Times.

do not Cummunicate this to aney one==do Not Indevor to find Me ought and you May Rest Satisfide I am your well wisher I-G.

Leeds 15th May 1812[45]

Y16 ❖ Late Spring or Summer 1812: Song fragment titled "How Gloomy and Dark Is the Day," Huddersfield vicinity

A very short song fragment recorded by Peel was composed some time after the disastrous assault on Rawfolds. In the aftermath of that greatest of Luddite failures, the croppers became more dismayed with collective action and turned to personal vengeance, political reform, or the millenarian or "chiliastic" despair described by Thompson as widespread during the period of industrialization.[46] More than any other Luddite text from Yorkshire, this song reflects the increasingly millenarian disposition of suffering workers whose efforts at self-help were coming to nothing and who waited for some external force to effect change.

Peel, *The Risings of the Luddites* 120.

❖   ❖   ❖

How gloomy and dark is the day
    When men have to fight for their bread;
Some judgment will sure clear the way,
    And the poor shall to triumph be led.

Y17 ❖ July 1812: Letter from "a well wisher" at Daypool to "The Secretary of State" at London

Although Yorkshire Luddites were more quickly and overtly moved to a political discourse than their Midlands counterparts were, and complained more frequently of "that blackgard drunken whoreing fellow called Prince Regent and his servants," the Home Office Papers contain very few threatening letters sent from Yorkshire to the regent and the cabinet. The following letter sent to the secretary of state from the vicinity of Hull, outside of the Luddite regions, is one example that affiliates itself with the Luddites, even though the writer claims to come from the West Country. Although its signatory claims to be a "well wisher," the letter hardly even qualifies as an attempt at a rhetorical duplicity.

What seems to be the original, printed in dark, clear letters, is preserved in the Home Office. The same handwriting that appears in the body of the letter directs it, "Haste/To the Secretary of State for the/Home Department/London." The words "Delivered without d" appear below the address: What follows the "d" has been cut off. A Home Office clerk dated its receipt, "1812 July."

H. O. 42/125.

❖ ❖ ❖

Daypool near Hull July

Sir,

I have too long been a dupe, to mischiefous men, by being led on, to mischief, in the west Country, and I have been guilty, of a many Crimes there, and have come here, by being deputed, for a very wicked purpose, even that, for which I now repent, & will have no concern, I am sent with others, to different parts of the Country, and especially where French Prisoners are many to some thousands, are already sworn in, to rise on a certain day, appointed in all parts of the Kingdom, on the 5th day of Novr next, the Luddites mean to rid themselves, of all their Enemys. They reckon on 50,000 French Prisoners, as helpers, as out of all that are sworn, amongs the French, not one did refuse.[47] On that morning, several, or many heads in London, are to be laid low, to cause a confusion, all the Mails, are to be stopt'd.

Castererleaah,[48] Liverpool, Gibbs, & several, are to fall, as fix'd on. Men are to go to all the places, where French Prisoners are, to assasinate the Gards, to let the Prisoners out, to join the Luddites, & then Mischief follows.

Tho' they appear quiet now, you are very much rong, if you trust to that. I have sent an account from here, where the arms are, in the Garrison, & what number.

But I repent, & will do no more, with them, but do you not be laid from Suspicion. Beware French Prisoners.

You need not advertize any reward for the writer of this to come forward because I won't tho' my conscience tell me to do this I will go no farther because by doing this I dare not return home. I wou'd not turn Kings Evidence for the World.

I will go so far as say that the Watch Word on that Day say 5th Novr next is to be LIBERTY AND LUDD, FOR EVER.

So no more from a well wisher N° 1175.[49]

Y18 ❖ September 1812: Song titled "The Devil Take the King," Birkby near Huddersfield

John Hog of Birkby, one mile north of Huddersfield, was charged in September 1812 with singing a seditious version of "God Save the King" after having objected to the singing of the ordinary version. Hog is identified variously as a Luddite and a malcontent in the different letters that dealt with his singing the song, which was forwarded to the Home Office in September 1812.

Versions of the song (certainly by no means a Luddite original), varying in completeness and somewhat in wording, appear in documents forwarded by Radcliffe, Lloyd, and another anonymous correspondent. The source for the text here is an anonymous letter.

H. O. 42/127.

❖ ❖ ❖

The devil take the King
Rid England of the King
God save us all
God damn his soul in hell
And throw him down to hell

The devil will serve him well
God save us all.

Y19 ❖ September 1812: Song by Charles Milnes, "You Heroes of England," Halifax

Occasionally, Luddite songs can be found outside of the usual primary source collections. Such a song is preserved in the prosecutor's brief for the crown case against Charles Milnes and William Blakeborough and has been reproduced with emendations in Thompson's introduction to the fourth edition (1968) of Peel's *Risings of the Luddites* (xiv).

Tried on 2 January 1813 at the York Special Commission, Milnes and Blakeborough were charged with larceny upon the statute 4 George II, cap. 32, for stealing lead from the roof of an untenanted garden house owned by the Dowager Lady Ibbetson in Halifax. One of the attorneys for the prosecution wrote on the brief for the case, "As it appears that the Lead was taken to cast into Bullets for Lud purposes it may be considered Evidence to produce a *song in the hand writing of Milnes* done in the presence of the Witness [Joseph] Taylor and delivered to him by the writer—it runs thus."[50] Joseph Taylor was a Special Constable for the West Riding and a spy who infiltrated the Luddite circles in the vicinity of Halifax. Taylor had asked Milnes for a copy of Milnes's song on 11 September 1812.[51]

The song follows a form of direct address that appears in the contemporary "Cropper's Song" as well as in an earlier song by Gerrard Winstanley, "You Noble Diggers."[52]

Rex v. Charles Milnes of Geldhill & William Blakeborough, Treasury Solicitor's Papers 11.813.2673, Public Records Office, Kew.

❖ ❖ ❖

You Heroes of England who wish to have a trade
Be true to each other and be not afraid
Tho'[53] the Bayonet is fixed they can do no good
As long as we keep up the Rules of General Ludd.

As we have begun we are like to proceed
Till from all those Tyrants we do get freed

For this heavy yoke no longer can we bear
And those who have not felt it ought to have a share.

And then they can feel for anothers[54] woe
For he that never knew sorrow, sorrow doth not know
But there is Cartwright and Atkinson also
And to shew[55] them justice sorrow they shall know.

Though he does boast of the deeds he has done
Yet out of our presence like a Thief he Does run[56]
It is the Laws[57] of England to stand in our defence
If he comes in our presence him we'll recompence.

Y20 ❖ 21 October 1812: Letter from "Enemie Anonimous" to "Ratclif," Huddersfield

After a brief hiatus during the summer of 1812, Joseph Radcliffe's efforts to discover Luddites attracted threatening letters again during the fall. Like several contemporary letters from the Midlands and Lancashire, the following letter to Radcliffe employs a "Bellingham trope," a threat accomplished through an allusion to the Liverpool man who, upset over having lost money in a Russian business venture and over the futility of his petitions for relief, assassinated Prime Minister Spencer Perceval on 11 May 1812 and became a popular hero whose actions were understood to symbolize public outrage at government policies. (Many of John Bellingham's letters to the government have been preserved in H. O. 42.)

Ironically, the author of this letter finds cause for hatred in Radcliffe's "Publick character," whereas Bellingham's grievance was distinctly private.[58] Clearly, a perfect correspondence between the Luddites' motives and actions and those of Bellingham mattered less to the writer than representing the political dimensions of resentment, hatred, and violence.

Radcliffe Papers 126/91. The letter is on a page of what appear to be copies of Radcliffe's correspondence.

❖ ❖ ❖

Huddersfield 21 October 1812
Ratclif

Sir,

I drop you this as a warning that I have for some time Eyed you as your Publick character act with so much injustice to almost every individual that has had the misfortune to come before you that I and my two Assocites is this hour your sworn Enimes and all his Magistes forces will not save you, for I dow not regard my own life if I can have reveang of you which I mos ashuredly will make myself another Jhn[59] Bellingham and I have the Pellit mad[60] that shall be wet in you Harts Life[61] Blood if I should dow it in the hous of God

I with hatered your sworn

Enemie Anonimous

Add. Joseph Ratclif Es[qr]

Millns Bridge

Y21 ❖ 29 October 1812: Letter from "Secretary to the Brotherhood" to Joseph Radcliffe, Milnsbridge near Huddersfield

Another October 1812 threat upon Radcliffe's life employs a rhetoric demonstrative of moral and religious motives instead of political or even trade concerns. Some people in the Huddersfield neighborhood still sympathized with George Mellor (arrested on 22 October and by the date of this letter jailed in York for the murder of the Marsden manufacturer, William Horsfall). The language of morality and moral struggle ("good and righteous," "glory," and "monsters") overrides even the language of political oppression ("tyrant" and "persicuteth") and completely replaces the juridical language of previous West Riding documents.

The letter is among the most difficult to read of all of the Luddite documents, largely due to the rough handwriting, the poor grammar, some missing words, the bleeding through of ink from both sides of each sheet, and the poor condition of the paper itself. The names of two persons mentioned in the letter prove especially difficult to decipher. The name that I render as "Whitehead" is probably the spy or informer whose deposition, which helped to indict several Huddersfield Luddites, appears in General Maitland's correspondence to the Home Office, preserved in H. O. 42/125. The name that I have transcribed as "Ferraby" is nearly indecipherable, but the name clearly begins with a capital "F" and ends with a "y." There was a Special Constable John Ferraby recruited for Secret Service in Yorkshire and Lancashire. His name appears in H. O. 40/2 in General Maitland's Secret Service expenditures for 30 August 1812.

Radcliffe Papers 126/95.

❖   ❖   ❖

Joseph Radcliffe Esq
Milns Bridge House
near Huddersfield

J. Radcliffe Esq

Unjust Judge

This is to inform thee that thy life will be taken from thee the very first oppertunity which will take place before the 2 of January 1813 for we will wa^{t}ch thee Both Day and But we will fulfill our promise to the Committee this is the last warning that thou will have from us thou wicked tyrant who persicuteth the Good and Righteous allso we are determined to murder 2 of thy wicked Servants Before the Expiration of this year I am ordered to give them this last warning But ther lives is determined on, I mean Ferraby & Whitehead for ther dilligence in hunting after our distrest Brotherhood both night and day for they are Both in there Glory which dragging our poor Brothers before the thou wicked man But though Meller be in York Castle we have thousands in this neibourhood left that shal much Glory to Rid the world 3 monsters and as sure as I have spoken the words thou with them will be destroyed Before the time they are in our poor Every week and thou will be watched closer than even Mr. Horsfall was is will be down [62] if in thy own Grounds and the persons suffer instant death for it for we shall Emortalise our reasons to further ages to Rid the world of such a monster as thou art till then I Remain thy mortal Enimey yrs Secretary to the
Brotherhood
October 29th 1812

Y22 ❖ 30 November 1812: Letter from George Mellor at York Castle to Thomas Ellis at Longroyd near Huddersfield

While imprisoned in York Castle, George Mellor attempted to pass a letter to a friend, Thomas Ellis[63] at Longroyd, containing advice for his cousin on what sort of testimony the family ought to offer at Mellor's trial. The letter was intercepted, and a copy came to Radcliffe enclosed in a letter from Henry Hobhouse at Lincoln's Inn.

Radcliffe Papers 126/127(a); H. O. 42/123, dated 30 November 1812.

❖ ❖ ❖

I now take the liberty of informing you that I am in good health, as by the blessing of God. I hope they will find you well. Please to give my respects to my cousin and tell him to stick fast by what he swore the first time before Ratcliffe and I hope his wife will do the same, that I left their House before 5 o Clock and I did not have any thing at their Hous, and if the Boy swears any thing else my cousin to contradict him and say he told him a different Story, that there had been a man and left them, and he did not know him, and as for the Girl she cannot swear any thing. I know that will harm me, and tell the Boys to stick by what they said the first time if not they are proven forsworn tell him and his wife, I hope they will befriend me and never mind their work for if I come home I will do for them. Remember a Soul is of more value than work or Gold. I have heard you are petitioning for a Parliamentary Reform and I wish these names to be given as follows G. M. Mark Hill James Haigh Joseph Thornton Wm Thorp Geo Rigge Saml Booth John Hodges C. Cockcroft James Brook Jos. Brook Geo. Brook James Brook C Thornton Jonathan Dean Jms Walker Joshua Schonefield Jms Cihorsfield[64] Thomas Smith James Storkey Anthony Walker Joseph Greenwood Thomas Green Benjamin Sigg Geo. Ludge Wm Hodgson Geo. Brook Wm Barnard Geo. Beaumont David Morehouse Wm Whitehead Joseph Fisher John Battley Jon Lamb Jon Shore Benjamin Hincliff Geo. Horten Jon^n Laild Jon Farrset James Whitehouse. Give my respects to all enquiring friends, and accept these few lines from your friend.

Y23 ❖ 1812: "Address to Cotton Weavers & Others," Huddersfield

One of the texts that Radcliffe included in his collection of Luddite papers is the "Address to Cotton Weavers & Others." Radcliffe gives no indication why an address directed to cotton weavers would have surfaced in the woolen districts, but the address is less about wool and machines than about the origin of hunger in political oppression. The Lockean argument that labor confers property rights upon the laborer was the basis for several Luddite texts, including this one, and it provided a language that enabled writers to make the leap from economic to political issues.

The only indications of the document's origin are a Huddersfield street address, "M^r [or M^{rs}] Alexander Burlington, Quay," and a Huddersfield postmark. Radcliffe includes in his own handwriting a year for the "Address," 1812. A Luddite oath follows the "Address," as in the Radcliffe Papers.

Radcliffe Papers I Appendix, Item 78, which was acquired in 1993 by the West Yorkshire Archives Service, Leeds.

❖   ❖   ❖

An Address to Cotton Weavers & Others

Friends and fellow Mortals, long & tedious has been the oppression that you are labouring under, & the prospect before you only tends to embitter y^r days, y^r existance will be shortened, & y^r many children will become fatherless if you tamely submit much longer to wear that yoke, & to bear that Burden which is intollerable for human nature to endure, frequently you have uselessly applied to Government, to Magistrates, & to Manufacturers, but all to no purpose—what then is to be done—will you still calmly submit to endure that Arrogance Tyranny and Oppression that hath so long been exercised over you—Will you suffer your Children to be tortured out of existance, by bearing the lashes of hunger & nakedness, & yourselves insolently degraded by those very men that are living in luxury & Extravagance from the fruits of y^r labour—there is no doubt but many of you are well assured that the present unjust, unnecessary and destructive war is the Cause of your present Calamity—who are they then that have always been Stedfast & Constant advocates for this War—have not the greatest part of our Manufacturors, not to say Magistrates, who are they who have made themselves Rich since the War's Commencement, they are a few in every principal Town through this distressed Kingdom. from whence did their riches proceed, Methinks I hear a Voice say, all riches proceed from the servile & feeble hand of slavery. Who are they that are in the full enjoyment of their own Labour. None, for the Rich & artificial great, Labour not, nor do they ever intend to do, in consequence of which the just rights of the servile slave is innocently and unjustly taken from him–Friends & fellow sufferers, how must justice be trampled under foot–how long must the natural rights of mortal man be held from y^r feeble sight, or how long will you bear your unparalelled suffering, & permit yourselves to be Robbed of more than four-fifths of the fruits of y^r labour–to solicit is in vain, to Petition is perfect Stupidity–as well might you solicit the Robber on the High way to give you back the property he had taken from you, or as well might you petition to head y^r Cause–You have but one life to lose. Death you must meet with, & to die with hunger is the most miserable, to Perish in the midst of that plenty that you have laboured for, is the most Dastardly–It is a Duty you owe to yourself & to the rising Generation, to put a stop to the unjust & lawless wheels of Tyranny–It is in y^r power and the immutable & unalterable Laws of Nature require it from your hands–It has often been said it is lawful & right for a Man to do what he will with his own–But this requires y^r serious consideration, in the first place you must determine what is a mans own, you must lay aside all Artificial Tyranical & unjust laws & simply look to the unerring Laws of Nature that are the same in all ages of the World. By so doing you will immediately see that nothing is justly a mans own but that he hath meritted by his own industry–but if you shew Lenity & admit that all is a man's own that he is in possession of, you will soon see that it is not right for him to do what he pleaseth with it–admitting it doth no harm to any Creature. But if it can be proved that his proceedings are injurious to Society, then Society hath an undoubted right to put a sudden stop to his Vile proceedings–But every thing is out of order through the whole– & the admission of one evil renders the Tyrant a pretence to plead the necessity of another–& thus the World has gone on for numberless generations--till at last the insulted & degraded slaves of Brittain are involved in the lawless & direful Whirlpool of Misery & Want. O', injured and degraded fellow sufferers, look around you & behold the rights you are deprived of - You who are as free born as your Vile oppressors–There was a fair Creation ready to recieve you the moment you came into existance. A fertile Land that ought to have cost you nothing but the pains of Cultivating it. But not an Inch on the habitable Globe is yours. Tyranny hath deprived you of it. Nor have you time to behold the fair & free Creation of heaven the wide realms of necessary Care before you, & despair & destruction invades y^r wretched dwellings–Can you then any longer bear to hear your innocent & helpless Children crying to you for food, or to behold them Clothed in filthy rags - & yourself treated with disdain and ridicule & scorn by those very men that are unjustly feasting on the fruits of your slavery. Can you bear with impunity to see you rights and priviledges thus trampled upon by a venal & profligate Band of Robbers. Insulted mortals, examine yourselves, and ask where are our rights that Bounteous Nature bestowed upon us. And you will see that they are fled from us for ever unless you Rise from y^r lethargy of Stupid Misery, and Boldly dare to tell your oppressors that you are determined to enjoy your natural rights–Viz–the fruits of your labour as these rights are founded in the unerring laws of the Great Creator

The Oath

I AB on my own Voluntary will & accord do declare and solemnly swear that I will never reveal to any person or persons, in any place or places under the Canopy of Heaven, the Name or Names of any Persons who compose this secret Committee, their secret proceedings, Meeting place, abode, dress, features, Connections, or any thing else that may lead to a discovery of the same, either by Word, Deed or Sign–under the penalty of being sent out of this World by the first Brother who shall meet me, My name & Character blotted out of Existance & never to be remembered but with contempt & abhorance, I further more do swear that I will use my best endeavours to punnish by Death any Traitor or Traitors, should any rise up amongst us, wherever I can find him or them, and though he should fly to the Verge of Nature I will pursue him with unceasing Vengeance, so help me God, and assist me to keep this my oath inviolable, Amen so be it

---

Y24 ❖ January 1813: Letter from "L. M." at Elland to "Cartlege Brow Bridge near Elland"

In the last weeks of 1812 and the first weeks of 1813, several threats were sent to Mr. Cartledge, described by Lieutenant Alfred Cooper of the West Suffolk Militia as the chief constable of Elland. In his letter, which encloses the threat below, Cooper says that Cartledge received many threatening letters, including one that said, "though Mellor had been hanged, he died *game* and there were many Mellors left to avenge him." Like some of the letters to Radcliffe, this letter is styled rhetorically from a friend. The mention of imprisoned "Enemy's" indicates the writer's concern for the accused murderers of William Horsfall and the Rawfolds attackers recently captured and jailed at York Castle. Like other letters from different regions, the focus on the implement of destruction ("the Ball his Cast that must take your life") is typical of the Luddite preoccupation with instrumentality, how something will be done—perhaps a response in kind to the change in methods of production wrought by machines. Compare the Nottinghamshire letter from "Joe Firebrand" to Messrs. Trevit, Biddles, and Bowler, transcribed earlier.

The letter to Cartledge was forwarded to Major General Acland at Wakefield with Lieutenant Cooper's 17 January 1813 letter from Elland, preserved in H. O. 40/2/3, Part 1. Acland probably forwarded both letters to the Home Office.

H. O. 40/2/4. It appears among documents from the West Riding from January 1813.

❖   ❖   ❖

Cartlege Brow Bridge near Elland

Mr Cartlege I take the opertunity of leting you now that your life his in great Danger you need not think that you have got all your Enemy's into prison has you may think the Ball his Cast that must take your life and that verey won with out you look Damd sharp and your officer likewise.

and your Friend, John Bedford that keeps your Company so much and Brings you news we keep a wach up on him has well has you on the 19th of December he was at Mrs Wilkisons a long with you and 15th at Halifax on the 19th we have Broke his Meshenery and will stop him verey soon take this for good

I Ham Your's

L. M. Elland

Y25 ❖ 12 March 1815: Letter to Radcliffe, Huddersfield

After the period of intense Luddism in Yorkshire had passed, the following 12 March 1815 letter was sent to Sir Joseph Radcliffe, who had lately been made a baronet. Most of the rhetorical evidence in the letter points toward its having been written by someone who was less concerned about ludding than with conveying insults to Radcliffe and implicating James Rourk and Samuel Brook in some trouble. It is likely that the letter is written in the duplicitous well-wisher vein, as it falls under the same category as those that say much, especially to incite fear and proffer insults, but convey little useful information.

Radcliffe Papers 126/136.

❖ ❖ ❖

Sir Joseph Ratcliff   March the 12

1815

Ludding is going to Start here again there has been A meetting of cropers at my house but I heard What the[65] Were on and I would not have them in my House The Way the are for Doing is to asemble in Private Houses and to Start out at a Certain Hour Ludders this time Will Die to a man the Determined to have Blood for Blood the Swear that the Will Shoot thee first old Bellsybub the Call thee and then Shoot the Rest of the Devils after Tom Atkinson Joe Atkinson Bradly mill Cartwright Frank Vickerman Taylor Hill Joe Hirst Marsh and every other Devil that loves Machinerry the Swear the both Shoot and Burn

But to Prevent all Disturbances order the Cavaldry or horse Soldiers to Padrole the Streets and order all lights to Be put out Before tin a Clock other ways thee have no Peace Depend upon much Blood Shed If Proper Steps be not observed James Rourk or Jemy the Gabler is their Principle man He Calls Himself Genral Lud Sir Joseph Ratcliff If thee Do not Send this James Rourk out of this Country the Will be Destruction and Blood Shed He Swears he Will Shoot thee Sir Joseph this James Rourk has been a Delegate to Leeds and all over the Country he lives Marthas Walkers / ould upperhead Row near Joshua Lockets Samuel Brook Croper Deighton near Mr Whitakers those ar Principal men of the Ludders do but Send those off all the others Will be quite[66]

Notes

❖ INTRODUCTION

1. Home Office Papers (H. O.) 42/123.

2. Letter from Nunn to Home Office, 6 December 1811, H. O. 42/118.

3. Malcolm Thomis, *The Luddites: Machine-Breaking in Regency England* (Newton Abbott: David and Charles, 1970), 11.

4. See J. L. Hammond and Barbara Hammond, *The Skilled Labourer, 1760–1832* (London: Longmans, Green, 1919), chap. 9; Frank Darvall, *Popular Disturbances and Public Order in Regency England* (London: Oxford University Press, 1934); E. P. Thompson, *The Making of the English Working Class* (New York: Vintage, 1966), chap. 14; Thomis, *Luddites* chaps. 1 and 6; John Dinwiddy, "Luddism and Politics in the Northern Counties," *Social History* 4.1 (January 1979): 33–63; Adrian Randall, *Before the Luddites: Custom, Community and Machinery in the English Woollen Industry, 1776–1809* (Cambridge: Cambridge University Press, 1991), chaps. 1 and 8; Brian Bailey, *The Luddite Rebellion* (New York: New York University Press, 1998), chap. 10.

5. Duncan Bythell, *The Handloom Weavers: A Study in the English Cotton Industry during the Industrial Revolution* (Cambridge: Cambridge University Press, 1969), 20–21.

6. Randall, *Before the Luddites* 1–2.

7. Charlotte Brontë, *Shirley, A Tale* (London: Smith, Elder, 1849); Phyllis Bentley, *Inheritance* (New York: Macmillan, 1932); G. A. Henty, *Through the Fray: A Tale of the Luddite Riots* (New York: Hurst, 1890); D. F. E. Sykes and G. H. Walker, *Ben O' Bill's, The Luddite: A Yorkshire Tale* (London: Simpkin, Marshall, Hamilton, Kenty, 1898); Ernst Toller, *The Machine-Wreckers: A Drama of the English Luddites in a Prologue and Five Acts* (New York: A. A. Knopf, 1923).

8. Randall has demonstrated the pervasiveness of what he calls a "teleological view of labour history," which, in one form "argues that Luddism took place only where labour

was not effectively organized" (Randall, *Before the Luddites* 150). That view, justly criticized, Randall describes as not only teleological but also tautological.

9. John Bohstedt, *Riots and Community Politics in England and Wales, 1790–1810* (Cambridge: Harvard University Press, 1983), 35.

10. Radcliffe Papers 126/114,West Yorkshire Archives Service, Leeds.

11. Robert Reid, *The Land of Lost Content: The Luddite Revolt, 1812* (London: Heinemann, 1986), 251, citing Edward Baines's report of the trial and execution in *Proceedings under the Special Commission at York* (Leeds: Baines, 1813).

12. E. J. Hobsbawm, *Labouring Men: Studies in the History of Labour* (London: Weidenfeld and Nicolson, 1964) 1.

13. Thompson, *Making of the English Working Class* 515; Thomis, *Luddites* 15.

14. Thomis, *Luddites* 15.

15. The original source for information regarding Nottinghamshire Luddism from March 1811 to February 1812, including the Arnold incident, is the "Brief Statement of the Transactions which have taken place from the commencement of the disturbances in the County of Nottingham and the Town of Nottingham" sent to the Home Office by two London police officers, Nathaniel Conant and Robert Baker, and compiled with the assistance of Nottingham Town Clerk George Coldham. The "Brief Statement" appears in H. O. 42/119. See also Russell, "Luddites" 55; Darvall, *Popular Disturbances* 64–66; Reid, *Land of Lost Content* 58. Thomis misprints the date of the Arnold action, recording it as 1812 rather than 1811 (Thomis, *Luddites* 75).

16. Darvall, *Popular Disturbances* 67.

17. The 24 November 1811 letter and the others cited in this paragraph appear in H. O. 42/117.

18. Several of the December 1811 newspaper negotiations are reproduced and discussed in the chapter on Midlands Luddism.

19. Craig Calhoun, *The Question of Class Struggle: Social Foundations of Popular Radicalism during the Industrial Revolution* (Chicago: University of Chicago Press, 1982), 187.

20. Bohstedt, *Riots and Community Politics* 3–5.

21. Randall, *Before the Luddites* 123–24.

22. John Mee, *Dangerous Enthusiasm: William Blake and the Culture of Radicalism in the 1790s* (New York: Oxford University Press, 1992), 8–9.

23. David Worrall, *Radical Culture: Discourse, Resistance and Surveillance, 1790–1820* (Detroit: Wayne State University Press, 1992), 4, 5.

24. James Epstein, *Radical Expression: Political Language, Ritual, and Symbol in England, 1790–1850* (New York: Oxford University Press, 1994), 5; quoting Thomas Paine, *The Rights of Man* (1792; reprint, Harmondsworth: Penguin, 1984), 42, 71–72.

25. Calhoun, *Question of Class Struggle,* 6–7.

26. Randall, *Before the Luddites,* 243.

27. The distinction between custom (or "the immemorial") and law is drawn by J. G. A.

Pocock in the first three chapters of *The Ancient Constitution and the Feudal Law* (Cambridge: Cambridge University Press, 1987).

28. Calhoun, *Question of Class Struggle* 60.

29. The various statutes are discussed in Hammond and Hammond, *Skilled Labourer*, 168–69.

30. Charter of the Company of Framework Knitters, of the Cities of London and Westminster, the Kingdom of England, and Dominion of Wales (15 Charles II.), Appendix No. 2, Report of the Select Committee on Petitions of the Framework Knitters, House of Commons, London, 1812; hereafter cited without pagination. A copy can also be found in the Guildhall Library, Ref. 16865-7, London. The special sufficiency of the charter for the framework knitters makes irrelevant, for the purpose of this section at least, the problem of differentiating between what we might call an originary document (a single text that anchors a practical discourse on a single temporal origin) and a constitutive document (one in what potentially is a series of texts that, like those that make up the English constitution, evolve a body of rights and discourse).

31. *The Rule Book of the Worshipful Company of Framework Knitters* (London, 1740), vi, notes that the company's power to enact all rules therein derives from the 1663 charter. Chambers notes that the Framework Knitters first sought, and received, a Charter of Incorporation from Cromwell's government in 1657, now in the Guildhall archives with the later charter. A 1655 petition for charter indicates that an "embryonic organization" had been functioning for some time until its membership had risen to a number warranting incorporation. See J. D. Chambers, "The Worshipful Company of Framework Knitters (1657-1778)," *Economica* (November 1929): 299.

32. William Felkin, *A History of the Machine-Wrought Hosiery and Lace Manufacturers* (1867; reprint, New York: Burt Franklin, 1967), 56; Chambers, "Worshipful Company of Framework Knitters" 299–300.

33. Charter of the Company of Framework Knitters; Hammond and Hammond, *Skilled Labourer* 259; Chambers, "The Worshipful Company of Framework Knitters" 302). Ironically, the charter initially benefited the wealthier masters, although smaller masters and assistants benefited more in the next centuries. See Chambers, "The Worshipful Company of Framework Knitters" 303, and George Unwin, *Industrial Organization in the Sixteenth and Seventeenth Centuries* (Oxford: Clarendon Press, 1904), 210–13. Many of these small masters and journeymen fled London, where enforcement of the rules was certain, to the Midlands (Hammond and Hammond, *Skilled Labourer* 221). Some of these same small masters and assistants who had opposed the rules of the company, especially those designating numbers of apprentices and length of apprenticeship, later appealed to the company rules and charter to halt the machinery practices of the larger masters.

34. At H. O. 42/118 is a summary of a cause tried in London at the "sittings" of the Framework Knitters Company. The document is undated and is not enclosed by any letter, but it obviously dates 1809 or after and follows a letter from the duke of Newcastle

to Ryder, dated 13 December 1811. The page immediately preceding the summary reads "No date [1811]." The summary also follows a list of "Delegates from the Country admitted Members and Deputies of the Company. Nov. 1806." The summary provides a clear indication that legal language was not at all unfamiliar to the framework knitters.

Framework Knitters Company

Wm Payne

a Framework Knr residing at Burbage in the Co. of Leicester.

Cause tried at the Sittings in London before Ld Jas Mansfield after Nichs Term 1808

Verdict taken for the Plt. on the 1st. 4th. 5h. Counts in the Declare with £53 Damages.

Motion in arrest of Judgt. KB Term 1809 Judgment arrested.

Declaration--Stated the Charter of Charles the 2d. to the Company and sundry By-Laws as applicable to the Actions, and contained, 6, Counts, Namely

1st.   That Deft exercised the Trade without making Proof of a 7 Years Service of Apprenticeship, and without having been first admitted a Freeman of the Society--Forfeiture every offence 30s./

2d.   That Deft exercised the Trade without having been admitted a Member--forfeit. 30s./

3d.   That Deft exercised the Art without making Proof of Service of 7 Yrs. Apprentsp. Dt. 30s./

4h.   That Deft having served an Apprenticesp of 7 Years to one Wm. Everitt, did delay for 3 Months to be admitted--Forfeit. 30s./

5h.   That Deft taught Thos. Main / not being his Child, or Apprentice lawfully bound, in the said Art. Forfeit. £50.

6h.   That Deft took T. Main an Apprentice, he Deft not having been approved of or allowed to be a Workhousekeeper. D: £5.

35. *Nottingham Review*, 6 December 1811 and 27 December 1811.

36. Darvall, *Popular Disturbances*, 138–39. See also P. Cunningham, *8 April 1813 Circular to Members of Parliament on the Repeal of Statute 5 Eliz. c. 4* (London, 1813).

37. Kirkpatrick Sale mentions the binarizing interpretations of the Luddite risings (economic-industrial versus legal-political), although he does not interrogate them. He writes, "On the question of how political (as opposed to merely industrial), or even revolutionary, the Luddites were, much has been written, most of it merely speculative." See Sale, *Rebels against the Future: The Luddites and Their War on the Industrial Revolution* (Reading: Addison-Wesley, 1995), 301n119. I argue that examining the documents written or relied upon by the Luddites themselves, rather than by authorities and informers corresponding with the treasury solicitor and the Home Office secretary, reveals a legalistic discourse that manages to bridge the political and the economic-industrial with confidence, if not always with grace and accuracy.

38. The authorities seemed to have feared Luddite appropriation of sanctioned discourses. Literacy—the very ability to identify, appropriate, and interpret legitimating documents and discourses that might be employed in the creation of a literate subculture—rated unusually harsh treatment by the authorities responsible for suppressing Luddism. Henry Hobhouse, sent by the treasury solicitor to prosecute the cases before the Special Commission at Chester, was especially interested in making an example of a literate cotton worker, Thomas Whittaker, simply because Whittaker was literate. Hobhouse writes, "The case on which I have the greatest anxiety is that of Whittaker, whom it appeared to me very important to convict, not merely on account of his crime, but because he is a man of superior ability and education and of proportionate influence among his confederates" (Hobhouse to John Beckett, 30 May 1812, H. O. 42/123).

39. "A True Copy of the Articles to be Observed by the Woolcombers in Great Britain," H. O. 42/130.

40. See, for example, Thomas Ollyffe's *The Young Clerk's Tutor Enlarged: Being a Most Useful Collection of the Best Precedents of Recognizances, Obligations, Conditions, Acquittances, Bills of Sale, Warrants of Attorney, &c.* (London: Battersby, 1717). Perhaps even the suspected writer of some of the Midlands Luddite documents might have had a vocational familiarity with legal forms. Reporting to the Home Office on events in Nottingham, Special Constable Conant writes, "There is a poor half starved dissolute & profligate fellow here who has been sometimes a hackney writer to the Attorneys, whose hand writing they have sometimes thought might be traced, in disguize, in some of the threatening letters received here, at an early part of the disturbances" (Conant to Home Office, 5 February 1812, H. O. 42/120).

41. *Nottingham Journal*, 28 December 1811.

42. This contrast with Yorkshire Luddism shall be developed at length later.

43. Wai Chee Dimock, "Class, Gender, and a History of Metonymy," in *Rethinking Class: Literary Studies and Social Formations*, ed. Wai Chee Dimock and Michael T. Gilmore (New York: Columbia University Press, 1994), 59.

44. Kenneth D. Brown, *The English Labour Movement, 1700–1951* (New York: St. Martin's Press, 1982), 82.

45. Hammond and Hammond, *Skilled Labourer* 264, quoting H. O. 42/120 (emphasis added).

46. Darvall, *Popular Disturbances* 207.

47. William Toone, *The Magistrate's Manual: Or, A Summary of the Duties and Powers of a Justice of the Peace* (London, 1813), 399.

48. Felkin, *History* 439; Hammond and Hammond, *Skilled Labourer* 266.

49. Bohstedt, *Riots and Community Politics*, 69–70, 72. By "communitarian," I mean to describe traditions, duties, practices, and ideals that are centered on a community defined by the geographical proximity of its members to each other and a commonality among them in economic, trade, or other social interests. I choose not to employ Anne Janowitz's otherwise very useful definition of communitarian—figuring "identity as emerging

from a fabric of social narratives, with their attendant goals and expectations." For one thing, her definition appears to have been constructed in opposition to her definition of individualism in a discussion of romantic theory. For another, her use of the attendant idea of embeddedness seems to presuppose an idea of entrenchment that I wish to avoid, especially in a chapter on Luddism in Manchester, where workers had little experience of embeddedness. On the distinction between "voluntaristic individualism" and "embedded communitarianism," see Anne Janowitz, *Lyric and Labour in the Romantic Tradition* (Cambridge: Cambridge University Press, 1998), 13.

50. John Foster, *Class Struggle and the Industrial Revolution: Early Industrial Capitalism in Three English Towns* (London: Weidenfeld and Nicolson, 1974), 31.

51. Bohstedt describes his "classic" model in the second chapter of *Riots and Community Politics* 27–68. A concise summary appears on p. 68.

52. Ibid., 126.

53. Bythell, *The Handloom Weavers* 2, 8.

54. On the one hand, see Bamford's description of the close interaction between a weaver and his master in *The Autobiography of Samuel Bamford: Early Days*, 2 vols. (London, 1849), 1:119–25. For a different view, describing the requisites for setting up as a cotton manufacturer and other information on those persons who were most likely to set up as manufacturers, see the discussion of David Whitehead and others in Bythell, *The Handloom Weavers* 30–31.

55. William Radcliffe, *The Origin of the New System of Manufacture Called "Powerloom Weaving," and the Purposes for Which this System Was Invented and Brought into Use, Fully Explained in a Narrative, Containing William Radcliffe's Struggles through Life to Remove the Cause Which Has Brought this Country to Its Present Crisis* (Stockport: J. Lomax, 1828), 10.

56. Bythell, *The Handloom Weavers* 31.

57. Bohstedt, *Riots and Community Politics* 126–31.

58. Ibid., 91.

59. Hammond and Hammond, *Skilled Labourer,* 58–60.

60. Ibid., 62–64.

61. Bohstedt, *Riots and Community Politics* 79.

62. Ibid., 75.

63. Ibid., 85.

64. H. O. 42/117.

65. Bythell, *Handloom Weavers* 25–27.

66. McConnell and Kennedy Papers 2/1/18/3/c–e.

67. See, for example, the letters from Robert Graham of Railton and Company in McConnel and Kennedy Papers 2/1/18/8.

68. Foster, *Class Struggle and the Industrial Revolution* 38–43.

69. Ibid., 48.

70. Ibid., 43.

71. Ibid., 38.

72. Ibid., 37; Hay Scrapbook, with jottings from March 1812, Chetham's Library, Manchester.

73. Thomis, *The Luddites*, 96; see also Wood's 28 April 1812 letter in H. O. 42/122.

74. Curiously, John Dinwiddy does not mention the letter in his article "Luddism and Politics in the Northern Counties," even though the letter would perhaps factor into his argument that Luddism was not part of a revolutionary, underground network but did share many features with Jacobinical organizations. See Dinwiddy's discussion of the Manchester Exchange riots in "Luddism and Politics in the Northern Counties" 43.

75. Dinwiddy, "Luddism and Politics in the Northern Counties" 60.

76. Dimock, "Class, Gender, and a History of Metonymy" 59; citing Kenneth Burke, *A Grammar of Motives* (Berkeley: University of California Press, 1969), 503–11.

77. Dimock, "Class, Gender, and a History of Metonymy" 59.

78. Randall, *Before the Luddites* 15.

79. Thompson, *Making of the English Working Class* 541.

80. Randall, *Before the Luddites* 263.

81. Thomis, *The Luddites* 170–72.

82. Randall, *Before the Luddites* 149–51.

83. Ibid., 20–23.

84. See Hammond and Hammond, *Skilled Labourer* 168–70; Randall, *Before the Luddites* 120, 201.

85. Randall, *Before the Luddites* 110–12.

86. Randall, *Before the Luddites* 131–32. Significantly, the Brief Institution also hired a solicitor, a "Mr. Wilmot." Perhaps Wilmot provided the cloth dressers with some of their familiarity with legal discourse (131–33).

87. Ibid., 175–76.

88. Hammond and Hammond, *Skilled Labourer* 184.

89. Randall, *Before the Luddites* 178–79.

90. Alan Brooke and Lesley Kipling, *Liberty or Death: Radicals, Republicans, and Luddites, 1793–1823* (Honley: Workers History Publications, 1993), 7–15.

91. Kirkpatrick Sale, *Rebels against the Future: The Luddites and Their War on the Industrial Revolution, Lessons for the Computer Age* (Reading, Mass.: Addison-Wesley, 1995), 119.

92. Thompson, *Making of the English Working Class* 530.

93. Sale, *Rebels against the Future* 119.

94. Thomis, *The Luddites* 86.

95. Thompson, *Making of the English Working Class* 530.

96. Sale, *Rebels against the Future* 119.

97. Thompson, *Making of the English Working Class* 530.

98. Randall, *Before the Luddites* 123.

99. H. O. 42/117.

100. Randall, *Before the Luddites* 242.

101. Ibid., 243. Randall provides a detailed summary of Jackson's efforts before Parlia-

ment on behalf of the cloth workers, deriving largely from Jackson's *The Speech of Randle Jackson, Esq. to the Committee of the House of Common Appointed to Consider the State of the Woollen Manufacture* (London: Randle Jackson and Joseph Gurney, 1806) and an anonymous pamphlet, *Observations on Woollen Machinery* (Leeds: E. Baines, 1803). The framework knitters, too, attempted to interpret the charter in their petition to Parliament in 1812.

102. Brooke and Kipling, *Liberty or Death* 10–11. Similar documents were found in April 1812 after a Luddite raid on Joseph Foster's mill near Horbury. Those documents were forwarded to the Home Office by William Hay and appear in H. O. 40/1.

103. Randall, *Before the Luddites* 28–29, 37.

104. Ibid., 278–79.

105. Ibid., 279.

106. Brooke and Kipling, *Liberty or Death* 8.

107. Ibid., 9.

108. Roger Wells has detailed the activities of the United Britons in Yorkshire. See *Insurrection: The British Experience, 1795–1803* (Gloucester: Alan Sutton Publishing Limited, 1983), 226–37.

109. Radcliffe Manuscripts 1.578; quoted in Brooke and Kipling, *Liberty or Death* 8.

110. Bohstedt, *Riots and Community Politics* 152.

111. Randall, *Before the Luddites* 269.

112. Thomis and Brian Bailey speculate that the two letters were written by the same author; however, no stylistic features are cited as reasons for their speculations. See Thomis, *The Luddites* 86, and Bailey, *The Luddite Rebellion* (New York: New York University Press, 1998), 49–50.

113. The same sort of containing maneuver is employed in the Nottinghamshire document titled "By the Framework Knitters, A Declaration" (M10).

❖ MIDLANDS DOCUMENTS

1. John Rule has usefully summarized the dispute in *The Labouring Classes in Early Industrial England, 1750–1850* (London: Longman, 1986), 369–75. Somewhat less useful, but more recent, is Brian Bailey's discussion in *The Luddite Rebellion* (New York: New York University Press, 1998), 144–53.

2. George Rudé, *The Crowd in History: A Study of Popular Disturbances in France and England, 1730–1848* (London: Lawrence and Wishart, 1981), 90.

3. Radcliffe Papers 126/46, West Yorkshire Archives Service, Leeds.

4. Point net, a type of mesh for hose, was first manufactured in 1776. None of the four men (Flint, Taylor, Morris, and Lindley) credited with the invention of the machine used to make it thought highly of the invention: "[A]lthough the mesh produced was the nearest approach to the long-desired lacey mesh and was of the regular honeycomb-shape, it, when wet, or even slightly damped, curled up and shrunk into a shapeless, stringy mass.

This was because it was made 'single press.'" Later, Rogers, a Mansfield stockinger, produced a doubled-pressed fast point net, which could be cut in any direction and would not shrink or "rove." By 1810 there were 1,500 to 1,800 such machines, 30 inches wide, in Nottingham, according to W. H. Webb in "The History of the Machine-Made Lace Manufacture," *Textile Recorder* (15 June 1916): 41–42. Making of the single press was an objectionable practice that motivated several of the Luddite documents transcribed here.

5. The two words following "By Order" appear to be an individual's name, the first name beginning with a T, the second with a D. Although the name appears to have been struck out or smeared, some letters are evidently risers, narrowing the range of possible names and suggesting "Thos." I am less certain that "Death" is a proper reading of the last name.

6. William Felkin, *A History of the Machine-Wrought Hosiery and Lace Manufacturers* (1867; reprint, New York: Burt Franklin, 1967), 232.

7. *Nottingham Journal*, 16 November 1811.

8. Roy A. Church and Stanley D. Chapman, "Gravener Henson and the Making of the English Working Class," in *Land, Labour and Population in the Industrial Revolution: Essays Presented to J. D. Chambers*, ed. Eric L. Jones and G. E. Mingay (London: Edward Arnold, 1967), 142.

9. Thomas Hayne of Nottingham, in a letter explaining to Secretary Ryder the problems in the town, remarks that the practice of reducing labor costs by paying workers in goods (thread, cloth, and occasionally other items) was "very ruinous to the Workmen and injurious to the trade at large." He continues: "When the Workmen receive this payment in goods, except in that part which may consist of the necessaries of life, they have no other means of turning these into money but by having recourse to the Pawnbroker, and we can pretty well estimate what such a man will leave for the Workmen" (Hayne to Ryder, 12 February 1812, H. O. 42/131).

10. Lord Newcastle seems to have held such a view, although with an emphasis on pacification before relief. In a 20 November 1811 letter to Richard Ryder at the Home Office, Lord Newcastle writes of the inhabitants of the vicinity of Mansfield, "They certainly are very much to be pitied and when every thing is perfectly tranquil and that they find themselves subdued by being obliged to submit to the Laws I hope we may be able by some means to relieve them" (H. O. 42/117).

11. In the *Nottingham Review* and the *Nottingham Journal*, the names appear in two columns.

12. John Russell, "The Luddites," *Transactions of the Thoroton Society* 10 (1906): 55.

13. "Town of Nottingham" Resolutions, *Nottingham Review*, 27 December 1811. In the same list of resolutions, the council also offered a reward for information about a "certain threatening Anonymous Paper, addressed to the Mayor, and received by him on Sunday the 8th of December Instant, intimating to him, that unless he complied with certain wishes express by the Author or Writer, it was intended on the part of the Author or Writer to commit Murder upon some Person or Persons therein described. . . ."

14. Russell includes notes on Transcript 3 intended to clarify some of the words and references in the letter. He says that "fugoffis" is "perhaps the same 'fog-office,' and used as a description of the meeting place of the special committee, by way of a gibe at the inability of the authorities, either by vigilance or reward, to discover perpetrators of outrages" (Russell, "The Luddites" 62).

15. Dr. John Willis was a physician specializing in mental diseases. Russell, "The Luddites" 62, notes that he had been called in 1811 to treat George III. That news had been reported in the *Nottingham Review*, 29 November 1811.

16. St. Luke's is a London hospital for the insane.

17. Malcolm Thomis, *Luddism in Nottinghamshire* (London: Phillimore, 1972), 18.

18. A seal (a circle enclosing an "S.") appears in the Russell transcription immediately to the right of "By order of / King Ludd."

19. Unfortunately, there has been a tendency to ignore or downplay the charter. Even though he professes a measure of sympathy with the Luddites, Kirkpatrick Sale describes the basis of stockinger claims as "*some charter* issued by Charles II in the 17th century" (emphasis added). See Sale, *Rebels against the Future: The Luddites and Their War on the Industrial Revolution, Lessons for the Computer Age* (Reading, Mass.: Addison-Wesley, 1995), 99. Brian Bailey mentions the charter only once and ascribes to the charter granted by Charles II the wrong date, 1657. See Bailey, *Luddite Rebellion*, 1.

20. J. L. Hammond and Barbara Hammond, *The Skilled Labourer, 1760–1832* (London: Longmans, Green, 1919), 259. The "endorsement" perhaps means nothing more than that the "Declaration" was sent to the Home Office without an enclosing letter identifying the sender.

21. Douglas has "Charles II."

22. Douglas has "28th."

23. Douglas has "III."

24. Douglas adds "as to."

25. Douglas inserts "by" following "to."

26. Douglas has "print." This is a material misreading on Douglas's part.

27. See later the open letter from "General Ludd" addressed to an "Unknown Stranger," returning goods stolen by some "Villinds" who had accompanied the general on a raid at Clifton (*Leeds Mercury*, 15 February 1812, and *Nottingham Review*, 7 February 1812).

28. Rutland's letter to Ryder also reports the result of posting the prince regent's proclamation and offer of reward for information: "I ought however to mention that soon after the Royal Proclamation was posted on the Church Door of Sheepshead in this County, a Handbill was exhibited at its side, stating that 'as the Government had offered a Reward of £50 for the conviction of offenders, there were 50 Bullets ready for the body of the first man who should give information.'" (5 January 1812, H. O. 42/119).

29. Many of the manufacturers who signed the 15 December 1811 "Resolutions" also are listed as signers of the 13 February 1812 proposals (transcribed later in the text). Most of

them appear to be small manufacturers and masters. The "Resolutions" include condem-
nations of payment in goods, disapproval (as "injurious to the Trade") of the manufacture
of single-press point lace net, and disavowal of two anonymous letters from "Friends of
Ned Ludd, and Friends to Reason and Justice."

30. Malcolm Thomis, *The Luddites: Machine-Breaking in Regency England* (Newton Abbott: David and Charles, 1970), 49.

31. The writer is attempting to spell out "two-course hole" and "single press." In the
manuscript, the writer seems initially to have spelled out "ole," then extended the "l" un-
derneath, and finally inserted, above a caret, "ole."

32. Roy Palmer, *The Sound of History* (Oxford: Oxford University Press, 1988), 104.

33. The papers are labeled: "1812 Jany 27. Statement of Outrages & from Nottingham, NB. This Statement was made out by the Police Magistrates during their Stay at
Nottingham with the assistance of Mr. Coldham the Town Clerk" (H. O. 42/119).

34. Full-fashioned work is a hosiery article that is woven in a single piece rather than
cut and resewn.

35. The line describes aspects of the process by which stocking material manufactured
on wide frames was made into hose. "Colting" refers to the practice of hiring workers, described as "colts" because of their lack of maturity and experience within the framework
knitting trade, who had not completed apprenticeships. "Cutting" and "squaring" refer to
the practice of using large pieces of wide-knit fabric and cutting them into smaller pieces,
which were sewn into hose.

36. Gravener Henson, *History of the Framework Knitters* (1831; reprint, Newton Abbott:
David and Charles, 1970), 315–18; Felkin, *History*, 174.

37. *Nottingham Review* 21 February 1812.

38. Thomis, *Luddites* 179.

39. In his letter to Ryder, Thomas Hayne explains that the "Two Course" involves two
operations in making the hole. The method approved by the trade is "6 Course requiring 6
Operations," resulting in a much more durable article (Hayne to Ryder, 12 February 1812,
H. O. 42/131).

40. This word in the manuscript is difficult to read. It could possibly be "be," although
the first letter resembles the writer's certain "d" more than it resembles the "b."

41. Contrast E. P. Thompson's version in *The Making of the English Working Class* (New
York: Vintage Press, 1966), 556.

42. Ibid., 187.

43. Samuel Whitbread, MP, was one of a number of supporters of reform and political
liberties affiliated with Sir Francis Burdett and H. G. Bennet in the House of Commons.
Whitbread was among those rumored in depositions (such as those of Barnsley weaver
Thomas Broughton) to be intending to lead a revolution or "general rising," of which
Luddism was thought to be a part (Thompson, *Making* 486, 580). Thomis mentions that
one writer—"from a lunatic fringe of people whose scare stories were not based on any real
attempt to assess their local situation but were the products of vivid or disturbed imagi-

nation"—reported from York on 15 July 1812 that "Burdett and Whitbread were providing great encourgement to the Luddites through their speeches" (Thomis, *Luddites* 83; citing H. O. 42.125, 15 July 1812). Regardless of the accuracy of the York letter, clearly, Whitbread was perceived to be friend to the oppressed textile workers. For information on Thomas Broughton, see Thompson, *Making* 578, Hammond and Hammond, *Skilled Labourer* 314, 325).

44. My own brief search for victims of Luddite attacks named in the Home Office Papers and in some of the histories does not indicate that any of the hosiers listed as having acceded to the Plain Silk Hands's proposals suffered the destruction of frames. A detailed study of the correlation between the hosiers' acceding to the proposals and immunity from Luddite attack could perhaps clarify the relationship between the Luddites and the Committee of Plain Silk Hands.

45. Craig Calhoun, *The Question of Class Struggle: Social Foundations of Popular Radicalism during the Industrial Revolution* (Chicago: University of Chicago Press, 1982), 60–61.

46. The word is barely legible, but it appears to end with a lowercase "l." Russell reads the word as "practicable" and the vertical line as an exclamation mark. The word could be "practicall" or "practicable," but the generally literate character of the rest of the letter indicates that Russell might be correct in reading it as he does.

47. Russell transcribes "Signed Joe Firebrand."

48. A. Aspinall, *The Early English Trade Unions: Documents from the Home Office Papers in the Public Record Office* (London: Batchworth Press, 1949), has "Henton," but the manuscript reads "Henson." "G. Henson" is certainly Gravener Henson, the Nottingham framework knitter who tried to advance the stockingers' claims through legitimate channels and who typically signed his name to his well-reasoned and carefully crafted texts. Compare his 11 February 1812 advertisement, "To the FRAMEWORK KNITTERS of NOTTINGHAM, THE COUNTY THEREOF and the TOWNS AND VILLAGES ADJACENT 666" (H. O. 42/120).

49. Aspinall's addition.

50. The manuscript seems to indicate that the letter preceding "Ludd" is "C," rather than the "N" that might be expected. Thomis reads it as "C" (Thomis, *Nottinghamshire* 43). It is unclear whether the letter in H. O. 42/120 was copied by a Home Office clerk, as many were. The letter's having been copied may explain the discrepancy.

51. By "wars," I refer to the practices of publishing a document and responding in the same print genre to that document. The Nottingham newspapers typically printed a single, anonymous poem in each issue. Most of the poems were celebrations of the season, reminiscences of times past, or eulogies for the British navy. The poem "Industry Distressed" was printed in the *Nottingham Review*, 6 March 1812:

INDUSTRY DISTRESSED.

A TRUE TALE.

How chang'd are the times! I've oft seen the day
    Of Christmas approach, free from frowns;

My creditor's bills with ease I could pay,
    With guineas, or shillings, or crowns!

Nor was the term, *Bankers*, in our village known,
    To mean more than hedger or ditcher,
That work'd on the margin of fields that were sown,
    Whilst his wife to the well took the pitcher.

But fine flourish'd paper has 'minished our coin,
    And rais'd our banks without fences;
And knaves with their *rag-money* often combine,
    Enough to distract a man's senses.

By frugal industry, I had made it my care
    To provide for the winter of age;
But unwarily caught in the bankruptcy snare,
    Nought now can my sorrow assuage.

My barrels that used to be stor'd with GOOD ALE,
    And wine which the elder produc'd,
Are worm-eat, and rotten, and not fit for sale,
    Having many years never been used.

And useless the stone, where the pig lay in pork,
    While others remain'd in the sty;
Nor hear we as once the carol or joke,
    When say round our large Christmas pye.

No more my old consort nor I meet the smile,
    This season was wont to produce;
Nor share in those visits which time so beguile,
    Such visits being now out of use.

Not a vestige remains of my once happy lot,
    The workhouse my refuge must be;
Must quit with reluctance my beautiful cot,
    So dear to my partner and me.

That cot, where my ancestors liv'd in repute,
    The spot where I drew my first breath;
such heart-rending thoughts, so sever and acute,
    A period will soon have in death.

But what makes my misery fully complete,
    My frame by NED LUDD has been broke;

Release from these troubles, kind death I intreat,
  But vainly thine aid I invoke.

But, hush! all rash thoughts which troubles create,
  I'll bow to adversity's rod;
With humble submission I'll yield to my fate,
  And happiness seek in my G O D.

52. The elided names are Eldon and Ryder.

53. Since the mid-eighteenth century, Tewkesbury hosiers had undersold Nottingham and Leicester by producing hose of inferior quality. On the conflict between Nottingham and Tewkesbury masters, which resulted in the Tewkesbury Act (6 George III, cap. 29), see Henson, *History* 359–71.

54. The tactic of opening at the post offices letters suspected to have been by Luddites or their sympathizers was practiced widely, having been advocated by Sir Frances Freeling of the postmaster general's office and by Nottinghamshire hosier William Nunn in a 19 December 1811 letter to the Home Office (H. O. 42/118). Other letters transcribed here were discovered in just such a fashion. On the government's use of the Post Office as a surveillance arm, see Kenneth Ellis, *The Post Office in the Eighteenth Century: A Study in Administrative History* (London: Oxford University Press, 1958), 60–70.

55. The phrase "nothing in hand" has a number of possible sources. Ecclesiastes 5 contains a passage about inequity in distribution of wealth, but the precise phrase in Ecclesiastes is "nothing in his hand" (Ecclesiastes 5:14, KJV), and it seems unlikely that the poet would misquote a Scriptural passage. Another unlikely source is Martin Luther's *Table-Talk*; however, the English translation containing the phrase "nothing in hand" is William Hazlitt's *The Table-Talk of Martin Luther* (London: H. G. Bohn, 1857), DCVI: ("When he [Satan] finds me idle, with nothing in hand, he is very busy, and before I am aware, he wrings from me a bitter sweat; but when I offer him the pointed spear, God's Word, he flies; yet, before he goes, makes a grievous hurricane"). It does not seem likely that a stockinger would quote from German.

Perhaps the most likely source is Samuel Rutherford's sermon "The Deliverance of the Kirk of God," in *Quaint Sermons of Samuel Rutherford, Hitherto Unpublished, with a Preface by the Rev. Andrew A. Bonar D.D.* (London: Hodder and Stoughton, 1885). Rutherford (1600–1661) was a Scottish Nonconformist pastor and political theologian, whose most famous work, *Lex Rex, or The Law and The Prince; a Dispute for the just Prerogatives of King and People*, outlined principles of constitutional government that were later embodied in the Constitution Settlement of 1690 and the United States Constitution. The passage in Rutherford's sermon touches upon some of the themes raised in the poem:

How shall this then be that Babylon shall be destroyed and we restored? The Lord answers this, that the deliverance is coming, but it would not come until that day that He had appointed for it. To teach the Kirk of God to give God that much—

as alas! He gets but little of that kind of us—that He will do for His own people at length, though not for the present, and to look to that word in Psalm 25:22, that the Lord will redeem Israel out of all his troubles, and Psalm 62:5: "My soul wait thou only upon the Lord, for my expectation is from Him," even to make God's omnipotence the object of their faith and of their hope, and learn to wait upon God only. "I would do that," says some, *"but I have nothing in hand."* But we must remember that all their stock is in God's hand who hope rightly in Him; for if they had anything in hand, it were not hope, as it is, Rom. 8:24: "Hope that is seen is not hope." But the thing which one sees not is properly the thing that he hopes for. And so the less we have in hand we have the greater reason of hope. That no man may be troubled with this, I have nothing for the present; but in such a case learn to believe in God, and then ye have the more. How many rich men are there in the world who have no more but only pieces of paper for all that they have, and yet men will account them rich, albeit there be not two pence in their purse. The hoper and onwaiter upon God is this way rich, yet all his sums are in God's hands, who pays His annual rents well, so that His annual rents they are better than the world's principal sum. ("The Deliverance" 152–77, emphasis added)

The sermon had circulated as a pamphlet during the eighteenth century.

56. Perhaps an allusion to a line in Byron's "An Ode to the Framers of the Frame Bill" ("Who when ask'd for a remedy, sent down a rope") as well as to the Frame Bill itself, which imposed hanging as punishment for frame breaking.

57. The quotation is from Alexander Pope's *Essay on Man*, Epistle IV:

Order is heav'n's first law; and this confest,
Some are, and must be, greater than the rest,
More rich, more wise; but who infers from hence
That such are happier, shocks all common sense.

58. One letter from Nottingham sheds some light on the proceedings below board before and during the March assizes. It comes from an informer who seems to hold a grudge against some of the frame breakers. Dated 26 February 1812, it is enclosed with a 1 March 1812 letter from General Hawker to the Home Office:

i have rote this that ou may kno sum of the frame brakers, thomas bukson the barber in owld basford and thomas willbore he lives upon the flat in new basford and mr dosley in owld basford and the maiser grines that stand stands in Nottingham Market against the change on a saturday grindin, thees is sum of the Worst of frame brakers, and is at all the frame brakin, and thomas Saxton in new basford is one of the head men at layin plans how to go on to get to them. the maiser grines live in sadby lane Nottingham, against the clock and hors, and Elias carnil in bulwel is the head man at the committe and he lay plans how they must proseed, and thay seen to Murder sum then that thay do not like and the way thay meen to Murder them is that when thay see them with a rope with a nouse in the middle of it, and one is to put it over is head and then thay pull it at each end of the rope til he is ded and thay meen to send sum delegates from bullwel and basford to Manchester to the Wevers thear. and all this is true as I have rote as true as thear is a god in heaven but you must Exques me putin my name to it, for I dar not. (H. O. 42/121)

Evidently, the letter had an effect, because William Carnell (or Carnill) was captured, imprisoned in Nottingham, and sent before Judge Bayley, then trying cases of machine breaking.

59. In the manuscript, the name is nearly illegible. Thomis's transcription of it, Byrnny, is reasonable (Thomis, *Nottinghamshire* 54).

60. What I have represented with the two closing brackets is actually one larger closing bracket encompassing both lines on the manuscript.

61. Thomis transcribes the closing as "Yours for Genl Ludd/a trueman." It may be that "true man" was a real name, as many framework knitters in the vicinity were surnamed "Trueman." See, for example, the 1814 letter from William Trueman to Bullock (H. O. 42/139, reproduced here and in Thomis, *Nottinghamshire* 77.

62. In the historical treatments of Luddism, there is occasional mention of the possibility that local militia sympathized with Luddite aims. The perception of local sympathy resulted in the government's posting militia units from Devon, Sussex, Denbeigh, and other remote areas to the various Luddite centers.

63. Large to Henson, 26 April 1812, Nottinghamshire County Archives CA 3984, I, 69, Nottingham.

64. Allsop to Large, 4 May 1812, Nottinghamshire Archives CA 3984, I, 84. Unfortunately, I have been unable to locate Large's "Last Dying Speech and Confession of Colting" to which Allsop refers.

65. The letter appears in the Nottinghamshire Archives CA 3984, I, 74, and in the *Records of the Borough of Nottingham* (Nottingham: Nottingham City Council, 1952), 8:142–43.

Leicester 30th April 1812

Dear Sir

Yours of the 20th I had an am happy to hear that matters are in a fare hair for succeeding I admire you plan and we fully acquiesce in it, You mention my petition being Blotched and really you do it so funny that I cannot help laughing at that and some other little matters which have come within my Knowledge very lately, but to the business you say I must look out for somebody to come to Town if called for now here I am lost we could sooner find a man than the money I was 5 Days in the Country last week and we have scarcely paid expenses we rather hope to get some in our Circular letter, if not we are stalled, Mr Toplas has sent us some large Bills which have been posted up against Colting and I again request you to get this insertion in the Bill in order that the act of the 5th of Elizb may be certainly extended to us. I have been informed that Mr Trantham Hosier of Nottm was shot on Monday night at his own door, report says that on Saturday last he <u>docked</u> his hands two-pence for pair and told them to tell <u>Ned Ludd</u> how true this may be I know not certain it is that this is not a proper time to irritate the public mind by gross Insults I dont know that the Hosiers of this Town mean to oppose our measures but many of them have discharged their hands from having anythingto do with it, You shall hear from me again soon

I am

Your respectfully

Thos Allsop

66. Hammond and Hammond, *Skilled Labourer* 269.

67. Rule, *Labouring Classes in Early Industrial England*, 369.

68. Chevening is a type of embroidery (Hammond and Hammond, *Skilled Labourer* 270n1).

69. Like the name "Balfour" the word that I have transcribed as "Patrina" is not en-tirely legible, particularly the character that appears to be "n."

70. Toplas was another member of the committee delegation.

71. Member of Parliament for Nottingham.

72. See *Luddism, 1811–1817, as illustrated by documents in the Nottingham City Archives*, Nottinghamshire Archives 67.01q, typescript, n.d., p. 7.

73. Later in H. O. 42/124 is a handwritten version of the letter, prefaced by the fol-lowing remarks: "The Author of the threatening Letter to Mr. Wood not having been yet discovered he publishes a fac simile of it in the hope that it may assist in the detection."

74. Felkin, *History* 239.

75. Consider, for example, the verses on a paper posted on the toll gates of the New Bridge in Manchester on 29 November 1800 and forwarded to the Home Office on 30 No-vember 1800 by the Justice of the Peace, Thomas Butterworth Bayley (H. O. 42/53):

No peace, No King
    to kill Billy Pitt it is no sin . . .
We will have a big loaf for a shilling
    or else the Justices we will be killing

76. Palmer cites the song as Derby Broadsides 8672, Derby Broadsides Collection, Derby Studies Library, Derby. Perhaps due to the song's being moved, Palmer's citation is no longer accurate.

77. Palmer's emendations, which improve the song for singing, hide the rough meter of the popular, laboring-class song. Compare Palmer's version of the first stanza and the chorus:

G o o d people I pray, now hear what I say,
And pray do not call it sedition;

For these great men of late they have cracked my poor pate:
I'm wounded, in a woeful condition.

Chorus

And sing fal lal the diddle i do,
Sing fal the diddle i do,
Sing fal the lal day.

78. Palmer has "Now it is not bad."

79. A reference to Burdett's imprisonment in the Tower for some time during 1810, an experience that Brian Bailey hints might have cooled Burdett's enthusiasm for reform, and which might explain the somewhat ironic treatment of Burdett in the song (Bailey, *Luddite Rebellion* 68–69).

80. There is earlier evidence of correspondence between Bristol and the West Riding of Yorkshire, where Luddism flared later. In the following letter from Bristol, the writer professes sympathy and solidarity with the cloth dressers of the Leeds.

The letter is reproduced in Aspinall, who notes, "The original letter, after being intercepted by the postal authorities, was sent on to its destination in order to prevent suspicion" (*Early English Trade Unions* 69n2). Such a tactic was not unusual and is advocated in a 25 June 1812 letter to Beckett from Freeling, regarding instructions for the postmistress at Strand to open suspicious letters (H. O. 42/124). The original source is a copy in H. O. 42/70, Charles Thomas to George Palmer:

> Bristol, 17 March 1803
>
> We received your kind letter the 5th instant, and am sorry to hear that you have so many enemies to contend with, as it must be very expensive to you when so many men is out of employ. Hope you have had liberal supplies from most towns in the kingdom; if you should be in want we have no objection of making you a small remittance. Hope you will in a short time be able to give us an account of your having met with good success, and be able to let the merchants and manufacturers know they are in the wrong, and be ashamed of their nasty mean conduct. We shall always be happy to hear from our brethren the cloth dressers of Leeds, as they are a set of men which ought to be esteemed, and I hope is by all trades. Gentlemen, wishing you health and respect, I remain you most obedient, Charles Thomas, President.

81. The "Bill" refers to the legal efforts of Gravener Henson and others to petition Parliament for relief in the stocking trades. The authorities, such as Stevenson, rarely distinguished Luddism from the more peaceful attempts by the stockingers to participate in public politics.

82. Few of the letter writers are known by name. In an 8 June 1812 deposition sworn before Reverend John Becher, John Cooper Kirk, an Arnold framework knitter imprisoned in Southwell, mentions an Arnold man named "Emmerson" as the writer of many of the letters signed "General Ludd." Some of the letters, he says, were put under doors by

George Lovat of Arnold (H. O. 42/124). "Emmerson," however, has not been completely identified.

83. Hammond and Hammond, *Skilled Labourer* 230.

84. Malcolm Thomis, *Politics and Society in Nottingham* (Oxford: Basil Blackwell, 1969), 38.

85. Perhaps the word might have been intended as "meretricor."

86. In the same issue of the *Nottingham Review*, on the same page as the letter from General Ludd, the Review Office commends Sir John Cope Sherbrooke, who is described as "Our Nottinghamshire Hero," for his success in the war against America, as reported in the previous Saturday's *London Gazette Supplement*, 8 October 1814. The *Nottingham Review*, 30 September 1814, quoted from the *London Gazette Extraordinary*, 27 September 1814, a report on the capture of Washington, an event in which, presumably, Sherbrooke took part.

87. In the manuscript, the word could be read as "have" but it perhaps makes more sense to interpret it as "hare," a version of "are" with an initial aspiration frequently seen in much of the phoneticized working-class writing from the Midlands and the North.

88. "Prizes" could be "prices."

89. The story of the Loughborough raid is told through witness accounts in Charles Sutton's *Reports of the Trial of James Towle, at Leicester, August 10, 1816, for Shooting at John Asher* . . . (Nottingham: Sutton and Son, 1817). See also Bailey, *The Luddite Rebellion* 116–20.

90. Charles Sutton, *Some Particulars of the Conduct and of the Execution of Savidge and Others* . . . (Nottingham: Sutton and Son, 1817), 3.

91. Ibid., 13. The man "who will soon be at large" is John Blackburn, called "Blackborne" in the Loughborough convicts' letters. See also John Crowder's 17 April 1817 letter to his wife, transcribed here.

92. The hymn is quoted in ibid., 13. Amos's version uses the first-person plural. A slightly different version, using the first-person singular, appears as number 786 in *A Collection of Hymns for the Use of the People Called Methodists, With a New Supplement* (London: Wesleyan-Methodist Book-Room, 1889).

❖ NORTHWESTERN DOCUMENTS

1. Letters in the McConnel, Kennedy and Company Papers for 1812 show continued demand for cotton twist, which the company was hard pressed to meet. The papers can be found in the John Rylands University Library, Deansgate, Manchester.

2. The letter appears in H. O. 42/121. See also the letter from Colonel Clay at Manchester to Ryder, 23 March 1812, H. O. 42/121.

3. E. P. Thompson, *The Making of the English Working Class* (New York: Vintage, 1966), 595; see also Duncan Bythell, *The Handloom Weavers: A Study in the English Cotton Industry during the Industrial Revolution* (Cambridge: Cambridge University Press, 1969), 189–95.

4. Lloyd to Home Office, 10 April 1812, H. O. 40/1/1. Lloyd also informs the Home Office that Wood's name appeared in the materials taken from the "Manchester 38," men tried on 27 August 1812 at Lancaster and acquitted of charges of illegal oathing (Lloyd to Home Office, August 1812, H. O. 42/127).

5. Kirkpatrick Sale, *Rebels against the Future: The Luddites and Their War on the Industrial Revolution, Lessons for the Computer Age* (Reading, Mass.: Addison-Wesley, 1995), 116.

6. H. O. 42/122, reproduced later in the text.

7. The incident is treated in Malcolm Thomis, *The Luddites: Machine-Breaking in Regency England* (Newton Abbott: David and Charles, 1970), 22, and Garside's letter to Ryder, 21 April 1812, H. O. 40/1/1 and 40/1/2.

8. Darvall, *Popular Disturbances and Public Order in Regency England* (1934; reprint, New York: Augustus M. Kelley, 1969), 91n5, citing H. O. 40/1.

9. The number "41" seems to be an addition written in a different hand.

10. "A stop" is inserted between the line ending "put" and the next line, directly under "put."

11. The "e" in "Sevility" overwrites an "i."

12. The "i" in "ruined" overwrites an "a."

13. A new line begins with "ing."

14. The writer probably means "curs."

15. On a separate page, in handwriting resembling that of the copyist of the Falstaff letter, a brief note identifies the persons who "will be looked to": "The Short hand are Penson Darwell Melling, Pinington and Battersly."

16. Thomis, *Luddites* 87.

17. "The Plague among the Beasts" is one of Aesop's fables. Several English editions of Samuel Croxall's translation of *The Fables of Aesop* were available in 1812. To give some idea of the letter writer's allusion, I reproduce here Croxall's version of the fable from Jean de La Fontaine, *The Fables of Aesop*, trans. Samuel Croxall (London: Cassell, Petter and Galpin, 1879), 343–44:

> A mortal distemper once raged among the Beasts, and swept away prodigious numbers. After it had continued some time without abatement, it was concluded in an assembly of the brute creation to be a judgment inflicted upon them for their sins, and a day was appointed for a general confession; when it was agreed that he who appeared to be the greatest sinner should suffer death as an atonement for the rest. The Fox was appointed father confessor upon the occasion; and the Lion, with great generosity, condescended to be the first in making public confession. "For my part," said he, "I must acknowledge I have been an enormous offender. I have killed many innocent sheep in my time; nay, once, but it was a case of necessity, I made a meal of the shepherd." The Fox, with much gravity, owned that these in any other but the king, would have been inexpiable crimes; but that His Majesty had certainly a right to a few silly sheep; nay, and to the shepherd too, in case of necessity. The

judgment of the Fox was applauded by all the superior savages; and the Tiger, the Leopard, the Bear, and the Wolf made confession of many enormities of the like sanguinary nature; which were all palliated and excused with the same lenity and mercy, and their crimes accounted so venial as scarce to deserve the name of offences. At last, a poor penitent Ass, with great contrition, acknowledged that once going through the parson's meadow, being very hungry and tempted by the sweetness of the grass, he had cropped a little of it, not more however in quantity than the tip of his tongue; he was very sorry for the misdemeanour, and hoped——. "Hope!" exclaimed the Fox, with singular zeal; "what canst thou hope for after the commission of so heinous a crime? What! eat the parson's grass! Oh, sacrilege! This, this is the flagrant wickedness, my brethren, which has drawn the wrath of Heaven upon our heads, and this the notorious offender whose death must make atonement for all our transgressions." So saying, he ordered his entrails for sacrifice, and the rest of the Beasts went to dinner upon his carcase.

18. One April 1812 letter describes the people who joined in the Luddite riot at Middleton on 20 April 1812: "One Thursday a numerous Body of People collected in Oldham, chiefly from Saddleworth and Hollinwood. From the latter Place they were almost all Colliers, which when united with the rude uncultivated Savages of Saddleworth formed an Assemblage of the most desperate Cast that can be imagined" (H. O. 40/1/1).

19. Daniel Burton was the owner of a Middleton mill that was destroyed by crowds from Middleton, Oldham, Saddleworth, and surrounding towns on 20 and 21 April 1812. "Goodier" is Joseph Goodair, the owner of Stockport mill that was destroyed during riots on 14 April 1812. Both Burton and Goodair used steam-powered looms in their mills. See Thomis, *Luddites* 22.

20. Thomis, *Luddites* 96; see also Wood's letter, 28 April 1812, H. O. 42/122.

21. Thomis, *Luddites* 26; Frank Peel, *The Risings of the Luddites, Chartists and Plug-Drawers*, 4th Ed. (London: Frank Cass, 1968), 53.

22. See Alfred Temple Patterson, *Radical Leicester: A History of Leicester, 1780–1850* (Leicester: Leicester University Press, 1975).

23. The word could be "five," but comparison of the letters to those of the "ive" in "Divel" suggests otherwise.

24. The final letter in "faile" and "saile" could possibly be a shortened "l," such as also appears in "well."

25. On Vansittart's role in the repeal, see Adrian Randall, *Before the Luddites: Custom, Community and Machinery in the English Woollen Industry, 1776–1809* (Cambridge: Cambridge University Press, 1991), 204–5. 5 Elizabeth, cap. 4 was repealed in 1814. On the statutes generally, see J. L. Hammond and Barbara Hammond, *The Skilled Labourer, 1760–1832* (London: Longmans, Green, 1919), 168–71.

26. Gravener Henson to Thomas Roper, 30 June 1812, Nottinghamshire Archives CA 3984, I, 145, Nottingham.

27. The "predecessor" to whom the writer refers is Spencer Perceval, who served as chancellor of the exchequer from 1807 until 1809, after which he was prime minister until his assassination in May 1812. His assassination caused the cabinet shuffle that resulted in Vansittart's becoming chancellor.

28. Also included with the letter to Blacow is the following handwritten sheet, in very large letters, posted in Liverpool about the same time as the letter. Nothing intrinsic to the letter associates it with Luddism, as the expressions therein are almost universal in Britain at the time. Only its connection to the "Iulius" Luddite letter sent to Reverend Blacow provides a reason to include it. The source is H. O. 42/123.

5000 For The
Heads of the Prince R
Lord Castlereagh and
Secrtary Ryder No Poppery
Britons Prepare for
Slaughter
Burdett our Captain
    for ever Huza

29. The underline is more of a flourish consisting of a series of short loops. On the left side of the page, on the same line as the name "Iulius," appears a symbol resembling a capital lambda with a chi superimposed. The significance of the symbol is unclear.

30. Keightley's name also has a flourish underlining it. The first name seems to be Archibald.

31. Roy Palmer, *Sound of History* (Oxford: Oxford University Press, 1988), 100. Compare the weekly wages (around ten shillings) of Midlands workers in plain silk, a grievance voiced in the open letter in the *Nottingham Review*, 20 December 1811, by the Derby Committee of Plain Silk Hands.

32. Palmer, *Sound of History* 100; Darvall, *Popular Disturbances* 7. In fact, the act did not go into effect until February 1811, although unsold cloth had been piling up in the Leeds Cloth Hall since 1810 (Thomis, *Luddites* 46).

33. The "w" in "weavers" is of a size between a capital and a lower case, perhaps underscoring a conclusion that the compositing of the bill was hasty and amateurish. No such problems appear in the later bill printed by Rogerson of Blackburn.

34. The "u" (selected by the typesetter but not turned upside down to create an "n") is more evidence of an amateurish printing job.

❖ YORKSHIRE DOCUMENTS

1. Letter, 22 January 1812, H. O. 42/119; Frank Darvall, *Popular Disturbances and Public Order in Regency England* (1934; reprint, New York: Augustus M. Kelley, 1969), 107; Malcolm Thomis, *The Luddites: Machine-Breaking in Regency England* (Newton Abbott:

David and Charles, 1970), 50; Kirkpatrick Sale, *Rebels against the Future: The Luddites and Their War on the Industrial Revolution, Lessons for the Computer Age* (Reading, Mass.: Addison-Wesley, 1995), 105.

2. On the arson fire at Ottiwells Mill and the resistance of Yorkshire croppers to the introduction of dressing machines to the region's woolen industry in the first decade of the nineteenth century, see Adrian Randall, *Before the Luddites: Custom, Community and Machinery in the English Woollen Industry, 1776–1809* (Cambridge: Cambridge University Press, 1991), 176. See also Brian Bailey, *The Luddite Rebellion* (New York: New York University Press, 1998), 12.

3. The story is told in D. F. E. Sykes and G. H. Walker, *Ben O' Bill's, The Luddite: A Yorkshire Tale* (London: Simpkin, Marshall, Hamilton, Kenty, 1898), 166–68.

4. Lesley Kipling, personal letter to author, 23 June 1999.

5. Palmer notes that the song has been recorded on Bill Price, *The Fine Old Yorkshire Gentleman*, Folk Heritage FHR038, 1972.

6. Frank Peel, *The Risings of the Luddites, Chartists and Plug-drawers*, 3rd ed. (Brighouse: J. Hartler, 1895), 51. Walker was one of the five Luddites hanged following the York assizes. He was discovered despite an attempt to evade the law by enlisting in a company of Royal Artillery at Woolwich.

7. See E. J. Hobsbawm, *Primitive Rebels: Studies in Archaic Forms of Social Movements in the 19th and 20th Centuries* (Manchester: Manchester University Press, 1959), chap. 2, especially 23–24.

8. Palmer has found a popular song, "The Gallant Poachers," which resembles "The Cropper's Song." Palmer is not certain which song predates the other but acknowledges that he can find no version of the poaching song dated as early as 1812. See Roy Palmer, *The Sound of History* (Oxford: Oxford University Press, 1988), 105, 316n. Regarding the tune, see Roy Palmer, "George Dunn: Twenty-one Songs and Fragments," *Folk Music Journal* 2.4 (1973): 276.

9. "Specials" refers to special constables appointed by the Home Office to assist the Yorkshire magistrates in suppressing the machine wrecking in the West Riding. Ironically, George Mellor's employer and relative, John Wood, was a special constable.

10. Palmer has "night *be* night" (*Sound of History* 106).

11. *Daisy Baines*, in *Huddersfield Weekly News*, 22 January 1881.

12. Lesley Kipling, personal letter to author, 23 June 1999.

13. Thomis, *The Luddites* 183.

14. W. B. Crump, *The Leeds Woollen Industry* (Leeds: Thoresby Society, 1931), has "Government."

15. Darvall, *Popular Disturbances* 111.

16. Thomis, *Luddites* 184.

17. Crump has "mispresented."

18. As earlier, Crump has "Government."

19. Crump includes a note on Mr. Hanson, summarizing his support for the workers

(Crump, *Leeds Woollen Industry* 230n). Hammond and Hammond provide a more detailed account:

> The leniency shown to the riotous [Lancashire] weavers was not extended to a man in a more prosperous condition of life, who was charged with having encouraged the strikers. Joseph Hanson, a colonel in the volunteers, who had stood as candidate for Preston and was popular with the weavers for his advocacy of the minimum wage Bill, rode on to the field during the monster meeting of May 25 [1808 at Manchester] and addressed the people in opposition to the wishes of the captain of the Dragoons. His own witnesses, citizens of respectable character, swore that he merely urged the people to go home peaceably, but witnesses for the prosecution, a sergeant, two corporals, and two of Nadin's constables, swore that Hanson had used inciting expressions. "My lads, your cause is good; be firm and you will succeed." "I will support you as far as £3000 will go, and if that will not do, I will go farther." "Nadin and his faction shall not drive you from the field this day." "I am sorry your Bill is lost. My father was a weaver, and I am a weaver, and I am the weavers' friend."

Hanson was sentenced in May 1809 to a six-month imprisonment and was fined one hundred pounds for having thus encouraged the strikers. The Lancashire workers offered to pay his fine by penny subscriptions, an offer he declined; nevertheless, "39,600 subscribers presented him with a silver cup." See J. L. Hammond and Barbara Hammond, *The Skilled Labourer, 1760–1832* (London: Longmans, Green, 1919), 81. See also Archibald Prentice, *Historical Sketches and Personal Recollections of Manchester: Intended to Illustrate the Progress of Public Opinion from 1792 to 1832* (London: C. Gilpin, 1851), 32–33. As John Dinwiddy points out, Hanson could not have led any rebellion in the Cotton Country because he had died in 1811. See Dinwiddy, "Luddism and Politics in the Northern Counties," *Social History* 4.1 (January 1979): 56, citing *Cowdry's Manchester Gazette*, 14 September 1811. Cf. Duncan Bythell, *The Handloom Weavers: A Study in the English Cotton Industry during the Industrial Revolution* (Cambridge: Cambridge University Press, 1969), 192.

20. The version in H. O. 40/1/1 has "passess an Act to put down all Machinery hurtful to Comonality."

21. See Depositions of William Hall and Joseph Drake, T. S. 11/812.2666, Treasury Solicitor's Papers, Public Record Office, Kew, London; Alan Brooke and Lesley Kipling, *Liberty or Death: Radicals, Republicans, and Luddites, 1793–1823* (Honley: Workers History Publications, 1993), 18–19; Radcliffe to Lt. Gen. Grey, 16 March 1812, H. O. 42/121.

22. At the bottom left is added "Delivered by Mr. Vickerman to Jos Radcliffe Esq."

23. Among the authorities, a similar fascination was manifested as a fear of correspondence between other Luddite regions and Nottingham. As late as 23 January 1817, Charles Mundy, writing to Lord Sidmouth from the vicinity of Loughborough, fearing a resurgence of Luddism, reports as a matter of great significance the arrival in Loughborough

of a man from Nottingham whose purpose it was to address the Loughborough Hampden Club (H. O. 40/3, Part 1).

24. As Robert Reid points out, Millbridge is not the same as Milnsbridge, Radcliffe's home three miles west of Huddersfield on the River Colne. Millbridge is a village six miles northeast of Huddersfield on the Spen. See Robert Reid, *Land of Lost Content: The Luddite Revolt, 1812* (London: Heinemann, 1986), 19n.

25. In their brief excerpt from the letter, Brooke and Kipling have "Sovrns [Sovereigns]," observing that it is "Jacobin terminology" (*Liberty or Death* 21). The handwriting is unclear enough that their reading might be correct.

26. Read as "spoke."

27. Reid, *Land of Lost Content* 100.

28. This approach was developed by Hayden White in *The Content of the Form: Narrative Discourse and Historical Representation* (Baltimore: Johns Hopkins University Press, 1987) and has been usefully employed in recent historical work such as James Vernon, ed., *Re-reading the Constitution: New Narratives in the Political History of England's Long Nineteenth Century* (Cambridge: Cambridge University Press, 1996).

29. Peel's *The Risings of the Luddites* contains a variation, appearing to combine the "Forster's Mill" and "Horsfall's Mill" songs. Peel reports of John Hirst, an acquitted Yorkshire Luddite, that "when engaged in rocking his grandchildren to sleep he invariably soothed them by crooning out an old Luddite ditty, every verse of which . . . ended with the refrain:--

Around and around we all will stand
And eternally swear we will,
We'll break the shears and windows too
And set fire to the tazzling mill. (270)

30. For a brief account of Cartwright's defensive preparations, see Reid, *Land of Lost Content* 106–7, drawing upon the York Special Commission records of Baines and Howell.

31. The writer appears to be attempting to spell "enough."

32. Frank Peel, *Nonconformity in Spen Valley* (Heckmondwike: Senior, 1891); E. J. Hobsbawm, "Methodism and the Threat of Revolution in Britain," *History Today* 7 (1957): 120; J. A. Hargreaves, "Methodism and Luddism in Yorkshire, 1812–1813," *Northern History* 26 (1990): 160–85.

33. Reid, *Land of Lost Content* 133.

34. Peel, *Risings of the Luddites* 218–19.

35. Thomis misreports the date of Horsfall's murder as 27 April 1812 (*Luddites* 184).

36. The excerpt for this version of the Luddite oath comes from a spy's report forwarded by Bolton magistrate R. A. Fletcher to Home Office Undersecretary John Beckett, 23 March 1812, H. O. 42/121. See also the oath included as part of the "Address to Cotton Weavers and Others" (Y23).

37. E. P. Thompson, "The Crime of Anonymity," in *Albion's Fatal Tree: Crime and Society in Eighteenth-Century England*, ed. Douglas Hay. (New York: Pantheon, 1975), 273.

38. Thompson, "Anonymity" 322.

39. Peel, *Risings of the Luddites* 56.

40. An abridged transcription, with several differences from the version given here, appears in Thompson, "Anonymity" 322.

41. The "attempt" described is probably the attempted murder of William Cartwright, owner of the mill at Rawfolds, near Hightown, on 18 April 1812.

42. Presumably, the man who "fel last nite" is Nottingham hosier William Trentham, shot on 27 April 1812, one night before the murder of William Horsfall, Marsden mill owner. George Mellor and two other croppers were convicted and hanged for Horsfall's murder. Trentham's attackers were never discovered, but, earlier, Trentham had received a letter (M30) complaining of low pay for women outworkers employed in chevening.

43. Thompson reads "Guelps." The word is a misspelling of "Guelph," and it adds a tone of British nationalism to the letter. Guelph was the name of a German noble family whose line of descent includes the British royal family ruling during the period. The writer appears to be commenting with disfavor upon the nationality of the Hanoverian royals, especially George "Juner," the prince regent. Additionally, the word "Juner" applied to both the Huddersfield Edward Ludd and the prince regent is a leveling stylistic device.

44. Contrast the 31 December 1812 letter to Joseph Radcliffe from "A friend to peace." The letter names several persons and gives fairly precise information about them (Radcliffe Papers 126/113, West Yorkshire Archives Service, Leeds).

45. On 14 June 1812, less than a month after Gott's receipt of this letter, Gibraltar Mill at Pudsey, just two miles west of Gott's home, was burned down. See Crump, *Leeds Woollen Industry* 72–73.

46. See E. P. Thompson, *The Making of the English Working Class* (New York: Vintage, 1966), 381–82.

47. Much of the correspondence in H. O. 42/125 treats the problem of French prisoners of war confined in distressed parts of England. Escapes posed one problem, but possible French sympathy for the plight of hungry English laborers caused more concern—a fact that the author of the letter from Daypool uses to advantage.

48. Apparently an attempt to spell "Castlereagh."

49. Immediately after the number is an equilateral triangle with a small circle inside, another small circle above, an "x" at the lower left, and a "v" at the lower right. The symbol appears on no other Luddite document that I have found.

50. There were four members of the prosecution team: J. A. Park, a barrister; John Lloyd and Jonas Allison, solicitors; and Henry Hobhouse, of Lincoln's Inn, who was supervising the conduct of the case on behalf of the Home Office. The handwriting on the brief does not seem to be Lloyd's or Hobhouse's.

51. Milnes also told Taylor that at the "rising" they would kill the officers of the local

regiment, after which the men would join the Luddites (*Rex v. Charles Milnes of Geldhill & William Blakeborough*, T. S. 11.813.2673).

52. Palmer, *Sound of History* 251.

53. Thompson has "Though"; however, "Tho'" appears clearly in the treasury solicitor's brief.

54. Thompson inserts an apostrophe, "another's."

55. Thompson has "show."

56. Thompson has "thief" and "does."

57. Thompson has "laws."

58. For discussion of the popular reaction to Perceval's death, see Thompson, *Making of the English Working Class* 570, and Asa Briggs, *The Age of Improvement* (London: Longmans, 1959), 157.

59. The word is almost illegible.

60. Read "pellit" as "bullet" and "mad" as "made."

61. The word is almost illegible.

62. "His will be done"?

63. Reid, relying upon the version in Mellor's own hand in the Home Office Papers, has the addressee as "Thomas Eddie" (*Land of Lost Content* 224). Such a reading is unlikely. Ellis is named in the 31 December 1812 letter to Radcliffe from "A friend to peace" (Radcliffe Papers 126/113).

64. The first two letters are unclear; perhaps the name is Schonefield, as the previous name.

65. Read as "they."

66. On Jimmy 'Gabbler' Rourk and Samuel Brook, both croppers from the area, see Brooke and Kipling, *Liberty or Death* 51. Brooke and Kipling also speculate on the possibility of a connection to Ireland.

Bibliography

❖ ARCHIVAL SOURCES

Derby Broadsides Collection, Derby Local Studies Library, Derby
Gott Papers, Leeds University Manuscripts, Leeds
Guildhall Library, London
Hay Scrapbook, Chetham's Library, Manchester
Home Office Papers, Public Record Office, Kew, London
Manchester Central Library, Local Studies Division, Manchester
McConnel, Kennedy and Company Papers, John Rylands University Library, Deansgate,
    Manchester
Nottinghamshire County Archives, Nottingham
Parliamentary Papers, Public Record Office, Kew, London
Radcliffe Papers, West Yorkshire Archives Service, Leeds
Treasury Solicitor's Papers, Public Record Office, Kew, London

❖ NEWSPAPERS

Huddersfield Weekly News
Leeds Mercury
Nottingham Journal
Nottingham Review

❖ PUBLISHED WORKS AND OTHER SOURCES

Aspinall, A. *The Early English Trade Unions: Documents from the Home Office Papers in the
    Public Record Office.* London: Batchworth Press, 1949.

Bailey, Brian. *The Luddite Rebellion.* New York: New York University Press, 1998.

Baines, Edward. *Proceedings under the Special Commission at York.* Leeds: Baines, 1813.

Bamford, Samuel. *The Autobiography of Samuel Bamford: Early Days.* 2 vols. London, 1849.

Bentley, Phyllis. *Inheritance.* New York: Macmillan, 1932.

Bohstedt, John. *Riots and Community Politics in England and Wales, 1790–1810.* Cambridge: Harvard University Press, 1983.

Briggs, Asa. *The Age of Improvement.* London: Longmans, 1959.

Brontë, Charlotte. *Shirley, A Tale.* London: Smith, Elder, 1849.

Brooke, Alan, and Lesley Kipling. *Liberty or Death: Radicals, Republicans, and Luddites, 1793–1823.* Honley: Workers History Publications, 1993.

Brown, Kenneth D. *The English Labour Movement, 1700–1951.* New York: St. Martin's, 1982.

Burke, Kenneth. *A Grammar of Motives.* Berkeley: University of California Press, 1969.

Bythell, Duncan. *The Handloom Weavers: A Study in the English Cotton Industry during the Industrial Revolution.* Cambridge: Cambridge University Press, 1969.

Calhoun, Craig. *The Question of Class Struggle: Social Foundations of Popular Radicalism during the Industrial Revolution.* Chicago: University of Chicago Press, 1982.

Chambers, J. D. "The Worshipful Company of Framework Knitters (1657–1778)." *Economica* (November 1929): 296–329.

Charter of the Worshipful Company of Framework Knitters. 1663. London: Guildhall Library. Ref. 16865-7.

Church, Roy A., and Stanley D. Chapman. "Gravener Henson and the Making of the English Working Class." In *Land, Labour and Population in the Industrial Revolution: Essays Presented to J. D. Chambers,* edited by Eric L. Jones and G. E. Mingay, 131–61. London: Edward Arnold, 1967.

A Collection of Hymns for the Use of the People Called Methodists, With a New Supplement. London: Wesleyan-Methodist Book-Room, 1889.

Crump, William. *The Leeds Woollen Industry.* Leeds: Thoresby Society, 1931.

Cunningham, P. *8 April 1813 Circular to Members of Parliament on the Repeal of Statute 5 Eliz. c. 4.* London, 1813.

Darvall, Frank. *Popular Disturbances and Public Order in Regency England.* 1934. Reprint, New York: Augustus M. Kelley, 1969.

Dimock, Wai Chee. "Class, Gender, and a History of Metonymy." In *Rethinking Class: Literary Studies and Social Formations,* edited by Wai Chee Dimock and Michael T. Gilmore, 57–104. New York: Columbia University Press, 1994.

Dinwiddy, John. "Luddism and Politics in the Northern Counties," *Social History* 4.1 (January 1979): 33–63.

Douglas, David C., ed. *English Historical Document, 1783–1832.* 12 vols. Oxford: Oxford University Press, 1959.

Ellis, Kenneth. *The Post Office in the Eighteenth Century: A Study in Administrative History.* London: Oxford University Press, 1958.

Epstein, James. *Radical Expression: Political Language, Ritual, and Symbol in England, 1790 – 1850.* New York: Oxford University Press, 1994.

Felkin, William. *A History of the Machine-Wrought Hosiery and Lace Manufacturers.* 1867. Reprint, New York: Burt Franklin, 1967.

Foster, John. *Class Struggle and the Industrial Revolution: Early Industrial Capitalism in Three English Towns.* London: Weidenfeld and Nicolson, 1974.

Hammond, J. L., and Barbara Hammond. *The Skilled Labourer, 1760–1832.* London: Longmans, Green, 1919.

Hargreaves, J. A. "Methodism and Luddism in Yorkshire, 1812–1813." *Northern History* 26 (1990): 160–85.

Hazlitt, William. *The Table-Talk of Martin Luther.* London: H. G. Bohn, 1857.

Henson, Gravener. *History of the Framework-Knitters.* 1831. Reprint, Newton Abbott: David and Charles, 1970.

Henty, G. A. *Through the Fray: A Tale of the Luddite Riots.* New York: Hurst, 1890.

Hobsbawm, E. J. *Labouring Men: Studies in the History of Labour.* London: Weidenfeld and Nicolson, 1964.

———. "Methodism and the Threat of Revolution in Britain." *History Today* 7 (February 1957): 115–24.

———. *Primitive Rebels: Studies in Archaic Forms of Social Movements in the 19th and 20th Centuries.* Manchester: Manchester University Press, 1959.

Jackson, Randle. *The Speech of Randle Jackson, Esq. to the Committee of the House of Common Appointed to Consider the State of the Woollen Manufacture.* London: Randle Jackson and Joseph Gurney, 1806.

Janowitz, Anne. *Lyric and Labour in the Romantic Tradition.* Cambridge: Cambridge University Press, 1998.

La Fontaine, Jean de. *The Fables of Aesop.* Trans. Samuel Croxall. London: Cassell, Petter and Galpin, 1879.

Luddism, 1811–1817, as Illustrated by Documents in the Nottingham City Archives. Nottinghamshire Archives 67.01q, typescript, n.d.

MacCalman, Iain. *Radical Underworld: Prophets, Revolutionaries and Pornographers in London, 1795–1840.* New York: Oxford University Press, 1993.

Mee, John. *Dangerous Enthusiasm: William Blake and the Culture of Radicalism in the 1790s.* New York: Oxford University Press, 1992.

Observations on Woollen Machinery. Leeds: E. Baines, 1803.

Ollyffe, Thomas. *The Young Clerk's Tutor Enlarged: Being a Most Useful Collection of the Best Precedents of Recognizances, Obligations, Conditions, Acquittances, Bills of Sale, Warrants of Attorney, &c.* London: Battersby, 1717.

Paine, Thomas. *The Rights of Man.* 1792. Reprint, Harmondsworth: Penguin, 1984.

Palmer, Roy. "George Dunn: Twenty-one Songs and Fragments." *Folk Music Journal* 2.4 (1973): 276.

———. *The Sound of History.* Oxford: Oxford University Press, 1988.

———. *A Touch on the Times*. Harmondsworth: Penguin Education, 1974.

Patterson, Alfred Temple. *Radical Leicester: A History of Leicester, 1780–1850*. Leicester: Leicester University Press, 1975.

Peel, Frank. *Nonconformity in Spen Valley*. Heckmondwike: Senior, 1891.

———. *The Risings of the Luddites, Chartists and Plug-drawers*. 3rd ed. Brighouse: J. Hartler, 1895.

———. *The Risings of the Luddites*. 4th ed. London: Cass, 1968.

Pocock, J. G. A. *The Ancient Constitution and the Feudal Law*. Cambridge: Cambridge University Press, 1987.

Prentice, Archibald. *Historical sketches and personal recollections of Manchester: Intended to illustrate the progress of public opinion from 1792 to 1832*. London: C. Gilpin, 1851.

Price, Bill. *The Fine Old Yorkshire Gentleman*. Sound Recording. Folk Heritage FHR038, 1972.

Radcliffe, William. *The Origin of the New System of Manufacture Called "Powerloom Weaving," and the Purposes for Which this System Was Invented and Brought into Use, Fully Explained in a Narrative, Containing William Radcliffe's Struggles through Life to Remove the Cause Which Has Brought this Country to Its Present Crisis*. Stockport: J. Lomax, 1828.

Randall, Adrian. *Before the Luddites: Custom, Community and Machinery in the English Woollen Industry, 1776–1809*. Cambridge: Cambridge University Press, 1991.

Records of the Borough of Nottingham. Nottingham: Nottingham City Council, 1952.

Reid, Robert. *Land of Lost Content: The Luddite Revolt, 1812*. London: Heinemann, 1986.

Rudé, George. *The Crowd in History: A Study of Popular Disturbances in France and England, 1730–1848*. London: Lawrence and Wishart, 1981.

Rule, John. *The Labouring Classes in Early Industrial England, 1750–1850*. London: Longman, 1986.

Rule Book of the Worshipful Company of Framework Knitters. London, 1740.

Russell, John. "The Luddites." *Transactions of the Thoroton Society* 10 (1906): 53–62.

Rutherford, Samuel. "The Deliverance of the Kirk of God." In *Quaint Sermons of Samuel Rutherford, Hitherto Unpublished, with a Preface by the Rev. Andrew A. Bonar D.D.*, 152–77. London: Hodder and Stoughton, 1885.

Sale, Kirkpatrick. *Rebels against the Future: The Luddites and Their War on the Industrial Revolution, Lessons for the Computer Age*. Reading, Mass.: Addison-Wesley, 1995.

Sutton, Charles. *Four Additional Letters, viz. One from William Towle to His Father; One from the Rev. E. T. Vaughan, to Towle's Brother; One from the Mother, and One from the Wife of William Withers, Addressed to Him Previous to His Execution*. Nottingham: Sutton and Son, 1817.

———. *Reports of the Trial of James Towle, at Leicester, August 10, 1816, for Shooting at John Asher; of Daniel Diggle, in the Shire Hall, at Nottingham, March 18th, 1817, for Shooting at George Kerry; Also of John Clarke, James Watson, Thomas Savidge, Wm. Withers, Joshua Mitchell, Wm. Towle, John Crowder, & John Amos, in the Castle, at Leicester, March 31st, and April 1st, 1817, for Firing at John Asher, in the Attack on Messrs. Heathcoat and Boden's*

Factory, at Loughbro'; Including a Variety of Interesting Particulars Relative to Samuel Caldwell alias Big Sam, John Disney alias Sheepshead Jack,---Hudson alias Aaron Daykin, Hill, John and Christopher Blackborne, and William Burton, who along with James Towle, and John Slater, were the whole of the Men Concerned in that Memorable Outrage. Nottingham: Sutton and Son, 1817.

———. *Some Particulars of the Conduct and of the Execution of Savidge and Others, Who Were Executed at Leicester, On Thursday, April 17, 1817; Including the Letters Which They Wrote to Their Friends, While under Sentence of Death.* Nottingham: Sutton and Son, 1817.

Sykes, D. F. E., and G. H. Walker. *Ben O' Bill's, The Luddite: A Yorkshire Tale.* London: Simpkin, Marshall, Hamilton, Kenty, 1898.

Thomis, Malcolm. *Luddism in Nottinghamshire.* London: Phillimore, 1972.

———. *The Luddites: Machine-Breaking in Regency England.* Newton Abbott: David and Charles, 1970.

———. *Politics and Society in Nottingham.* Oxford: Basil Blackwell, 1969.

Thompson, E. P. "The Crime of Anonymity." In *Albion's Fatal Tree: Crime and Society in Eighteenth-Century England,* edited by Douglas Hay, 255–344. New York: Pantheon, 1975.

———. *Customs in Common.* London: Penguin, 1993.

———. *The Making of the English Working Class.* New York: Vintage, 1966.

———. *The Poverty of Theory, or, An Orrery of Errors.* London: Merlin, 1978.

Toller, Ernst. *The Machine-Wreckers: A Drama of the English Luddites in a Prologue and Five Acts.* New York: A. A. Knopf, 1923.

Toone, William. *The Magistrate's Manual: Or, A Summary of the Duties and Powers of a Justice of the Peace.* London: N. p., 1813.

Unwin, George. *Industrial Organization in the Sixteenth and Seventeenth Centuries.* Oxford: Clarendon Press, 1904.

Vernon, James, ed. *Re-reading the Constitution: New Narratives in the Political History of England's Long Nineteenth Century.* Cambridge: Cambridge University Press, 1996.

Webb, W. H. "The History of the Machine-Made Lace Manufacture." *Textile Recorder* (15 June 1916): 41–42.

Wells, Roger. *Insurrection: The British Experience, 1795–1803.* Gloucester: Alan Sutton Publishing, 1983.

Wesley, John. *A Collection of Hymns for the Use of the People Called Methodists, With a New Supplement.* London: Wesleyan-Methodist Book-Room, 1889.

White, Hayden. *The Content of the Form: Narrative Discourse and Historical Representation.* Baltimore: Johns Hopkins University Press, 1987.

Worrall, David. *Radical Culture: Discourse, Resistance and Surveillance, 1790–1820.* Detroit: Wayne State University Press, 1992.

Index

References to Luddite documents are indexed only when the references appear separate from the documents themselves